FROM YOUR AFFECTIONATE SON

The Civil War Letters
of
Frederic Henry Kellogg

Compiled by his great-granddaughter
Kathi Mac Iver

Mac Iver, Kathi
        From Your Affectionate Son
        The Civil War Letters of Frederic Henry Kellogg
ISBN 0-9651272-0-6

Printed in the United States of America 1996

First Edition

Dedicated to Mama and Uncle Bud who brightened their grandfather's last years. Safe in the leafy mulberry tree, they recited his curse words, giggling at the forbidden syllables. They sat at his feet and heard all about tearing up the Georgia railroads. They marched smartly across the big front porch, singing "Rally 'round the Flag, Boys" and "If you wanta have some fun, Jine the Cavalry."

Acknowledgements
Many thanks to the people and organizations who helped make this book possible: Dr. Richard Sommers and staff at the U. S. Army Military History Institute, Carlisle Barracks, Pa.; National Archives, Washington, DC.; Firelands Historical Society and Museum, Norwalk, Ohio; DeWitt Historical Society and Museum, Ithaca, NY; Recorder's offices of Huron County, Ohio; Tompkins County, NY; Marion County, KS; McPherson County, KS; Harvey County, KS; and DeKalb County, Ill; Shasta County Library, Redding, CA; Shasta College Library, Redding, CA; Sutro Library, San Francisco, CA; Special thanks to Becci, current protector of the letters; Asa and Gwen, for hours of copying; Lee, for editing; Tom, for explaining military terminology; Rob for solving computer glitches and Pat, for his love and constant support.

BACKGROUND

Frederic Henry Kellogg inadvertently discovered run-away slaves in a neighbor's cellar while playing hide-go-seek with his little brothers. Pondering, he realized his childhood was over. War was imminent, as people were saying. Fred was only eleven. He dreaded going onto the battlefield so young. Still, other Kelloggs, as young as six and eight, had done so in the War of the Revolution. They beat the drums and carried the flags. Boys not much older shouldered muskets along with their fathers and grandfathers. Though he trembled to think of it, when the time came, Fred would go to war. And proudly.

Ten years passed before South Carolinian P. G. T. Beauregard fired on Ft. Sumter and war was declared. Fred enlisted in the Fifteenth Illinois Volunteer Infantry. He was two months shy of his twenty-first birthday.

The first months brought frustration and disillusionment for Fred Kellogg. Rather than best an enemy for the preservation of the Union his forefathers had established, he and his fellow soldiers wandered from place to place, expecting a charging Rebel force. Instead, they found empty battlefields strewn with the smoking remains of wagons and buildings and the ghoulish sight of the dead and dying, both friend and foe. Yet, Fred cheerfully accepted what each day had to offer, knowing that tomorrow might bring the promised glory.

Later, after joining the Third Ohio Volunteer Cavalry, Fred found a cherished esprit de corps, organization, and more than enough battle action to last a lifetime.

Frederic Kellogg's letters give a comprehensive picture of the life of a soldier who found something interesting in every situation. He reflected on the beauty of the countryside and the horrific battles that became historic. With dry humor, he wrote of officers and campmates, brawls and pranks. Food, weather or living conditions might be "top rate" or "the worst I ever did see." Fred reported all of it with an optimistic outlook.

The discolored pages are quite legible, considering the uncomfortable writing positions sometimes necessary. Except where vital for clarity, Fred's handwriting style, capitalization, punctuation and grammar have been preserved in transcriptions as they appear in the original letters. His spelling was left as written. Almost without exception, he spelled names of officers, cities and battlefields correctly; he saw these printed repeatedly in newspapers. Many simpler words, misspelled in early letters, were corrected later. Some words (carry, which, receive, expect, beautiful) he failed to master. He was not sure of quit, quiet and quite. And though he tried a dozen ways, the word "since" remained a mystery to the end.

He separated the "a" from words such as ago, about, and around, (a go -- a bout -- a round) and added an "a" before going and fighting, (agoing -- afighting) This seems to have been acceptable, at least in the area where he had lived in Illinois. These words have been left as he wrote them, carrying down though the decades the accent and flavor of a 19th century farm boy's speech. Here and there he omitted a word, an obvious oversight. That word was inserted in brackets.

Letters, the mainstay of every soldier, were especially important to Fred. His father, Doctor Moses Curtis Kellogg, moved his wife and ten children from Newfield, New York to North Fairfield, Ohio, then heartlessly abandoned them. Fred was not quite seven years old. Life without father had its heartache, but the family learned to cope. Elizabeth Swartwout Kellogg, a strong-minded, yet sensitive woman, was active in church and community and well-known for her poetry. She proved quite capable of being both mother and father to her children. Though their livelihood was the Ohio farm where Moses had left them, Elizabeth guided her sons into professional careers and her daughters into good marriages.

The other children managed to put their father out of their minds. Fred, however, longed for him continually. He remembered the days when he rode along in the buggy, his small feet propped on the scuffed, black medicine bag, accompanying Moses on his calls around the country. All through his growing up years, Fred refused to believe Papa did not intend to come back to them.

After a ten-year absence, a letter from Moses asked his boys to come live with him in Illinois. Fred left at once, elated at the prospect of being with his father once again. An excited twelve-year-old Frank went with him. Brother Romeyn rebuffed the invitation with disgust.

Fred was quickly disillusioned. Papa had another wife, Mary, and a step-son who had taken the place in his father's life Fred thought was reserved for him. Fred left his father's house and struck out on his own.

The war, and being a soldier, gave Frederic Kellogg a chance to make contact with his mother again, and the rest of his family.

Fred's letters to his mother begin tentatively and reveal an increasing attachment to this woman he had run away from five years earlier. His first letters are signed with only his name or "your son." It was five months before he was able to sign, "Your loving son." Many of his letters closed with "Your Affectionate Son," a popular phrase of the day. He seems eager to keep his mother informed of his well being. Perhaps he regretted his lack of correspondence while living in Illinois.

Three of Fred's brothers -- Lyman, Romeyn and Frank -- served in the Civil War.

Lyman Mack Kellogg (Lyme), was fourteen years older than Fred, and a West Point graduate, class of 1852. Lyman and his wife, Caroline Sturges, had served at several western posts. In 1857 Lyman became disgruntled and resigned from the Army. With war looming nearer, however, he raised and drilled a regiment of volunteers in his home territory of Norwalk, Ohio. As noted in Fred's first letter home, Lyman re-enlisted in the Eighteenth Regiment, Regular United States Army. He served as aide to General David S. Stanley. Later, Colonel Lyman Kellogg commanded the Eighteenth Regiment in the battle of Jonesboro, where he was severely wounded. In 1877 Lyman succumbed to his injuries. He was fifty years old.

Edgar Romeyn Kellogg (Rome) was two years younger than his brother, Fred. According to Rome's obituary, recorded in the annals of the Firelands Historical Society, Norwalk, Ohio, he "lay aside his law books and took up the call of his country." He chose the unit his brother Lyman had raised, the Twenty-fourth Ohio Volunteer Infantry. It wasn't long, however, before Rome decided his chance for action and promotion lay with the Regular forces. He resigned the Volunteers and re-enlisted in the Sixteenth United States Infantry. Well suited to army life, Romeyn advanced swiftly. He would see thirty-eight years of active service, reaching the rank of Brigadier General. His hand-written "Recollections of Civil War Service" are in the U. S. Army Military History Institute at Carlisle Barracks, Pennsylvania.

William Francis (Frank) Kellogg had just turned sixteen, the spring of 1861. No one considered him old enough to go to war. No one, except Frank. Before summer ended, he ran away and enlisted. He was assigned to Battery B, 2nd Light Artillery Regiment of Illinois Volunteers.

Two other brothers did not serve. Thirty-six-year-old Oscar Eugene (Ock) Kellogg had been a prominent lawyer in Norwalk, Ohio many years. He and his wife, Mary Elizabeth Williams, had two daughters. Bessie was only a toddler. Young Clara wrote letters to her Uncle Fred.

Theron Hotchkiss Kellogg (Bubby), a law partner with Oscar, was twenty-nine when the war began, still unmarried, though he would take a wife (Frances Ann Ester Penfield) in January 1862. Tacit references in family records indicate Theron might have been what we would now consider a conscientious objector. Comments in Fred's letters lead one to believe he was agitated with Theron's civilian status, as well as his attempts to "boss" little brother from afar.

The family history book states that sister Nancy Cornelia Kellogg was married to Major Elijah B. Hall of the 130th Ohio Volunteer Infantry. Other than his mother, Nan seemed to be Fred's most faithful correspondent. Indeed, with a husband and four brothers all at the front, Nan must have kept the mail carriers very busy with her cheerful letters to all.

Records are unclear but it is possible that Ebenezer Price, husband of sister Mary Floyd Kellogg, served for a short time towards the end of the war.

Fred's oldest sister, Martha Mack Kellogg (Mrs. Clark Chapin Sexton) had been married fifteen years, had four children and would have two more.

Fred wrote consistently of family members, often using their nicknames. Because of the numerous Marys, he referred to his sister as Mary Price (her married name) and to Oscar's wife as Mary Ock. Interestingly enough he did not mention Mary, his stepmother, by name -- only that he had a letter "from Illinois." He does mention his father from time to time, but does not say much about him. Moses did not enlist, but followed the army as a surgeon. Since he was sixty years old at the beginning of the war, this was rather remarkable He stayed near his sons when he could. It is hard to determine whether Fred was appreciative of his father's nearness or would have preferred his father stay out of his life.

Fred, Lyme, Rome and Frank were often within miles of one another, in spite of being in different branches of service. They kept track of each other as best they could, sharing news of visits and letters with their mother. The brothers became very close as the war erased the difference in their ages and the years spent apart. For several days after Fred was wounded at Shiloh, Rome stayed with him and cared for him. Because they all suffered from a severe lack of money, if one brother had an extra ten or twenty dollars, he sent it to Oscar, who acted as banker.

Anyone who needed it was welcome. Of course, they all understood, their Mother's needs would come first.

Albert Kellogg, often mentioned in Fred's letters, was one of Fred's many cousins, originally from Newfield, New York.

Others mentioned were acquaintances, officers and campmates.

After the war Elizabeth Swartwout Kellogg gave her son's letters to Fred's wife, Jane Hudson Kellogg, who in turn, passed them on to their granddaughter, Katherine Cosette Kellogg McIntosh.

The letters are presented here by Fred's great-granddaughter, Kathi McIntosh Mac Iver, as a lasting tribute to one "Affectionate Son" -- Frederic Henry Kellogg.

FREDERIC HENRY KELLOGG

This photograph was taken in De Kalb County, Illinois, soon after the war ended. Fred served in the Fifteenth Regiment of the Illinois Volunteer Infantry. He was assigned to Company H, commanded by Captain Morton D. Swift. Regiment Commander was Colonel Thomas J. Turner.

Taken from "The Patriotism of Illinois" by T.M. Eddy, D.D., published 1866.

FIFTEENTH ILLINOIS INFANTRY

The 15th Regiment was organized at Freeport, in April, 1861, and mustered into the United States service May 24th.

On the 1st of June, the regiment proceeded to Alton, where it remained till the 1st of August, when it went to Jefferson Barracks, Missouri. It then went to Rolla, Missouri, where it arrived in time to cover General Sigel's retreat from Wilson's Creek. On the 1st of October the regiment marched to Tipton, where it joined General Fremont's grand army, and began a campaign in Missouri. Near Sedalia it assisted in the capture of 1,300 of the enemy. Thence it marched to Otterville, where it went into winter quarters on the 26th of December, remaining there till February 1, 1862. On the 7th of the latter month it was ordered to St. Louis, whence it proceeded to Fort Donelson, arriving on the morning of the surrender. Here it was assigned to Hurlbut's "Fighting Fourth Division." It then went to Pittsburg Landing, being the first regiment to disembark there. At the battle of Shiloh, on the 6th of April, the 15th was in the first line of battle, with the 77th and 53d Ohio regiments on either flank. At the first fire of the rebels, the Buckeyes broke and ran, and the enemy was soon on both flanks of the 15th, which bravely stood its ground for an hour, and until entirely cut up. It was the final charge on the 7th, led by General Grant in person, which gave our army the victory. In this battle the 15th lost 252 men killed and wounded.

It was in the advance on Corinth, when Colonel Turner, who had been absent on account of severe illness, again assumed command, but was obliged to give it up after the evacuation of that place.

After the evacuation of Corinth, the 15th marched to Grand Junction and Holly Springs, and on the 21st of July arrived at Memphis.

It was here, at Holly Springs (or La Grange) on July 8, 1862, that Fred became ill of typhoid fever. He was hospitalized in Memphis. Soon after, he was sent home to Illinois to recover and was discharged, ending his service with the 15th Illinois Infantry.

Camp Scott Ill
Freeport May 21
AD 1861

Dear Mother,

      I rescieved your letter on Friday night last but have not had time to answer until today. I was very glad [to] here from you and all the rest. It was no news to here that Rome and Lyme had volunteered because I exspected it.[1] I feel sory for Ock and Nancy[2] haveing there things stolen but such things will happen. I recieved a letter from Mary Price[3] yesterday and in closed was one witch you had wrote her and one that Nancy had wrote her to. You all seamed worrid about me but dont abit. I am with a good crowd and enjoy my self good enough. We have a good camp here and plenty to eat and coffee to drink and I am in with as good boy as can be. His name is Charley Champlin and there is a number of boys from Rockford and other Places. I know Johnethan Owen, Alferd Heart and others to numerous to mension. If Rome has not gone a way tell him I am afine and in as good spirets as any man in the regement and am called the best man in the regement at a wrestle. I just wrote Mary answer to her letter. they are all well or was yesterday. I dont [know] but I shall go and see them soon. Nan wrote to Mary that she wrote me at Cairo. I must write to her and I shall write to Frank[4] as soon as I finish this and as I have nothing more to write a bout I will quit. but you need not give yourself any trouble a bout me.
Direct care of Capt M. D. Swift Freeport Ill
from your Son
Fred Kellogg

---

[1] Fred's brothers, Edgar Romeyn Kellogg and Lyman Mack Kellogg.
[2] Brother Oscar Eugene Kellogg and sister Nancy Cornelia Kellogg Hall. Details of robbery are unknown.
[3] Sister Mary, Mrs. Ebenezer Price.
[4] Youngest brother, William Francis Kellogg, age 16, living with their father, Dr. Moses C. Kellogg and step-mother, Mary, near Genoa, Ill. He also spent time in Rockton, Ill. with sister Mary Price and family.

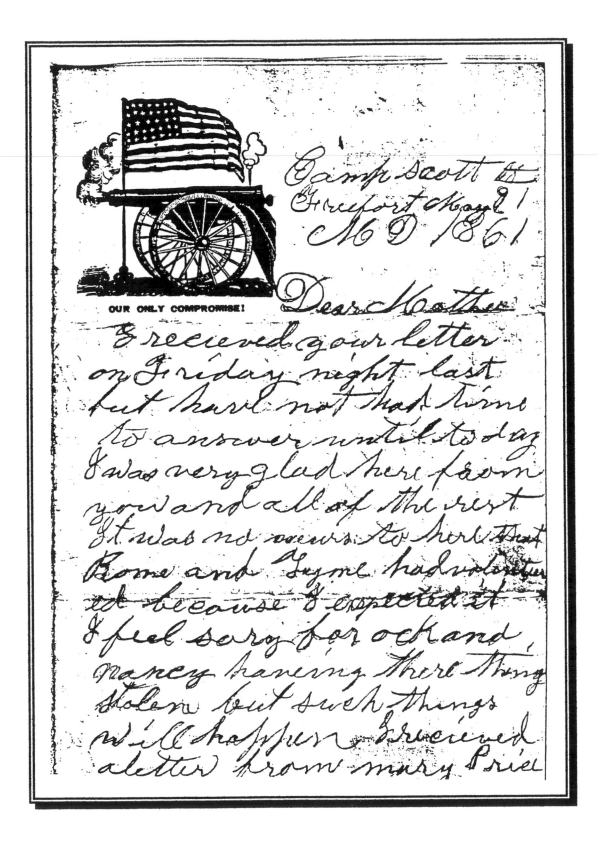

OUR ONLY COMPROMISE!

Camp Scott &
Freeport May 21
MD 1861

Dear Mother

I recieved your letter
on Friday night last
but have not had time
to answer until to day
I was very glad here from
you and all of the rest
It was no news to here that
Rome and Zyme had volunteer
ed because I expected it
I feel sory for och and
Nancy haveing there things
stolen but such things
will happen I recieved
a letter from mary Priel

Mother,

I have made avery nice hart out of red and white clay. I wanted to send it to you.   I had a chance to do so but the fellow went a way when I was on duty. he lives only 4 miles from [you]. Erastus Mead [is] his name. so I will send a little one not so nice.

from
Fred Kellogg

Camp Scott
Freeport

June 13, 1861

Dear Mother

I rescieved your kind letter to day and as I have time to write I will answer it now.   I wrote Rome a few days a go. I hear the boys saying that we will go a way from here next weak the first. it may be so and it may not. you wanted to know how I am aliving. I can [tell] you that I never enjoyed my self better than I have in this place so far and I weigh 15 pouns more than I did when I left Fathers. my weight now is 149 pounds. I am fat and saucy and they all say the best man in the regiment at a wrestle. I think you have no need of fear of Romeyn for he will go it all right. I had a letter from Mary and Frank 10 days a go. they were all well then and I heard from them yesterday. Frank is at Rockton yet. I shall write to Rome to morrow. The number of our regiment is 15 company 6th. I had a letter from Mt. Morriz[5] yesterday. they want I should come out there before I go a way but I am a fraid I cant. I would like to go first rate. I dont know of any thing more to write and so I will stop.

From your son.
FH Kellogg

---

[5] Mt. Morris, Ill.

Mother
I have made a very nice hart out of red and white clay I wanted to send it to you & had a chance to do so but the fellow went a way when I was in duety he lives only 4 miles from Erastus Mead his name so I will send a little one not so nice

from
Fred Kellogg

Alton[6]
June 20, 1861

Dear Mother
        I will now answer your letter. The reason I did not answer before
we was exspected to leave. we are at Alton on the Mississippi River. Our
Camp ground has no name and it dont deserve any. the stumps are as
thick as can be. There is five regiments of us here. There is a good many
secessionest a bout here. one of the guards was fired at night before last.
We heard firing of cannons from down the River last night. We dont
know the cause. We have to be very carefull here. the regiment that was
here had poison fed them. none killed but some hurt. they are now at
Cairo.[7] We dont exspect to have [to] stay here long and we are all eager
to get into action. Albert Kellogg, uncle thans Boy is in the Peoria
regiment the 17th. I see him yesterday. he is a good looking fellow.
When you write direct 15th regiment Capt M D Swift H Company
Illinois volunteers. I ought to write to Rome but I dont know the number
of his regiment or company. We have jest been out drilling to see witch of
the regiments gets their equipments this weak. Cherries are ripe here and
they are aharvesting there wheat. I think that corn is backward. what
I have seen any way. it is very warm here to day. the sweat is adroping
off from my face. We shant live here as well as we did at Freeport. we
dar not buy milk of the people here. Our Company went down to the
river and had a good swim. there is only one of our company sick now.
I must write to Father to day. he was at Freeport twice to see me. he was
there on monday. we started tuesday morning and got here Wednesday
morning. today is Thursday.
                                                    From you son
                                                        Frederic H Kellogg

I will write as often as I can and all I can and to all I can.

---

[6] Alton, Illinois is located across the Mississippi River from St. Louis, Missouri.
[7] Cairo, Illinois was the site of a large military hospital. Later, Fred's father, Moses, served as a
surgeon there.

MISSOURI, 1861

When Fred Kellogg and his companions joined the army, they expected to go east to defend Washington. Fred may have envisioned camping on the shores of the Potomac river in the shade of the capitol building with its half-finished dome, daring the Sons of the South to cross the waters. Perhaps he even anticipated crossing the river himself and routing the Rebels from Richmond, putting a timely end to the conflict.

Therefore, he must surely have been dismayed to find himself on the banks of the mighty Mississippi, looking across to the state of Missouri. Who cared about Missouri?

Actually, there was much to care about in Missouri.

The Missouri River, running east across the state, and the Mississippi River, snaking along its eastern border, were vital for transporting troops and supplies. Both Federal and Confederate forces were determined to control these waterways. Iron and other minerals abundant in the southeastern corner of the state were needed by both sides. An United States Army arsenal was situated in St. Louis. The Confederacy States coveted the arsenal, but President Lincoln and Union Generals demanded it remain in Union hands.

Fighting in Missouri had begun seven years before Lincoln declared war. Planters had moved to Missouri, bringing their slaves to toil in the fields. When the Kansas/Nebraska Act passed in 1854, their right to own slaves was in jeopardy. Only the success of the Confederacy could preserve their way of life.

Others, Union men to the core, had come from New England, Ohio and Illinois. They were adamant about Missouri's loyalties going with the North.

Missouri "Border Ruffians" rode into Kansas to influence the soon-to-be state's politics. Riders from Kansas retaliated. Pro-slavery Missouri militia battled New England abolitionists. Indians fought with the Rebel forces. Home guards tried to keep outlaws at bay. Slaves struggled to find their way out of the clutches of their masters.

Had he known the confusion, frustration and devastation of all these warring factions, Fred Kellogg may well have been more than dismayed.

Alton Camp Pope
July 1 th   1861

Dear Mother

I just resceived your kind letter and was glad to get it too for it was the first one I have had scence I have been here. You wanted to know how I am Equiped. I have got a good blanket. Charley Champlin has one to and he has got an oilcloth blanket witch does for us both so I thought I would not buy one. We have a fatugue uniform and a dress suit so we are very well off for clothing. We have got tow wollen shirts apiece and drawers too. We only have 560 muskets for our regiment[8] yet they are the old United States musket thow we are to have the enfield rifle soon for the whole brigade. as for the living part I think that [we] live very well. the peopple fetch in cherrie pies and green apple pies and ripe apples witch we buy and all kinds of garden sence the Colonel gives passes to those whom we buy of to come in the camp. there was one of the privates of the 17th reg drumed out[9] of the camp this morning for stealing 2 dollars of one of his companions and sent home. good enough for him. there is a good many of the boys punished prety hard for geting drunk and fighting and raising the devil generaly.   some I feel sory for and some I dont. Wrote to Rome the other day and yesterday I wrote to Mary Price.

Albert Kellogg is sick with the mesels. I think that he is a very fine boy. Well mother I [dont] know of anything more to write about, so I will quit.

Give my [*word omitted*] to all the good looking girls any how.

From your son
Frederic H Kellogg

You may tell Nanie I have [not] for got her if I did answer her letter.

---

[8] A regiment is composed of approximately one thousand men.

[9] A ceremony in which dishonorably discharged men were marched past a formation of their comrades to the dire drum beat known as the Rogue's March.

Map 1

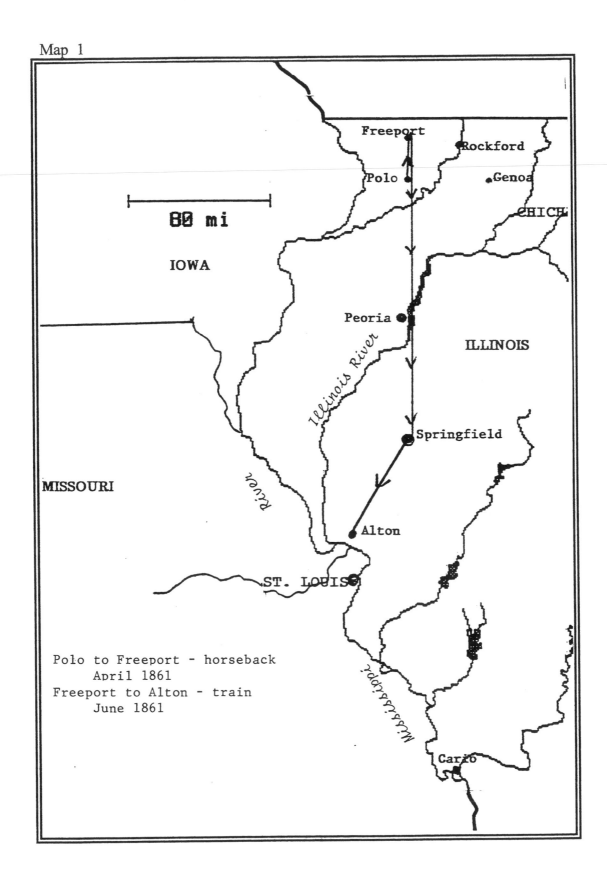

Alton Camp Pope
July 5th 1861

Mother

As all of the boys are awriting I thought that I would write a few lines to you. We held a selabration in the fore noon yesterday and in the after noon the Colonel gave us liberty to go where we had a mind to go. the most of us went down to Alton witch is about 3 miles from camp. I should think there was 3000 of us. we all came back to camp at sundown they made things rattle while they were down there.

Our Colonel started for Washington last night. he is agoing to try and get this regiment sent to virginnia. I hope he will for we have been here long enough. there is some nice orchards here. Well it is a prety nice country a round here. This fore noon our 2d lieut took us out to drill and then he took [us] out in the woods and let us drill in the shade for 2 hours. I like such drills my self for I always did like [to] sit in the shade. There is not much [to] write a bout now. I have heard nothing from any of our [family] but you cience I have been here. I suppose they are all well. I know I am any how. I would like to here from Rome but if he dont want to write he need not. I shant cry a darn bit. I have wrote 2 letters to him and have had none cience. I have wrote to Mary Price and had no answer either. they may go to hell. I shant [write] any more to them till I get one from them. I see Mrs. Shores from Rockton the morning I left freeport. she said that Mary was complaining that I did not write. I [wrote] her four letters and got two from her. it is all right. Our boys are most all well. there is a few sick.

I will have to close for diner is ready. I had a letter from Macks[10] folks the other day. they are all well. there was one of our reg drumed out of camp day before yesterday for bad conduct. there is a good many gets in the guard house. I never was yet nor I never was away at roll call nor I never was spoken to yet for not doing right. Give my best respects to all who deserve them.

from your affectionate son
Fred H Kellogg

---

[10] The Mack family is mentioned several times. Possibly they were the ones living in Mt. Morris, Ill.

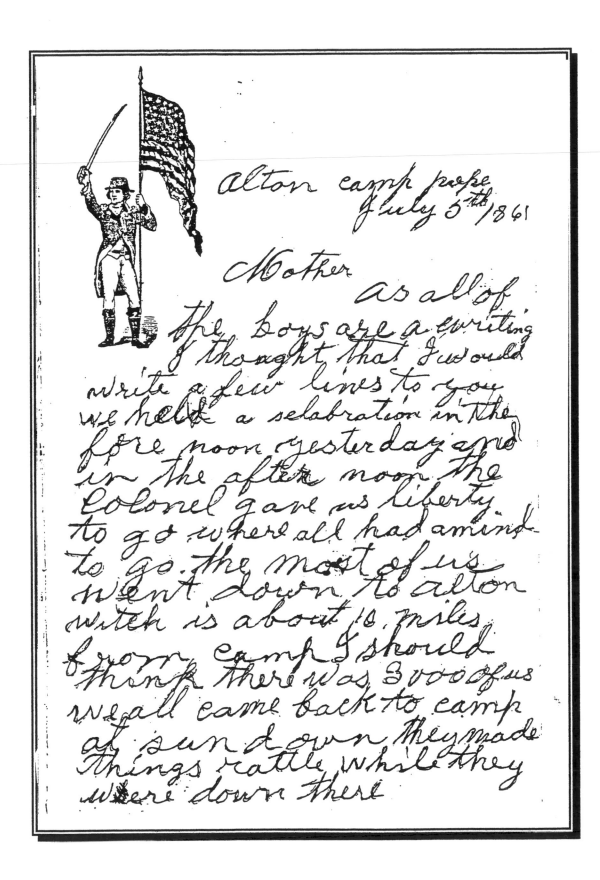

alton camp pope
July 5th /861

Mother
    as all of
the boys are a writing
I thought that I would
write a few lines to you
we held a selabration in the
fore noon yesterday and
in the after noon the
Colonel gave us liberty
to go where all had a mind
to go. the most of us
went down to alton
witch is about 15 miles
from camp I should
think there was 3000 of us
we all came back to camp
at sun down they made
things rattle while they
were down there

in lurning over the paper I made a misstak and commenced on the wrong
one

Alton Camp Pope
July 10th 1861

Dear Mother

I rescieved yours of the seventh today and was glad to hear from
you and I am glad to hear that Rome[11] has got an office for I think he
will perform the duties right. he has not wrote to me yet. it may be that
he has not rescieved my letters. if he has not it is strange. I have had no
letters only from you and one from Lydia Mack. You wanted to know if
we had religious service. on the sabbath we all go that is a mind to go in
the fore noon down to alton. in the after noon we have preaching here on
the campground. Our Chaplin is a very smart man and a good one. We
have had 5 dollars and 10 cents for pay while in the States service.
I lent $3.60 to some of the boys that did not join until we were sworn in
the u. s. service. I have got some paper and 8 postage stamps and 15 cent
all in money. We will get our pay in about 10 days. I have not entirely
[run] out of [money] yet. I have spent a good deal for papers and novels
for to read. Albert Kellogg has been very sick for nearly three weaks.
he is ageting better now. he is down at alton. he says he has good care
taken of him. there is women who attends to the sick in his company
from Peorie. The 20th reg left here last friday and went to st louis to
guard the arsynal. our reg had the offer but would not take it. I am glad
we did not for we enlisted to fight not to guard but I dont believe we shall
ever get where there is eny fighting thow we may have fighting to do our
selves. There is a good many sick of 17 reg. There is but a few of our reg
that are sick. there is plenty of nice apples brought here in camp.

Give my love to all from your son
Fred H Kellogg

---

[11] Romeyn was serving with the 24th Ohio Volunteer Infantry in West Virginia at this time and
had been promoted to Second Lieutenant

2 fore noon down to alton in
the after noon we have
preaching here on the camp ground
our Chaplin is a very smart
man and a good one.
we have had 5 dollars and 10
cents for pay while in the
states services I lent $3,60 to
some of the boys that did not
join untel we were sworn
in the u.s. service. I have got
some paper and 8 postage stamps
and 15 cent all in money
we will get our pay in about
10 days I have not entirely
out of yet I have spent a
good deal for papers and
novels for to read
Albert Kellogg has been
very sick for nearly three
weaks he is a geting better now
he is down at alton he says
he has good care taken of

Camp Pope Alton
July 17, 1861

Brother Theron
        I rescieved your letter this forenoon and as we dont have to drill
this after noon because it is so warm and I have time I will answer it now.
I was very glad to get your letter for it is but few that I do get. You say
I must write to Romeyn. I have wrote him three letters and have
rescieved none in return. I dont think it is paying buisness to pay postage
on letters and get no answers and I have wrote 3 to Mary and two to
Frank and two to Father and they dont any of them answer. I think when
they hear from me again they will know it. Your advice is very good.
I thank you for it but as to gambling that is not allowed in camp and card
playing is not allowed in our company and I have not played a game of
cards science I enlisted in service nor I dont intend too and so to drinking
liquor I see the affects of that without haveing anything to do with it. the
most of our company went down to the river to day to swim and two of
them got drunk and have caused a grate deal of excitement here this after
noon and some trouble between our Co and Co E and I think there will be
some fighting between them if they [don't] disband. the boys are all
excited. I have been pulled off from my seat 3 times while writing this.
they are all lively fellows and we would fight for one another like
brothers and if Co E dont look out they will find it so. I had a letter from
Nan a few days a go and I answered it. We are all in good health and
geting busy as the devil. The boys are acarriring on so I cant think of
anything more to write so I will stop. My love to all

                                        from your
                                        Brother Fred Kellogg

PROTECT IT!

Camp pope Alton July 17
1861

Brother Theron
I reseieved
your letter this forenoon and
as we dont have to drill
this after noon becaus it is
so warm and I have time
I will answer it now. I wos
very glad to get your letter
for it is but a few that
I do get you say I must
write to Romeyn I have wrote
him three letters and have
reseieved none in return
I dont think it is paying
buisness to pay postage on
letters and get no answers

Mexico Missouri
July 24th 1861

Dear Mother

I rescieved your letter last friday at alton but we were on our rode to st. Charles Mo. We got to St. Charles about 3 oclock saturday morning. sunday after noon we were ordered to strike our tents and march. we got down to the depot and our orders were countermanded and we marched back to our camp ground. we had to start a gain and come to Mexico 100 miles southwest[12] of St. Charles. there was an Ill. reg. here be fore us. they had all the fun. they kill a bout 40 secessionest in this part of the country. none in this place I believe but there is a good many of them here but they dare not say anything. I dont think that we shall stay here long. I hope not. I see in a Mo. paper that our troups got drove back at Mannassas Junction va and good many of them killed and taken prisoners. We had one of our sargents of our company drowned while going from Alton to St. Charles. he was drownd at the mouth of the Mo [Missouri] river jest as our boat had turned up the Mo river. We had gone 60 rods. he fell over board. he kept above water till he came where the two rivers [Missouri River and Mississippi River] meet. Then he [reached] out and the man in the boat tuched his head as he went down the the first time witch was the last. I got a letter from Rome the same time that I got yours. I have not answered it and dont know when I can so when you write to him you tell him that I have had his letter and would have answered it if I could. I only [have] one postage stamp[13] and canot send but one letter and you are the first Mother. you will not here from me as often as you have unless we leave here for there is no mail and we are in the enemys country now. but I will write to you as often as I can. there is but half of our regiment here but we exspect them all here tonight. I think that our regiment will be divided up in small parties and then go ascouting but I dont know. you will know more of me from the papers[14] than I shall know myself.

---

[12] Mexico is located northwest of St.Charles, not southwest as Fred wrote.

[13] Shortage of stamps and writing materials was universal and is often mentioned in Fred's letters.

[14] Thanks to the telegraph and a new invention called "shorthand writing" the folks on the homefront were extremely well informed of the activities of their men at war. Every newspaper had a reporter following his hometown unit, often a local man who had known each soldier from childhood. His telegraphed reports were published before letters could reach home.

The New-York Times.

VOL. XIII—NO. 3794.　　　　　NEW-YORK, FRIDAY, NOVEMBER 20, 1863.　　　　　PRICE THREE CENTS.

IMPORTANT FROM EAST TENNESSEE

The Rebels Advancing upon Knoxville.

THE PLACE COMPLETELY INVESTED.

HEAVY SKIRMISHING YESTERDAY.

The Position Very Strongly Fortified.

THE REBEL FORCES UNDER LONGSTREET.

Knoxville, Thursday, Nov. 17.

The enemy began skirmishing from their position on Kingston Road, at 10 this morning. Our advance alone, composed wholly of mounted infantry and cavalry, occupied the position, under command of Gen. Sanders, and each man fought like a veteran.

At noon the enemy opened with artillery at short range, their battery protected by a large house. Benjamin's battery was the only one which replied, occupying the chief fortification, half a mile in front of and to the right of the town. A desperate charge was made by the enemy about 3 P. M. Our men were protected by a barricade on the crest of the hill. Gen. Sanders was severely wounded, and was borne from the field.

We yielded the position, and fell back about a third of a mile to a stronger one. We have lost about one hundred, one quarter of whom were killed. The enemy had completely invested the place, but Gen. Burnside will defend it to the last man, and it is believed successfully. The troops are in the best spirits. Every important point is fortified, and confidence prevails that we shall whip the enemy out.

A MORE DETAILED ACCOUNT.

Knoxville, Tenn., Tuesday, Nov. 17.

Gen. Longstreet, after crossing the Tennessee on Saturday morning, 14th inst., was attacked in the afternoon by Gen. Burnside, who drove the advance guard back to within a mile of the river's edge by nightfall.

LATE FROM CHATTANOOGA.

Correspondence of the New-York Times.

Chattanooga, Monday, Nov. 16, 1863.

REPORTS FROM REBEL SOURCES.

Atlanta, Friday, Nov. 13.

THE ARMY OF THE POTOMAC.

Cavalry Skirmishes at Germantown Ford—Great Scarcity of Contrabands—The Army Doing Well Off.

Washington, Thursday, Nov. 19.

THE HEROES OF JULY.

A Solemn and Imposing Event.

Dedication of the National Cemetery at Gettysburgh.

IMMENSE NUMBERS OF VISITORS.

Oration by Hon. Edward Everett—Speeches of President Lincoln, Mr. Seward and Governor Seymour.

THE PROGRAMME SUCCESSFULLY CARRIED OUT

PRESIDENT LINCOLN'S ADDRESS.

Fourscore and seven years ago our Fathers brought forth upon this Continent a new nation, conceived in liberty and dedicated to the proposition that all men are created equal. [Applause.] Now we are engaged in a great civil war, testing whether that nation, or any nation so conceived and so dedicated, can long endure. We are met on a great battle-field of that war. We are met to dedicate a portion of it as the final resting-place of those who here gave their lives that that nation might live. It is altogether fitting and proper that we should do this. But in a larger sense we cannot dedicate, we cannot consecrate, we cannot hallow this ground. The brave men, living and dead, who struggled here have consecrated it far above our power to add or detract. [Applause.] The world will little note nor long remember, what we say here, but it can never forget what they did here. [Applause.] It is for us, the living, rather to be dedicated here to the refinished work that they have thus so far nobly carried on. [Applause.] It is rather for us to be here dedicated to the great task remaining before us that from these honored dead we take increased devotion to that cause for which they here gave the last full measure of devotion; that we here highly resolve that the dead shall not have died in vain. [applause] that the Nation shall under God have a new birth of freedom, and that Government of the people, for the people and by the people, shall not perish from the earth. [Long continued applause.]

Three cheers were then given for the President and the Governor of the States.

GOV. SEYMOUR'S SPEECH.

GREAT BRITAIN AND AMERICA.

Welcome to Rev. Henry Ward Beecher.

Demonstration at the Brooklyn Academy of Music.

A GREAT SPEECH:

His Impressions of British Feeling Toward America.

An immense audience assembled at the Academy of Music, Brooklyn, last evening, to welcome and hear the Rev. Henry Ward Beecher. The meeting was under the auspices of the War Fund Committee, the entire proceeds to be devoted to the Sanitary Commission. Rev. Dr. Storrs made an eloquent address of welcome to Mr. Beecher, who, on his appearance, was most enthusiastically greeted. When quiet was restored Mr. Beecher spoke as follows:

MR. BEECHER'S ADDRESS.

DEPARTMENT OF THE GULF.

ARRIVAL OF THE CREOLE FROM NEW-ORLEANS.

The Attack upon Gen. Washburn's Column.

Our Entire Loss Six Hundred and Seventy-seven.

The steamship Creole, Capt. Thompson, arrived yesterday morning from New-Orleans, bringing dates to the 10th inst.

THE DELAWARE ELECTION.

The Union Ticket Overwhelmingly Successful—Smithers, for Congress, Walked the Course.

Wilmington, Thursday, Nov. 19.

I would like to hear from you once in a while but I [dont] know as your letters would come to me and I dont [know] as you will get this. We are in a good country but water is scarce here. We are all well and all are crazy to know the truth of the battle in Virginnia. if you write to me direct 15 reg Co H. Illinois volenteers Missouri. well I cant think of anything more to write so I will quit. give my love to all.

from you son
Frederic H Kellogg

I got a letter from Theron and one from Nan while at Alton and answered them but I did not know then that we where agoing to leave alton so soon.

Map 2

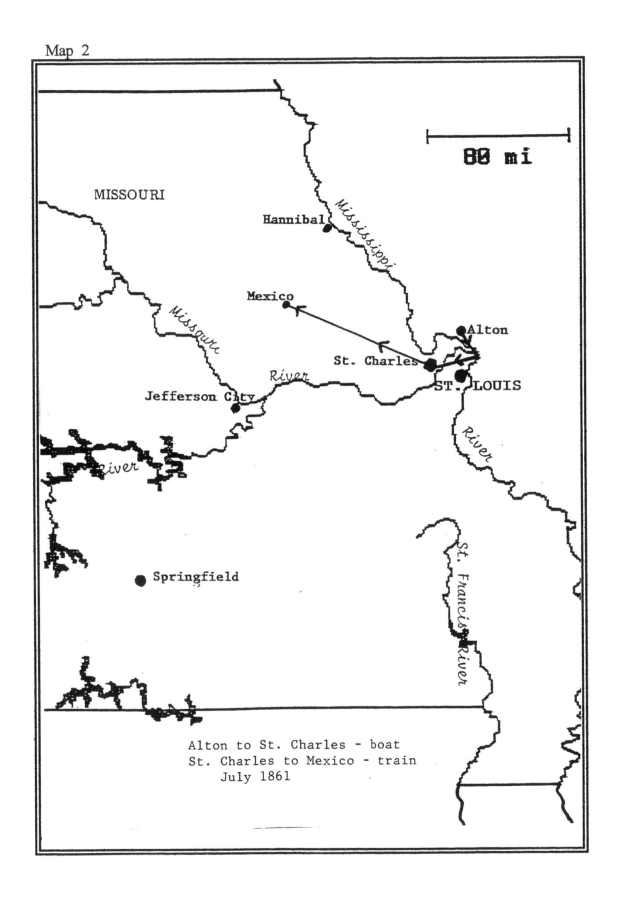

Mexico
July 28th 1861

Dear Mother

As to day is sunday and one of the boys says he will pay the postage on all the letters that I want to write to my mother I will write you a few lines and tell you what I had for breakfast. I took some flour, warm water and salt and made some pan cakes. we had fresh beaf and I had a good meal. we have had nothing to eat cience we left Alton but hard bread[15] and bacon. the boys took a barl of the bread last night and drumb them out of camp with the rouge march and throwed them a way[16]. there is one company of sappers and miners[17] here, one Co of flying artilery, six Co of cavalry and the 21th reg of Illinois boys and our bully 15th. Heckers Chicago duch regiment left here day before yesterday. We shall leave here this after noon for another campground a bout 3 miles from here. company A of our reg is out ascouting now. they went thursday. I wrote to Rome yesterday and to Macks folks. I have just been and heard some singing by some slaves that come into camp. I believe it is natural for the Black devils to sing. the boys have fun with them. you can send your letters to me but you will have to direct Co H. 15 reg. Ill Vol. Mo. by St louis and then I will get them. when you write to Frank tell him not to enlist for he is not old enough, for it is a bad place for boys. I liked soldering while at Freeport and Alton but here I dont like it none of the best but I supppose it will be better as soon as we get settled a gain. we have a little more privilages here than we did at Alton for we can go a mile from camp without a pass. We have not drilled any for two weaks. I am agetting fat and lazy. I weigh 150 pounds and am in good health and as strong as a horse. One of the sappers died friday. the most of the boys are in good health and all are anxious to get into a fight. There is now plenty of good sugar coated hams here for us soldiers and good flour. We have rice and beans, tea and coffee too. I don't think we shall starve. I have not heard anything from Frank or Mary Price yet. I am a lying on my belly while writing this for this is the only way we have to write. Well I have wrote all I can think of to write so I will stop. give my best respects to the folks.

from your loveing Son.
Frederic H. Kellogg

---

[15] A cracker commonly known as hardtack. Early in the war it was distasteful to the soldiers who were accustomed to fresh bread. Later on, they would learn to scrape away the worms and mold, and to fry it or boil it, anything to make it edible.

[16] What a droll statement! The activity itself must have been hilarious!

[17] Sappers are explosive experts. Miners laid explosive mines in roadways and fields to deter the enemy.

"we have had nothing to eat cience we left Alton but hard bread. the boys took a barl of the bread last night and drumb them out of camp with the rouge march and throwed them a way"

KELLY MAGLADRY-TOTEN 96

Jefferson Barracks[18] Mo.
Aug 6th, 1861

Dear Mother,

I will try and let you know a little of what I have been doing cience I last wrote you from Mexico, Mo. last sunday the 4th day of Aug we left Mexico for hannibal sixty miles distance a foot. it was awfull warm. we had no trouble as was exspected. We see some 4 or 5 secessionest on horses but they run for the woods. the left wing of our Reg. and 2 Co.s of the 21th Ill. Reg. and 2 peices of artilery, 300 cavalry that is all there was of us but I think the rebles might as well run. We were told all the way through that we would be attacked 5 miles a head but we had no such good luck as to be attacked. We arrived at hannibal wednesday the 7th at 11 o clock. orders arrived there 2 hours before us so we went right on the boat and arrived here yesterday at noon. how soon we shall leave here I dont know but we dont exspect to stay here long. the right wing of our reg is or was at fulton 25 miles south of mexico. we shall go to pilot knob[19] as soon as our reg gets to gether a gain. We exspect to anyway. it is only 10 miles from here to st louis. the boys stood there march very well. we marched nights very well but sunday we crost a prairie 8 miles and it [was the] warmest day I ever saw I think and no wind stiring. there was 3 or 4 of the boys droped down. one came very near dieing. We are right on the bank of the Mississippi. a very prety place but what I have seen of Missouri I dont like. there some places that I like but as a general thing it is damb miserable State. I guess if all of the southern states are no better than this I dont think they are worth fighting for. there is a bout 500 of the boys in the river now. We are to have our rifles today. the boys are all in good spiretes. some say that we will go to Birds point. When you write direct Co H, 15 reg. Ill. vol. Missouri via St louis. I had a letter from Frank and Father while at Mexico. Frank is at Fathers now.   Well Mother this all the paper that I can get so I cant write anymore. give my love to all. I got a letter from you and Theron while at Mexico. tell Theron I will answer his as soon as I can but when that will be I dont know. so good by

from your son
F. H. Kellogg.

[18] A historic military supply post, established in 1826.
[19] Pilot Knob is near Ironton in the mining district south of St. Louis. Bird's Point is a strategic lookout on the Mississippi River, across the river from Cairo, Illinois.

Map 3

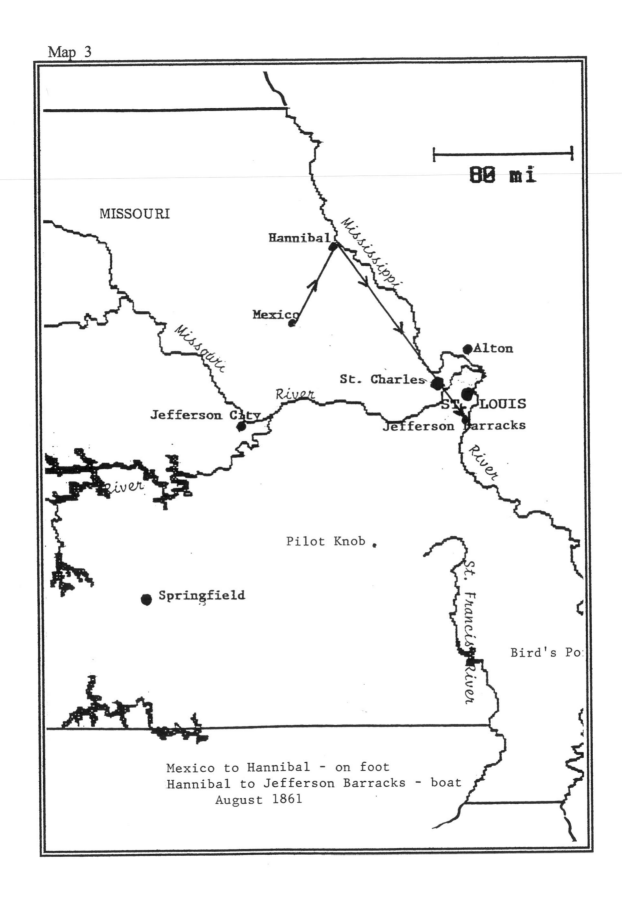

MISSOURI

Hannibal

Mississippi

Mexico

Alton

St. Charles

ST. LOUIS

Jefferson City

Jefferson Barracks

River

Pilot Knob

St. Francis River

Springfield

Bird's Po

Mexico to Hannibal - on foot
Hannibal to Jefferson Barracks - boat
August 1861

80 mi

Rolla Missouri
Camp Rolla Aug 15th 1861

Dear Mother

We are now 110 miles southwest of St. louis. I rescieved your letter last monday night but I have not had time to write you before. I got one from Nan and one from Father and Frank all at the same time. I answered Nannies and Fathers while at the Barraks. I had not had them mailed ten minutes when we were ordered to get ready for a march. We left on tuesday and got here last night. We went to St. louis on the boat and there took the cars for this place. we are camped a mile and a half from Rolla in the woods or barons. there is four reg.s here and four more to come from Jefferson Barracks and General Seigles[20] will be here to morrow with what soldiers he has left. I suppose you have heard a bout the battle and gen Lyon's deth. I have seen a number that was in the Battle. they all say that there was from 4,000 to 8,000 of the rebles killed, and 600 killed and 200 wounded of our men. We had 7,000 engaged in the Battle and there was 21,000 of the rebles in arms and they had 8000 more that had no arms. I here a good many differnt storys about there taken prisoners on both sides but we shall know all a bout it soon for Siegles will be here soon. McCullough[21] says he will take Rolla and then St. louis. we do exspect to be attacked here but they will get hell when they make the attack. there is 5,000 rebles 50 miles southeast of here and McCullough is between here and springfield with over 90,000. McCullough says our men killed man for man and that they fought like devils. We got ten dollars pay to day. I will get my likness taken[22] tomorrow and send it to you. that is if I can get to town. Nannie sent me six postage stamps and Father sent me 12. the sight of them did not make me mad. I ought to write to Theron and will soon. When we left Freeport I weighed 149 1/2 pounds now I weigh 135. I am well but not so fat as I was. it is a geting dark so I will have to stop writing.

From your affectionate son
F. H. Kellogg

---

[20] Franz Sigel was a Colonel at the time, but promoted soon after.
[21] Confederate General Ben McCulloch.
[22] Meaning, "have a photograph made."

THE BATTLE OF WILSON'S CREEK

In February of 1861, a rough, red-bearded little man wearing a worn-out captain's uniform arrived in St. Louis from Ft. Riley with his company of weather-beaten regulars. Nathaniel Lyon had volunteered to organize and train troops to serve the Union. Twenty years out of West Point and a rabid abolitionist, Lyon had a deep-seated hatred for the Missouri Border Ruffians. He recognized the disastrous consequences should the United States arsenal at St. Louis be captured by the Southern supporters, and took it upon himself to move arms and ammunition to safety in Illinois and to reinforce the guard at the arsenal.

Pro-Confederate Governor Claibourne Jackson tried to take the arsenal in May 1861. Failing, he retreated to southwestern Missouri accompanied by former Governor Sterling Price and the new Missouri State Guard. They joined General Ben McCulloch and his 12,000 men. Lyon, commissioned Brigadier General at the opening of the war, pursued them, leading 5,000 Union soldiers.

Lyon defeated a Confederate unit near Springfield on August 2, 1861, but realized he was outnumbered. Unwilling to give up, he chose his ground carefully, thoroughly instructed his commanders and launched a two-pronged surprise attack on August 10th. The enemy rallied swiftly, driving back the Yanks and securing the eastern side of Wilson's Creek. Colonel Franz Sigel led his St. Louis German-American volunteers in a flanking attack. He might well have won the day had it not been for confusion over who was friend and who was foe. Neither army was equipped with standard uniforms. The Texicans wore civilian clothes. Both sides were augmented with small groups of volunteers from far-flung places, wearing the colors of their choice. Sigel allowed a group of gray-clad men to come too close to his line. Sigel assumed the men were a Company from Iowa, assigned to him. Instead, they were Confederate. The rebels opened fire, causing a panic filled retreat. Now the rebels advanced in full strength against Lyon, defeating him on a ridge that came to be called Bloody Hill. Nathaniel Lyon was killed, the first general officer to fall in the war.

Union casualties totaled 1317, the Rebels, 1230, not nearly as many as indicated by rumors received by Fred and his companions.

Rolla Missouri
Aug   Sunday the 20, 1861

Dear Mother
        I will try and write you a few lines to let you know how I am.
        I got a letter from Nan last night and it was a good one too. I have
got my picture taken. I send it to you in this. it is a good likeness of me
for there is nothing wright or wrong. the hat is wrong side to.[23]   I did
not notice it but it is all right. There is nothing new to write a bout. Seigle
has got here with his men. they look hard dirty Raged and tired. they all
say that we had only 400 killed and 600 wounded. 80 to 100 taken
prisoners and that the rebles had from 4 to 5000 killed and we got 65 of
them prisoners and our men burnt their bagage and wagons and made
good their retreat for Rolla but Gen Lyons is no more. They all say that
McCullough is a gentleman and a man of honor.[24]
I have just wrote to Nan and I am tired of writing so I will wind up and
I want to write to Joel Carle and there is nothing to write about.
all are well and good spirits

                                        from your Son
                                            Frederic H Kellogg

Give my love to all of the folks.

---

[23] Photography was brand new. Fred did not realize the image was in reverse, putting his hat on
the "wrong" side.
[24] An amazing statement about a confederate officer! Did he mean to write "not" a gentleman?
Or was it meant as a satirical remark, an attempt at humor regarding a man who had badly
defeated the Union troops? Could they have actually admired the demeanor of the man, even if he
was the enemy? If so, few Union soldiers agreed.

Map 4

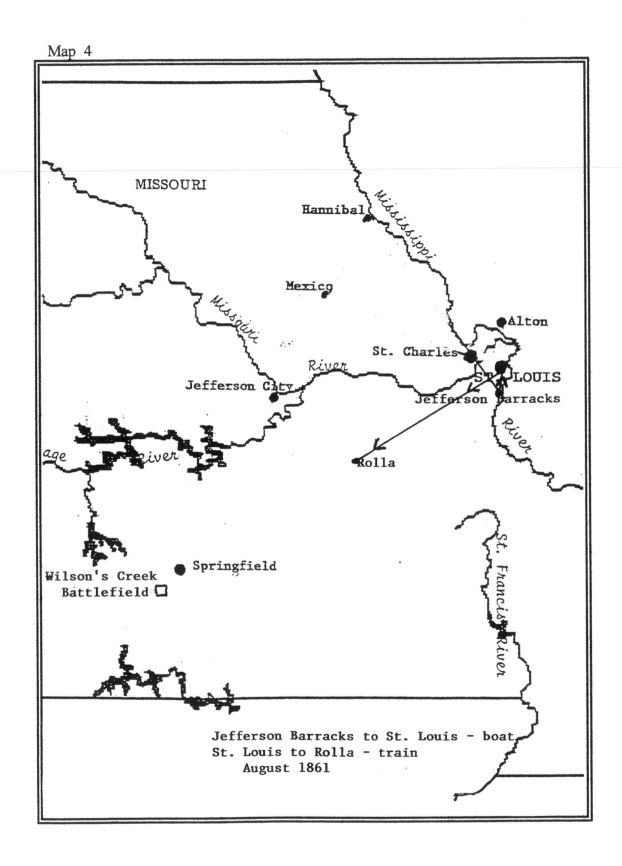

MISSOURI

Hannibal

Mississippi

Mexico

Alton

Missouri

St. Charles

River

ST. LOUIS

Jefferson City

Jefferson Barracks

River

Rolla

age   River

St. Francis River

Springfield

Wilson's Creek
Battlefield ▢

Jefferson Barracks to St. Louis - boat
St. Louis to Rolla - train
August 1861

Camp Rolla
Aug 28th 1861

Dear Mother

I will try and write you a few lines to let you know how I am and why I did not write before. I have been quit sick and so I did not write and I am not well yet though I am geting better slow. I was taken with the diarie and I had some feaver. I am very weak yet but dont you give your self any trouble a bout me for if I was very sick I should go to fathers. I could go there in 30 hours. I had a letter from Martha and Clark[25] a few days a go and one from Mary Price and I have not answered them yet. I shall try and answer them tomorrow and I ought write to Frank, Father and Nancy too and several others. there is nothing new to write about here. The scouts report McCullough moveing from Springfield to this place. We are ready for him. We have four 32 pounders[26] mounted here and we are clearing off the ground here so as to have a fair sweep at them when they do come. when you write a gain tell me where Romeyn is so I can write to him. we have got a very good campground here and water plenty only a half mile from camp. there is 10 or 12000 soldiers here. I believe that I wrote you we had gotten 10 dollars pay when I last wrote you. We exspect to get all of our pay the last of this month or the first of next. if we do I will send you 10 dollars. there is a good many sick here now. there has been only one deth from sickness in our regiment and he was left at Jefferson Barracks sick and cience died. Our first Lieut went home day before yesterday sick. he was very sick too.   cience I have been writing here there has been as many as a dozen come in and say Fred how do you feel. I tell them I feel better and then they say you look darn peaked. I suppose I do. My head aches very hard now so I will close. Give my love to all. I will write again soon but dont you worrie a bout me.

From your affectionate son

Frederic H. Kellogg

---

[25] Oldest sister and her husband Clark Sexton.
[26] Cannon.

Camp Rolla aug 28th 1861

Dear Mother

I will try and
write you a few lines to let you
know how I am and why I did
not write before I have been
quit sick and so I did not
write and I am not well yet
though I am geting better slow
I was taken with the diarie and
I had some feaver. I am very
weak yet but dont you give
your self any trouble a bout
me for if I was very sick I
should go to Fathers, I could
go there in 30 hours I had a
letter from Martha and Clark
a few days a go and one from
Mary Price and I have not
answered them yet

Camp Rolla
Sept 6th 1861

Dear Mother

I rescieved your kind letter a few days a go but I have been unwell for some time so I did not write til I got well a gain. I am well now and on duty to day acarriring water   I rescieved a letter from Nan a day or two ago. I answered it yesterday. We are aliving now first rate. we had a large box of cakes and preserves and good Bread from Polo and Asa Kayce a boy that tents with me he got a large fruit cake and as good a one as I ever see. I had my share of it. We are having good times here now. We are amaking fortifications and have got 4 32 pounders mounted and ready for what ever is needed of them. You say that you dont think that my likeness looks like me. I will have another one taken when I can with my cap on. I think it will be beter. I have not heard from Father or Frank cience I came here.   I shall write to Frank to day. there is ten men out of each company aworking on the fortifications. We had out a picket guard last [night] to guard the railroad. some of the boys went 97 miles from here on the cars and came back this morning. about 500 men of the 14th Ill. reg. went out from [here] last sunday about ten miles where there was a bout 6 or 700 rebles and attacked them but the rebles would not stand fire. we had two men wounded. we got two men of the rebles prisoner and supposed to have killed a number with our cannon. all is quit here now.   there was 600 of cavalry came in here last night from St. louis. I see that the papers report Jef Davis[27] as being dead but we dont believe it here. When you write tell [me] where Rome is if you know so I can write to him. I got a letter from Macks folks last night. they are all well. Your letter left there on the 27th and I got it on the 29th. I have not been out of camp but once cience we came here but I am agoing a round some now that I am well. there is plenty of fruit here and as nice peaches as I ever see and some very good apples. there is four of our Co sick now. I believe I wrote all so I will stop.

from your loving Son.
Frederic H. Kellogg

---

[27] Jefferson Davis, President of the Confederate States of America.

the rebles would not stand
fire we had two men wounded
we got two men of the rebles prisioners
and supposed to have killed a number
with our cannon. all is quiet here
now. there was 600 of cavalry
came in here last night from
St louis. I see that the papers report
Jef Davis as being dead but we dont
believe it here when you write tell
where Rome is if you knows o I can
write to him - I got a letter from
Macks folks last night they are
all well. your letter left there on
the 27th and I got it on the 29th.
I have not been out of camp but once
exence we came here. but I am a
going a round some now that
I am well. there is plenty of fruit
here and as nice peaches as I ever
See and some very good apples.
there is four of our co sick now

Camp Rolla
Sept 14th 1861

Dear Mother

I will try and write you a few lines as I have nothing ealse to do. all is quite here at present excepting that the boys are acleaning up now for sunday. I rescieved a letter from Theron this morning. I would answer it but he said he was agoing to Columbus this weak so I thought I would answer it to you. there was a funeral here last sunday and another to day both from Co K. there is a good deal of sickness here at present. there is four of our Co sick now though not dangerous. I have got over my sickness and now all right a gain. I was sick for a bout 3 weeks not so I could get a bout. there is no drilling here now and has not been any for some time. We are aliving now on the top shelf. good bread, sugar coated hams, potatoes, and fresh beaf every other day and we buy butter for 15 cents a pound. to day I bought some honey. it was nice and good peaches are only 20 cents a bushel and by going out in the country one can get them for nothing. there was a little skirmishing the other day betwene the home guards and the rebles a bout 20 miles from here. the home guards killed 30 of the rebles and took 7 prisoner and some 20 or 30 horses. the rebles then left.

It has been raining here for 3 days but this after noon it is very pleasant and looks as if it had cleared off. I see that Gen. Rosencrace has drove Floyed from his camp.[28] Charley or I buy a paper every day so we get all the news. I had a letter from Nancy the other day. she is well. I have not heard from Mary Price latly nor from Frank. I esxpect a letter from Frank to night. there is a grate many sick in the 111th Ill. reg. hospital. I guess our reg. is in the best health of any here. Father wrote me in his last that he thought some of going in John Farnsworths[29] cavalry reg. as surgeon. if he does and they come to St louis Charley and I will try and get trancefered into that reg. if we can. our troups are ageting down the river slow but shure.

---

[28] This is probably a reference to a campaign in the Kanawha Valley in West Virginia. General William S. Rosecrans, an Ohio native, had not yet reached enough prominence to be mentioned in historic reports of the battle. However, brother Romeyn was under Rosecrans command. Therefore, Fred undoubtedly read the newspaper details very carefully, knowing his mother was doing the same. The brief statement shows none of the pride and concern he must have felt for his brother.

[29] John F. Farnsworth, an Illinois man who had charge of the 8th Illinois Cavalry.

Camp Rolla sept. 14th
1861

Dear Mother

I will try and
write you a few lines as I have
nothing ealse to do. all is
quite here at presant excepting
that the boys are a cleaning up
now for sunday I receieved
a letter from Theron this morning
I would answer it but said he
was a going to columbus this weak
so I thought I would answer it to
you. there was a funeral here last
sunday and another to day fouth
from Co. K. there is a good deal
of sickness here at presant there
is four of our co. sick now.
though not dangerous I have

Sunday the 15th   I have jest come from meeting and we had a good surmon. We got a new cap and a large bleu over coat and a rubber blanket to day and a new pare of shoes and stockings and we exspect to have a new uniform soon but as to geting our pay we cant tell any a bout that. we had ten dollars when we first came here witch Freemont[30] firnished himself. I have got 65 cents left yet.

I did not get a letter from Frank last night for the mail did not come in from St louis. I see in last nights paper that they were a fighting in the northwest part of the State but I suppose you hear the news as soon as we do here. One Co of each reg. here went out from here some 20 miles and we heard this morning they had got 30 head of cattle, ten negroes and a lot of mules and wagons.

it looks now as if we were agoing to have another rainy night and I guess we will. the boys are all buisy amarking their own coats and rubber blankets. all is quite here to day.

> from your son
> Frederic. H. Kellogg

---

[30] John Charles Fremont, the "Path Finder" explorer (1840's), Senator, 1856 Presidential candidate. While in charge of U.S. Department of Works, he was removed from office because he ordered the confiscation of rebel property including slaves. At the time this letter was written, he held the rank of U.S. Army Major General and had been sent to Missouri by President Lincoln to "take hold of the west."

got over my sickness and now all right a gain. I was sick for a bout 3 weaks not so but I could get a bout. there is no drilling here now and has not been any for some time. We are a living now on the top shelf good bread sugar coated hams potatoes. and fresh beaf every other day and we buy butter for 15 cents a pound to day. I bought some honey it was nice and good peaches are only 20 cents a bushel. and by going out in the country, one can get them for nothing. there was a little skirmishing the other day betwene the home guards and the rebles a bout 20 miles from here the home guards killed 3 of the rebles and took 7 prisoner and some 20 or 30 horses the rebles then left

Rolla   Sept 30th 1861

Dear Mother,

I will try and write you a few lines to let you know we have had a
march saturday last. We started west at four oclock in the after noon.
We went 6 miles. three or four wagons were upset. our tung and reach
[were] broken so that we did not start on sunday until ten oclock and
when we got on the banks of the Gasconade river we got orders to come
back to Rolla and take cars. we got back to our old campground at dark
last night. we are now a waiting for cars to come to take us a way but
where to I dont know. there was 3 regs of us a going out west and all
ordered back. one reg. left here on the cars last night. it is the worst
county here I ever see. I suppose you know that we are in the country of
the Ozark Mountains and it is an awful mountainous country too.
I suppose you have heard of the 14th Ill reg having a smash up on the cars
on their way from here to Jefferson City. If Frank is not at Rockton when
you get this[31] I would like to have you write to him and tell him I would
write to him and Father but I have no money nor postage stamps so I cant
write any more letters untill we get our pay witch we ought to have soon
and when you write to Nancy tell her I have rescieved a letter from her
and that I can not answer until I get some money. within one hour after
we got in camp last night there was as many as 50 hogs killed. our
colonel says that the boys will have to pay for them but we thought that a
little fresh pork would eat good and so it did. When you write me tell me
if Theron is Captain of a Company.[32]   Direct your letter to St louis and
I will get it. Tell Mary if she wants a nice name for her babe to name it
Lydia or Maria or Ida. a name that is short and sweet. Tell Lyme to be
a good boy and keep his nose clean. tell Ebb I have seen enough of
Missouri to think it is damb poor State and if the rebles can live here they
had ought to let them alone for White men cant do it. Well I dont know
of any thing more to write so I will stop. I will direct this to Mary so if
you are not there she can read it. from your loving son
                                                        Fred Kellogg

---

[31] At this time, Fred's mother, Elizabeth, was in Rockton, Illinois with her daughter Mary (Price)
who was expecting a baby. Lyme was Mary's small son, named for his Uncle Lyman Kellogg.
Ebb was her husband, Ebenezer Price.
[32] Theron was not in service. This remark was apparently sarcasm. Big brother must have had
advice that Fred did not appreciate.

postage stamps so I
cant write any more
letters untill we get
our pay writch we
ought to have soon,
and when you write
to nancy tell her I have
received tow letters from
her and that I can not
answer until I get some
money, within one hour
after we got in camp last
night there was as many
as 5 0 hogs killed our
colonel says that the boys
will have to pay for them
but we thought that a little
fresh pork would eat good
and so it did, when man
write me, tell me if Theron
is Captain of a company
Direct your letter to St louis

Direct to St louis, Mo Co H   15 reg. Ill.Vol.

Tipton Missouri
Oct 7th 1861

Sister Mary,

     I will try and write you a few lines to let you know where and how I am. we are at Tipton Mo. 40 miles west of Jefferson City. we arrived here last night at 12 o clock. We left Rolla last Friday night in open cars and arrived at Jefferson City the next morning. we had a nice time for it rained all of the way and rained all day Saturday. we were in Jefferson City until yesterday noon (Sunday) when we left for this place. there is a good many soldiers here to night and there is 90 pieces of cannon here and two regiment of cavalry and Tottons[33] regiment of artilery will be here to night, but how many regiment of infantry I dont know. this place is all most disserted for they were most all secessionest. there was a Co. of them raised in this place. I saw some fellows that belong to the Northwestern rifle regiment[34] one of the same Co. that Louis Chestain is in. he said that Lew was well and all right and was cook for the Co. Saturday night our reg. took lodging in the Statehouse at Jefferson City. they say that we are to have our pay before we leave here. if we get it I will send you my likeness. I got a letter from Romeyn last Friday night. it was wrote the 25th of Sept. he was well but had had no pay yet either. I see in the paper that his reg. or a part of it was engaged in a Skirmish with the rebles. I hear that we are agoing to move right on South after Price.[35] I hope so. Gen. Hunter[36] has command of us. I believe Gen Seigles is at Georgetown with some ten or 15 thousand men 30 miles west of this place. the northwestern reg. is there. Freemont and his staft will be here to morrow morning so I hear any way.

---

[33] General Joseph Gilbert Totton had a colorful military and engineering life before the Civil War began. A West Point graduate, class of 1805, he was an old man (73) in 1861, but was still active and considered one of the best.

[34] The 44th Regular Infantry Illinois was known as the Northwestern Rifle Regiment.

[35] Confederate General Sterling Price, nicknamed "Old Pap".

[36] Union Maj. Gen. David Hunter. He had commanded troops at Manassas. At Lincoln's request, he became second in command under Fremont. The President felt Fremont, explorer and politician, needed assistance from a man with more military experience.

Map 5

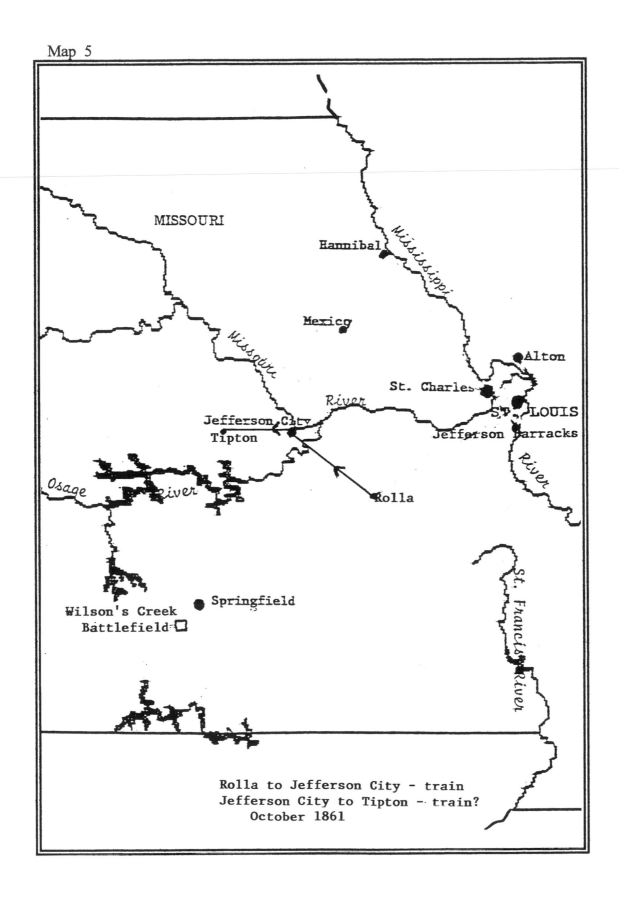

Rolla to Jefferson City - train
Jefferson City to Tipton - train?
October 1861

After supper and a good one too. we had hot buiscuit, hot coffee and butter and frid ham. good enough for a soldier. the boys are all in good spirits to night and the band is playing dixeyland. This town is full of tents, horses, mules, wagons and provisions.

if Mother is not with you when you get this wish you would send it to her or write to her and tell her where I am and that I am all right. if you could see the cannons here and cavalry you would say that it looks like war.

Well I am wrote out and so I will stop
Give my best respects to Ebb and Lym.[37]

from your brother
Frederic H Kellogg

---

[37] Interesting, but perhaps not surprising, that Fred makes no mention of Mary's pregnancy or a new baby. Family records do not give the birthdate of Mary's baby, nor a full name...only "Bessie", probably a nickname for Elizabeth, her grandmother's name. It may possibly have even been another Mary Elizabeth. If so it was the fourth or fifth in the family!

DIXIE

The tune "Dixie" or "Dixie Land" was written in 1859 by Daniel Decatur Emmett. Emmett, born in Ohio, was a white minstrel who often performed in black face. He wrote the song as entertainment, an exaggerated picture of life in the South. The song rapidly gained wide popularity. Reportedly it was a favorite tune of Abraham Lincoln. The lively tempo lent itself to marching and the Yankees stepped along happily to its beat. The verses are still familiar to all Americans.

> I wish I was in the land of cotton.
> Old times there are not forgotten,
> Look away, look away, look away, Dixie land.
>
> Chorus:
> Then I wish I was in Dixie, Hooray! Hooray!
> In Dixie land I'll take my stand to live and die in Dixie,
> Away, away, away down South in Dixie.

As war clouds gathered, many Southerners came to resent the lyrics. One such was Albert Pike, born in Boston, yet aligned with the Southern homeland of his wife. He wrote another version of the lyrics, all but forgotten today, but dear to many hearts during the terrible strife. There were many verses, only one of which shall be reprinted here.

> Southrons, hear your country call you!
> Up! lest worse than death befall you!
> To arms! to arms! to arms! lo Dixie!
> Lo! all the beacon-fires are lighted,
> Let all hearts be now united!
> To arms! to arms! to arms! lo Dixie.
>
> Chorus:
> Advance the flag of Dixie! Hurrah! Hurrah!
> For Dixie's land we'll take our stand,
> And live or die for Dixie!
> To arms! to arms! And conquer peace for Dixie!
> To arms! to arms! And conquer peace for Dixie.

Warsaw [Mo.]
Nov 15th 1861

Dear Mother

It has been a long time cience I wrote to you. We have been to Springfield and now are on our way back to Tipton. When we started for Springfield the first day we went 20 miles. then our company were ordered back to Tipton to guard a train of provisions through We were there a bout a weak 23 of us had to drive teams to Springfield. I drove one myself. We had fun a going but it was not so funny acoming back. When we were at Springfield there was 122 regiments there. I see the dead horses that were killed there by Freemonts cavalry and saw the place where they burrid some 60 rebles. We got there Friday at noon and started back Saturday morning at daylight.

Nov 21th. I now will try and finish this letter. we are now at Tipton. We got here the 19th but I have not been very well and so I did not write. We are exspecting to leave here soon but I cannot tell where we shall go. Tell Rome that I got his letter yesteday and when we were at Springfield I got one but it was a month old and I got one from you and one from Mary Price and one from Father and I have answered any of them not yet. I had a letter from Frank yesterday. he is well and likes his company.[38] My companion Charley Champlin was taken very sick here before we went to Sprinfield and I got him a furlough and he went home. but he was near dead when he got home and was not expected to live when his sister wrote me. he is or was one of the best boys I ever saw. We may go to fort Leavenworth Kansas but we dont know yet where we will go but you will see by the papers where we go. our regiment is the first regiment in the first Brigade and first division under Major Gen Turner who was our Colonel. Hovey is our Brigadier Gen.

from your affectionate son
Fred Kellogg

---

[38] Despite family advice to the contrary, Frank enlisted in Co. B of the 2nd Light Artillery Regiment, Illinois Volunteers. He was sixteen years old.

ACTION IN MISSOURI, AUTUMN 1861

Lexington, Missouri fell to the Rebels in mid-September. In retaliation, Union General John Fremont ordered the destruction of Confederate supply depots in Oscelo. Oscelo was burned to the ground. Confederate Generals Price and McCulloch bribed the Five Nations Indian tribes to fight with them. They freed slaves, raided homes, and ruined crops, leaving the countryside destitute. Wires from a worried Washington flooded Fremont's office.

Fremont claimed a great victory near Springfield, hoping to gain back lost favor with the President. Lincoln, however, had already made up his mind. On November second, orders were delivered to Fremont announcing he was being replaced by General David Hunter.

On assessing the steadily deteriorating situation, Hunter ordered a general retreat to the north. Disgruntled, Lincoln replaced him, within a month, with General Henry M. Halleck.

Halleck, author of "Elements of Military Art and Science", spent many a midnight hour pondering and sketching battle scenes. He prided himself on devising plans and issuing orders. Many of his schemes, however, looked better on paper than in action. Men were ordered back and forth from one area to another, expecting to reinforce this unit or relieve that one, but inadequate directions and misjudged distances made it difficult for replacements to locate the fighting in time to assist. Commanders in the field had no clear idea what was required of them. They operated on rumors and misinformation. Once encountered, the Rebels were totally unlike the enemy Halleck's mind had created. Union officers reported repeatedly, "They are evasive, striking like lightning and then fleeing." "The enemy would not stand." "They appear from nowhere and are gone before we can form a battle line."

Fred, and hundreds of men like him, had traveled more than one thousand miles by train, boat, wagon and on foot, had seen the aftermath of battle after battle, but had not yet personally faced an enemy. Morale fell to its lowest point. Dozens of discouraged men deserted.

Sedalia
Dec 18th 1861

Dear Mother
   I will write you a few lines to let you know that I am a live and well. I rescieved your letter of the 8th yesterday and was very glad to hear from you. I got one at the same time from Frank. He is well. he said he had got no pay yet so I reckond he had no money and so I sent him 5 dollars. Mother it must be my letters to you are miss carrid for I think I have rescieved all of your letters and I know that I have answered them all. but I have not answered all of Nans but in every letter I get there are compaints of my not writing and I know that I have answered all with two exceptions and thoes are to Nan. I have made up my mind if there [is] much more fault found I will not be so perticular about answering as I have been. We are now expecting to have a fight soon. We are having as nice weather as I ever saw in my life and the worst weather we have had for camp was in Oct. Frank writes is is prety cold there at camp Butler. you want to know if I have comfortable clothes. I have more than I can put in my knapsack. I have two suits all through and two good blankets. yes I have seen the most of Missouri and it a most damb miserable state. if I owned the best farm in it I would not want my friends to know it. there [are] from 2 to 600 rebles at Lexington they say and a lot more at Osceloa. there has two divissions gone to one or the other but I dont know witch and we are under orders to march at a moments warning.[39]
                          from your son
                                    Fred Kellogg

Brother Rome[40] I have not time to write to you to night. it is now ten o,clock and the boys are araising hell now. they up set my ink and so I have to write with a pencil You wanted to know how I like the Generals. I can tell you that I have never seen any of them only Hunter and the prospect of our having a fight is as good as it was last Spring I think.[41] I will write to you as soon as we get to any place.   Fred

---

[39] Apparently there was no battle. The Regiment went into winter quarters until February 1, 1862.

[40] This letter accompanied one to Fred's mother. This would have the period of time between Rome's resignation from the Ohio Volunteer Infantry and re-enlistment in 16th U. S. Infantry, Co. B, First Battalion.

[41] A bit of bitterness Fred could express to his brother, but not to his mother.

Map 6

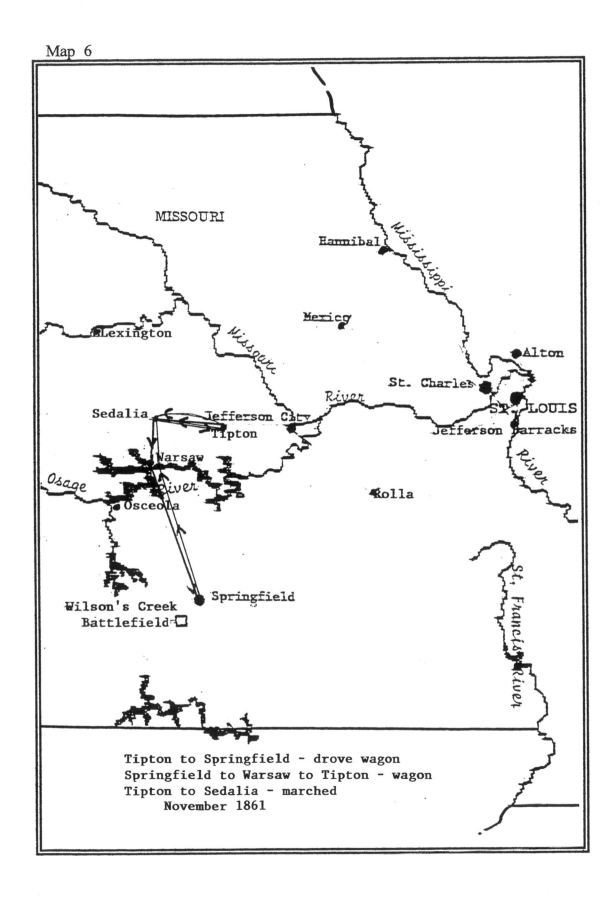

Tipton to Springfield - drove wagon
Springfield to Warsaw to Tipton - wagon
Tipton to Sedalia - marched
        November 1861

Fort Donalson
Tennessee, Feb 18th 1862

Dear Mother,

I now take the opportunity to write you a few lines. We left Otterville Mo. the 6th of this month. We marched to Jefferson City, 60 miles. There took the cars. went to St. louis. there took the boat for fort Donalson. We arrived here sunday 5 hours after the surrender of the fort. I have been over the battle ground. it is an awfull sight. We got 12,000 prisoners with the fort and yesterday 3,000 more who came to reenforce the fort not knowing that the fort was in our possession. Our loss is from 1500 to 2,000 killed and wounded and the rebles loss 3,000. Floyed, Pillow and Johnson[42] crossed the river and flead with 3,000 men saturday night. they cant brag about bull run any more. You will learn more from the papers than I can tell you so I wont say any more. I got a letter from Rome when we came through St. louis. he said he was out of money and he hadnt been paid cience he had been with there. I would send him some money if I thought he would get it. I dont think he is over 60 miles from here. I hear that Beuals[43] forces are a marching this way. if so we may see one [an]other. Frank is at Cairo. I see his comrade today. he says Frank is geting fat as a fool. there was 12 of the Co that Frank is in volenteered to work on the morter boats to help take this fort but they did not get here in time.

Mother when you get this write to Nan and tell her I will answer her letter of the 9th when I can but I cant get no paper nor envelopes now. but Mother I will write to you as often as I can. if you want to write to Frank Direct care of Major Strolbrand 2nd Ill. battalion, Ill. artilery, Cairo. I sent my likeness to Mary and one to Nancy from Otterville.

Direct as before to 15th reg. Ill. Vol. via St. Louis

from you loving son
Fred Kellogg.

---

[42] Confederate Generals John Buchanan Floyd, Gideon Pillow, and Albert Sidney Johnston.
[43] Union Major General Don Carlos Buell, commander of the Army of the Ohio. Rome's unit, the Sixteenth   U. S. Infantry, was under this command, thus prompting Fred to believe his brother would soon be nearby.

Map 7

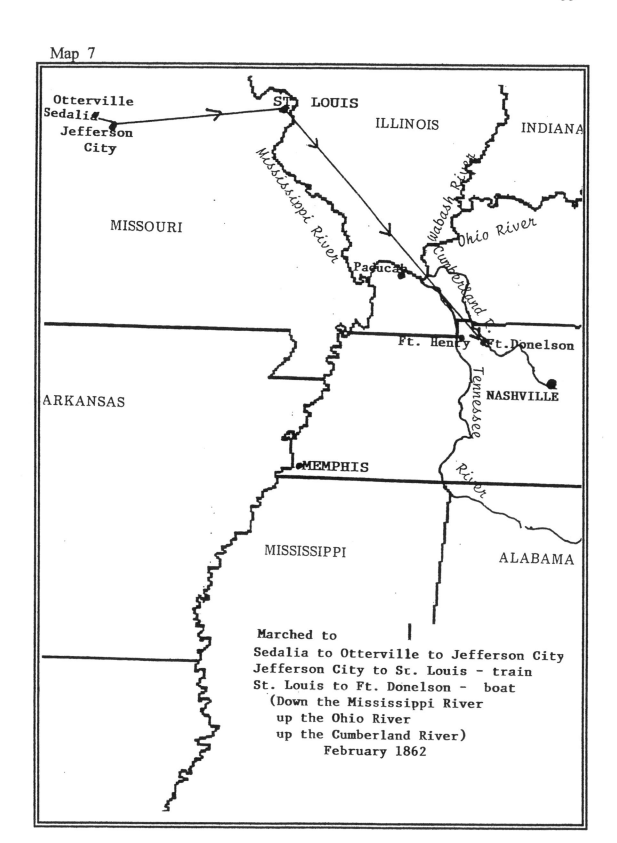

Marched to
Sedalia to Otterville to Jefferson City
Jefferson City to St. Louis - train
St. Louis to Ft. Donelson - boat
 (Down the Mississippi River
   up the Ohio River
   up the Cumberland River)
      February 1862

WESTERN TENNESSEE THEATER OF WAR

Fred's mother must have been surprised to find him so far afield when she finally received his letter, after two months silence. Fred was probably pretty amazed himself.

Had Kentucky seceded as its sister states expected, the line between North and South would have been formed by a natural barrier -- the Ohio River. However, Kentucky had strong Union support as well as Confederate. Therefore, the line zigzagged from town to mountain to railroad junction -- difficult to define and more difficult to defend.

Two waterways flowing into the Ohio River provided wide-open routes to the South for Union troops. The Cumberland River led directly to Nashville. The Tennessee ran the length of the state into Mississippi and across Alabama. General Albert Sidney Johnston, entitled "General Commanding the Western Department of the Army of the Confederate States of America" was well aware of this hazardous situation. He urged haste in strengthening Ft. Henry on the east bank of the Tennessee and Ft. Donelson on the west bank of the Cumberland. Also on Johnston's mind was the protection of a railroad located just south of the forts that ran from Memphis, providing transportation and supplies for Confederate troops.

On January 19, George Thomas, as yet a little known leader under General Don Carlos Buell, defeated the Rebels at Mills Springs, east of the mouth of the Cumberland River. Ulysses S. Grant, one of Halleck's least trusted generals, was commanding forces near Cairo. Encouraged by Thomas' victory, Grant determined to take Ft. Henry. He requested Admiral Andrew Hull Foote to accompany him with four of his gunboats. The ironclads were new, their guns untried. The Rebels had seeded the river with mines, another unknown commodity. With a few trial and error shots Grant and Foote positioned the boats within reach of the fort's defenses, just short of her gun's range.

Confederate General Lloyd Tilghman watched in horror, knowing his fort was doomed. On February fifth, he sent all but a few of his men across twelve miles of swamp ground to Ft. Donelson.

A bitter wind blew and icy rains turned to snow as Grant's troops approached on both sides of the river and the naval guns blasted away. Tilghman held off for two hours, then surrendered to Naval officers who sailed into the fort on the flood swollen river.

Grant continued on and destroyed the railroad bridge across the Tennessee River. Now he was ready to conquer Ft. Donelson.

Donelson, however, was forewarned and better prepared. Also, it was situated on higher ground, giving her guns a better angle at the ironclads. Within hours all four were crippled, drifting helplessly back down the Cumberland River. Undaunted, Grant positioned his troops in an arc, completely surrounding the fort. They pushed steadily, squeezing the Rebels into the river.

An argument between three Confederate leaders, left General Simon B. Buckner in charge of the fort while Generals John B. Floyd and Gideon Pillow fled across the river, along with Nathan Bedford Forrest, the Confederate Cavalry leader whose exploits Fred would come to know well.

Simon Buckner and Grant were old friends. Buckner had once loaned Grant money when he was down and out. He expected Grant to show him leniency. He sent a message inquiring about surrender terms, the first such message in the war. Buckner was stunned by Grant's reply, "No terms except an unconditional and immediate surrender can be accepted."

The surrender took place at the inn of the tiny town of Dover, with very little pomp or ceremony. Buckner was sent north as a prisoner of war.

The victory set church bells pealing throughout the North. The Union had a new hero. "Uncle Sam" Grant of West Point days was now known across the country as "Unconditional Surrender" Grant.

As Fred states in his letter, his unit arrived five hours after the end of the battle of Ft. Donelson. Frank's regiment also was too late to fight. Rome and Lyman, with their units, were marching from Kentucky to aid Ft. Donelson. Upon hearing of the victory there, their orders were countermanded.

As the Union forces surged southward, however, all four brothers would soon see plenty of action.

Fort Donelson, Tennessee   Dover March 3d 1862

Dear Mother   I rescieved yours of the 22th today and one from Theron dated
the 25th I think he lied a little. he said that you had not had a letter from me in
8 weaks. weather you have or not I have wrote you as many as six at least.
he says he has rescieved no letters from me this winter. well I have wrote him
twice. you wrote that Frank said that we have gone to Fort Henry. he was
mistaken but I suppose we shall soon see that place for we are under marching
orders now and I hear that we shall go to morrow. The report is that we shall go
from here to Fort Henry and there take the boat and go up Tennessee river.
I suppose that Rome passed up the river here for Nashville 4 days a go. I wrote
to him yesterday and also to Frank. Theron wanted I should write all what has
happened cience I last wrote you. We have had nothing to do yet. I know of
nothing that has been done at this [time] except of a few thousand men that
have been sent from here to Fort Henry. there had I should think from 50 to
60,000 of Gen. Buels army passed up the river by here within the last few days.
I understand that Buel has 180,000 men at Nashville. I should think that he
would do something soon. The distance from here to Fort Henry is 12 miles
witch we will have to march soon through the mud witch is very deap. the mud
in Ohio is nothing to the mud of Tennessee. It rained all day yesterday and to
day it is atrying to snow and the wind blows a Jimie cane from the North. there
has just passed 3 boats loaded with soldiers for Nashville. When you wrote you
thought I was sick. I got a cold at Otterville and I was a little sick for a day or
two but now I am as harty as a buck. In one of your letters some time a go you
wanted to know how Albert Kellogg was. he belongs to the 17th Ill reg. his
reg. is here, But he is at Fort Henry. he was wonded last summer at the Battle of
Frederick town in the arm so that he has no use of it. I have not seen him cience
we were at Alton Illinois. Well it is so damb cold and the [wind] blows so that I
cant think nor write. I thought that I would write a long letter this time for the
Devil only knows when I shall write again. But Mother I will write to you as
often as possible. But Bubby[44] thinks that I might write a grate deal oftener
than I do. if he dont like it let him go and soldier a while and I'll not complain if
he writes all the time. Well I suppose you want to know how we are aliving. I
will tell you: we have hard bread and meat for breakfast, pancakes for dinner
and tea or coffee witch we want and once in awhile we get a mess of potatoes. O:
I for got we all ways have plenty of beans and harmeny and salt beaf.

[scrawled initials for signature]

---

[44] Theron's nickname.

Map 8

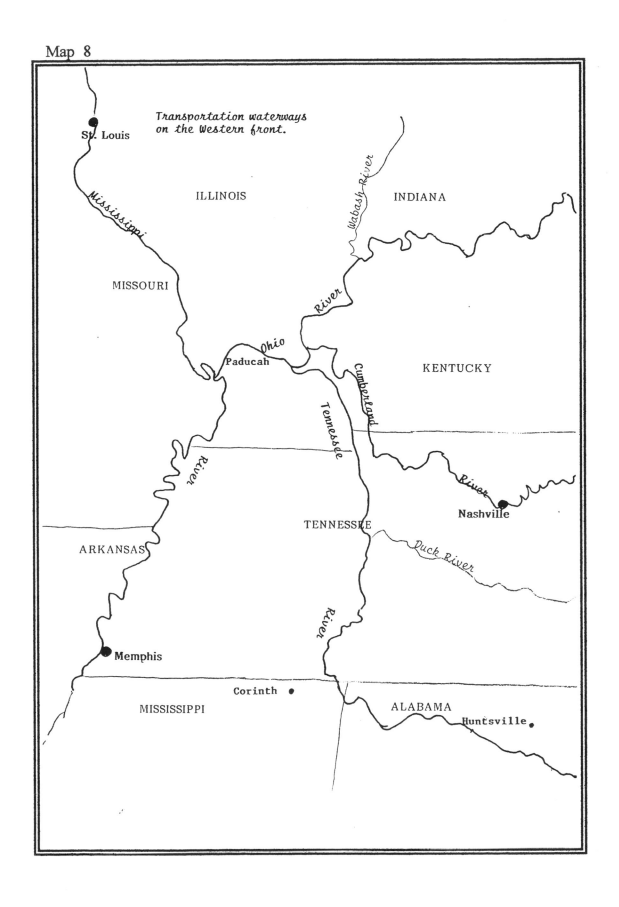

Fort Henry Tennessee
March 8th 1862

Dear Mother
        I will write you a few lines to let you know where and how I am
and that Frank in only 2 miles from here and I cant get to see him.
Yesterday I was only a half a mile from him and didnt know he was
there. if I had I would have seen him sure. I am sure that I will see him
either here or where we land. there is 50 boats here now and they are all
loaded with soldiers and how many reg. there is yet to take the boats
I know not. But I hear that there is near 100,000 men to go with this fleet.
We got the news last night that Mannasses gap was taken by Gen.
Mc Clelan[45]   the [mail] goes at 12 so I have no more time to write.
But I will write as often as possible.

                                                        Fred Kellogg

---

[45] Union General George B. McClellan. Both battles at Manasses or Bull Run (July 1861 and
August - September 1862) were Confederate victories. Soldiers everywhere were hopeful
McClellan would meet the Rebels on that site once more, this time claiming victory. This hope
led to constant rumors.

Fort Henry Tennessee
March 8th 1862

Dear Mother

I will write you
a few lines to let you know
if I here and how I am, and that
Frank is only 2 miles from here
and I cant get to see him,
yesterday I was only a half a
mile from him and I didnt know
he was there if I had I would have
seen him sure; I am sure that
I will see him either here or
where we land. There is 6 J boats
here now and they are all loaded
with soldiers. and how many Regt
there is yet to take the boats I
know not. But I hear that there
is near 100. 000 men to go with
this fleet. we got the news last
night that Mannasses gap
was taken by Gen McClelan.
the gees at 1 so I have no more
time to write. But I will write
as often as possible. Fred Kellogg

Camp near Pittsburg, Tennessee
March 18th 1862
In the wood 1 1/2 miles from the river

Dear Mother

     As I have got time I will write you a few lines to let you know that I am a monge the liveing. I believe my last to you I wrote from Fort Henry. We left Fort Henry the 9th and went on board of the Alleck Scott. the fleat started up the river the 10th. a part of them landed at Savannah and a part landed here yesterday and day before. We landed yesterday. there has been some little skirmishing done here but no hard fighting as yet and they may not be but the supposition is that there is to be a battle fought near here. At least their pickets are very bold. our pickets cought one Capt. the other day and killed one other reble. they wounded four of our men and killed 3 horses in that shirmish. there is two boys of Co B of our reg. missing. it is supposed they are taken prisoners. they went out in the woods and have not got back yet any how. I suppose you would like to know what kind of a camp we are in. Well I will tell you. We are in the woods and near a nice spring and in a butifull dry place and the weather is warm and pleasant. peachtrees are in bloom. This warm day puts me in mind of home while siting here in the sun a writing of the times when I was a little boy with Rome and Frank and running through the woods.
There has been no trouble with the picketts ceince night before last. I have not seen Frank yet but he is or was with the fleet when they left Ft. Henry so I heard. I cant write any news for [I] dont know of any. when we get a paper it is a weak old or more. I had a letter from Nan 2 days ago. She sent me two envellops with stamps on and paper in to write on. She seasms to think more of us than we do ourselves.   I hope I shall be able to repay the kindness back some time. Well I must go to the guard house for I am on guard today and it is all most time for my relief to go on.

Your affectionate son
Fred

Direct Co. H 15 reg.Ill. Vol. Hurlberts[46] Division Tenn.

---

[46] Stephen A. Hurlbut, leader of the "Fighting Fourth Division".

PITTSBURG LANDING

This letter and the next are written from Pittsburg Landing, an insignificant spot on the western bank of the Tennessee River about halfway between Savannah, Tennessee and the Tennessee - Mississippi border.

Grant, now a major general, tenth-ranking man in the U.S. Army, was leading his army to Corinth, Mississippi where he expected to wage a battle against Johnston's Rebel forces. He hesitated at Pittsburg Landing to wait for the rest of his armies to arrive from Paducah and Nashville.

Grant made no attempt to establish defenses -- their stay was temporary; the enemy, miles away. There were no facilities for housing or feeding men. Fred and some thirty thousand men with him, camped wherever they could find a suitable spot -- not an easy task. The area was less than five miles square. Except for a few farms and orchards, it was covered with trees and undergrowth. Half a dozen flowing creeks snaked along, leaving the terrain difficult to maneuver

Fred observed the build up of troops, heard stories of pickets skirmishing and prisoners taken. A battle must be eminent. But, for the moment, Fred sat among the peach blossoms, remembering a time long ago when he played in woods such as these with his little brothers.

Those same brothers were making their way up the river and across the Southern Tennessee countryside. None of them could know what the next days would bring. None of them knew of the little church nearby that would ultimately give its name to one of the most devastating battles of the Civil War.

Shiloh.

Camp near Pittsburg Tennessee April 5th 1862

Dear Mother

We are ten miles up the river from Savanah, twenty three miles from Corinth. there is now from 75 to 100,000 men here and they still keep coming. there was a recornortoring party of the rebles some 3000 strong made an attack on us yesterday but they had to scatter in a hurry. the fireing lasted nearly two hours. We had one Major one Lieut and 8 privates killed. There was 20 of the rebles killed and ten taken prisoners. the skirmish caused some excitement. our reg. was called out at 6 o'clock last evening. We marched two miles and then were ordered back. We got back to camp at half past eight. We got a little muddy. it rained a little yesterday enough so as to make it muddy and slipery. the report is that the rebles have from 60 to 70,000 at Corinth headed by Old Beauraguard[47] and that they are being reenforced all the time so I think we shall have a chance to fight either here or at Corinth and soon too. The report is that Buel is at Savanah with his command and is crossing the river today. I had a letter from Frank some two weaks a go. it was wrote the 12th of March. he then was at Columbus Ky.[48] I have not heard from Rome cience the 31th of Jan. If Buels force is at Savanah he and Lym must bouth be only ten miles from here and if so I may by chance see them. Tell Theron that I have rescieved his letter witch he wrote me the 13th and 14th of March and that I will answer it when I have postage stamps to spare. We are having fine weather. the trees are a leaving out and the woods are full of flowers. I have not had a letter in some time from anyone. I dont see why I dont get one from Nan for she generaly writes to me every weak and I believe I have answered the most of them and if I do not she does not complain and she all ways writes a good cheerful letter witch does me good to read. I suppose that I shall get no more letters from Theron for he seemes to have his feelings hurt from what I wrote to you but if he is so foolish as that I dont care. Mother you need not worry a bout us boys for if we do have to fight we can do it as well as others and if we get killed it is no worse for us to die than for others. As soon as anything happens I will write you again. Give my best respects to all inquirering friends. I will write as often as I can.

From your loveing Son   Frederic H Kellogg

---

[47] Confederate Pierre Gustave Toutant Beauregard, Commander of the Army of Mississippi.
[48] Frank had followed the same water route Fred had made. His unit, 2nd Ill. Artillery had arrived at Pittsburg Landing.

Map 9

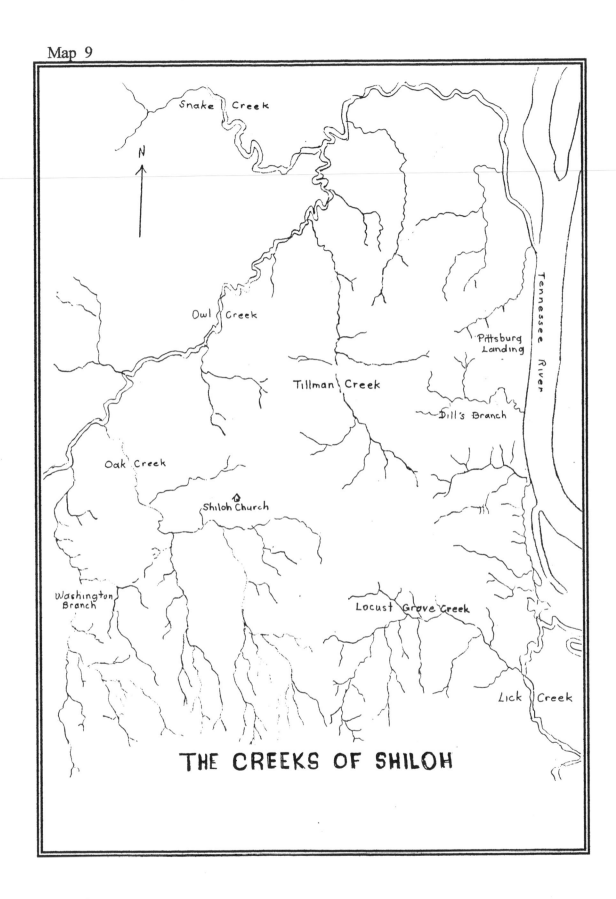

THE CREEKS OF SHILOH

[*This letter was written by Romeyn Kellogg*]

                                            Pittsburg Landing, Tenn
                                            April 9th, 1862

Dear Mother:

     Of course you will have read all the details of the desperate battle
fought here Sunday and Monday last. I have not time to give you
anything approaching a description of the conflict and slaughter -- indeed
I could not describe the scene to you had I nothing else to do. I can only
tell you than I am "as good as new", and Fred has only a slight wound in
the hand and a little furrow in one cheek. His gun saved his life. A ball
struck it, with sufficient force to knock it out of his hands and lay him on
his back. he was loading and had his piece in front of him. Bull's Run,
Springfield, Donelson and a half dozen more respectable fights combined
would not amount to more than a skirmish when compared with this
engagement. Our men were driven back by the overwhelming numbers
of the enemy all day Sunday clear to the river bank, and would have been
cut to pieces but for the timely arrival of General Buell with several
divisions who turned the scale this morning. By four o'clock in the
afternoon we had the enemy routed.

     The Bridage that I'm in -- Genl Rousseau's[49] -- landed early in the
morning on Monday and marched immediately into the fight. I hope the
rebles will now lay down their arms for I at least have "supped full of
horrors", and I have no desire to see men knocked down like ten pins
again, if it can be honorable avoided. Lyman was not in the battle; his
division did not arrive in time. Goodbye. I am writing this in Fred's tent.
I did not find him, nor hear of him until the day after the battle.

                                            Your Son
                                            Romeyn

---

[49] Union Brigadier General Lovell H. Rousseau. Sunday morning, April 6th, Rome heard the
first canons of the battle of Shiloh. His Regiment was 23 miles east of Savannah, having
marched well over 200 miles from Munfordville, Ky. They hastened their march to Savannah
and were taken by boat to Pittsburg Landing.

Pittsburg Landing, Tenn,
April 9th 1862

Dear Mother:

    Of course you
will have read all the details of the
desperate battle fought here
Sunday and Monday last.
I have not time to give
you anything approaching
a description of the conflict
and slaughter—indeed I could
not describe the scene to you
had I nothing else to do—.
I can only tell you that I am
"as good as new"—and Fred has
only a slight wound in the
hand, and a very little furrow
in one cheek. His gun saved
his life. A ball struck it,
with sufficient force to

THE BATTLE OF SHILOH

That first Sunday morning in April, Fred and his campmates woke to find the "Sunny South" had turned bitter cold with howling winds, icy rains and snow. Above the wins a more fearful noise roared -- cannon, gunfire and that eerie Rebel yell the Yanks had heard about. What they had hoped for, and dreaded, had finally happened. They were under attack by forces they had believed were in far off Corinth. Bugles blared. Lieutenants shouted orders. Men grasped their rifles and stumbled to their feet. Battle lines formed bore little resemblance to those on the practice field. Officers had no battle plan; their leader, General Grant, was warmly content in a river front mansion ten miles away.

An exuberant Beauregard, from his post in the little church called Shiloh Chapel, urged his field commander, Albert Sidney Johnston onward with much optimism and little direction. The Rebels had marched from Corinth, eating their three day rations the first day and discarding coats and blankets on a sunny afternoon. Now they were bone-tired, cold and hungry. But Johnston had told them, "The eyes and hopes of eight million people are on you." That thought drove them onward. It was their chance to expel the evil mercenaries from their beloved homeland. Some 50,000 Rebels followed their own firing into the area already congested by 30,000 Yankees.

Yesterday's pink peach blossom haze became a veil of dirty gray gunpowder smoke. Yesterday's bird song air was torn with screams of terror and the ravings of the dead.

Trees, tangled vines, broken ground and overflowing creeks became obstacles -- hindrances, separating men from their forces. Units became so mingled that leaders found themselves commanding men they had never before seen. One elite Southern battalion came on the battlefield in their dress blue uniforms. Mistaken for Union soldiers, they were fired on by their own Confederate comrades. At first opportunity they reversed their coats. The white silk linings glimmered through the trees, badly shaking Yankees who thought they were the ghosts of death.

Johnston took a minie ball just below the knee and bled to death before help could reach him. Beauregard had lost a friend and his best commander. It weighed heavy on his heart. Still, he felt his troops had prevailed and he sent a jubilant wire to Jefferson Davis claiming a complete victory.

At dark, thunder replaced the boom of the cannons and rain fell in torrents. Men sought shelter in vain, most sleeping among the dead.

Grant, disgusted that he had allowed himself to be caught so unaware, considered his circumstances. Some ten thousand men had run at the first sound of battle, too scared or cowardly to fight. Grant discounted them. A man was soldier material or he was not. And no man knew which until his first battle. Other men became soldiers that day and Grant was inordinately proud of them.

Benjamin M. Prentiss' battalion held their position in a low cut road long enough for the Rebels to call the area "the hornet's nest." Eventually surrounded, Prentiss sadly surrendered his 2000 survivors. W. H. L. Wallace fell; his battalion fled in terror. Stephen A. Hurlbut (Fred's commander) was left without protection and forced to retreat. The other three battalions, commanded by Lew Wallace, John A. McClernand and William Tecumseh Sherman, had taken severe losses. They were down to half their strength.

To a lesser man than Grant, it was a hopeless situation. But Don Carlos Buell and his army were forging up the river at this moment. Tomorrow, the tables would be turned and the victory prematurely claimed by Beauregard would belong to Grant. He hunched under his poncho to sleep beneath an oak tree while the rain poured down and the gunboats in the river tossed their booming shells ashore, every quarter-hour, all night long.

Dawn brought new hope -- and Buell, with 20,000 fresh troops. The Yankees fought through sudden showers and steamy sunshine. Then the wind came up out of the north turning the rain to sleet and dropping huge hailstones. No matter. They pushed on.

By mid-afternoon Beauregard knew it was over. One by one the Southern battalions began their withdrawal. The valiant leader who had promised them to "water our horses in the Tennessee River" was dead. The Rebels' short-lived victory vanished, their spirit, gone. They retreated to Corinth.

Of the 100,000 soldiers engaged in this first major battle of the war, roughly one in four were killed, wounded or captured, a total of 23,741 men. The total American casualties in all three of the nation's previous wars, The Revolution, The War of 1812 and The Mexican War were only 23, 273. These facts were sobering to say the least. Especially since this battle gained little and meant nothing. Except for one thing. Those men destined for soldiers, from North or South, would fight fiercely and stand firmly for the cause they had chosen.

Pittsburg Landing
April 11

Dear Mother

by mistake I did not mail this as I thought I had done. I suppose you have had all the news of the battle. we went out with 500 men Sunday morning and returned with 200 less (our reg.) 50 killed and 152 wounded. the most of our officers was killed or wounded. We had 32 killed and wounded out of our Co. only 4 killed dead on the field. Charley Champlin my companion was shot through his leg. there was 5 out of my mess and one killed. Rome has been with me the most of the time cience the battle.[50] he thinks we live better than they do. I have not seen Lyme but Rome saw him yesterday. his camp is a bout a mile and a half from here. I will write again as soon as I can.

from Fred Kellogg

I rescieved two letters from you yesterday.

---

[50] At what point in the battle Fred was injured cannot be ascertained from his letters. It must have been unusual for Rome to stay with him for several days, in spite of being in a different unit and, undoubtedly, having duties of his own. Though Fred's injury was not severe, Fred may have suffered from shock and emotional damage, causing Rome to feel he needed care and companionship. The brothers had not seen each other since Fred and Frank had left Ohio to live with their father in Illinois -- five years before. Those few days together must have been precious to both of them.

Map 10

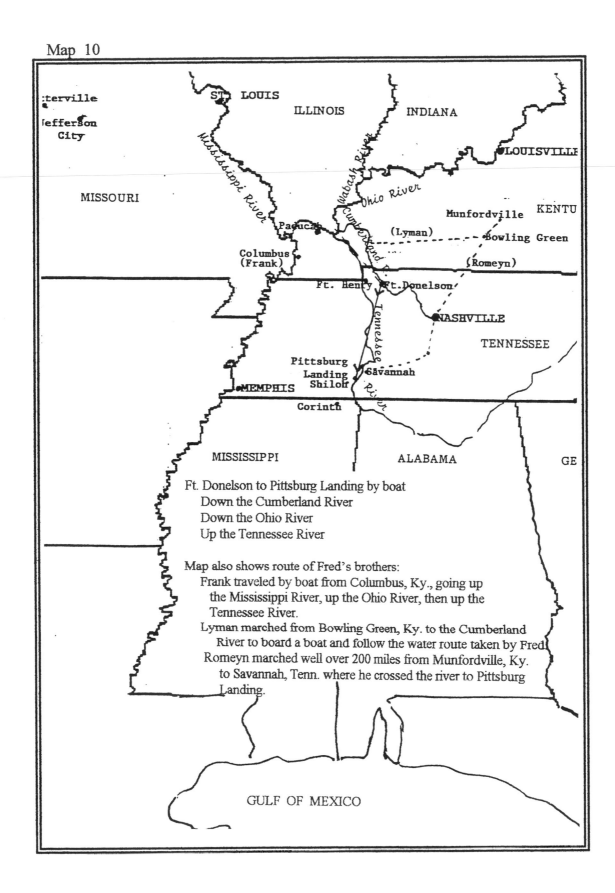

Ft. Donelson to Pittsburg Landing by boat
Down the Cumberland River
Down the Ohio River
Up the Tennessee River

Map also shows route of Fred's brothers:
Frank traveled by boat from Columbus, Ky., going up
the Mississippi River, up the Ohio River, then up the
Tennessee River.
Lyman marched from Bowling Green, Ky. to the Cumberland
River to board a boat and follow the water route taken by Fred.
Romeyn marched well over 200 miles from Munfordville, Ky.
to Savannah, Tenn. where he crossed the river to Pittsburg
Landing.

Camp near Corinth
Mississippi, May 12th 1862

Dear Mother

I just rescieved your letter and one from Nan too and I was very glad to hear from you bouth. The big battle is not yet fought but it soon will be. our arms are now loaded and stacked in line of battle and we are a waiting for the rebles to pitch in. We are exspecting that they will attack us. the picketts are constantly fighting and I think we shall have fighting to do soon and it maybe before night but they will not surprise us this time. but I do believe that they will fight like devils. We have been called out in line of battle 4 or 5 times. night before last we work all night digging rifle pitts. our army is advancing slow but sure I hope. You wanted to know where Charley Champlin is. he is at Cincinattia Ohio in the Marine Hospital and he will get well and not lose his leg. I saw Lyme a few minuets a bout 2 weaks a go. he was not very well then. I have not seen Rome sience I last wrote you. I will write to you as soon as this battle comes off a gain.
I know nothing of Frank but suppose he is here.[51] the weather now is warm and pleasant. We had a nice time a weak a go yesterday and today amarching in the rain and had no tents at night. Wheat here is headed out. We have plenty of fresh mutton and pork and sum beaf. there is plenty of hogs and sheep here but not much of anything else. I pitty thous who are to be wounded in the coming battle for the weather is so warm. I wrote a letter to Mary Price yesterday.

Well I cant think of anything more to write so I will quit. My best respects to all.

from your Son
Fred Kellogg

Co H 15th Ill. Vol. Hurlberts Division Tenn via Cairo

---

[51] Though neither Fred nor Romeyn had seen him, Frank (2nd Ill. Light Artillery) fought in the battle at Shiloh and was now moving toward Corinth.

We had a nice time a week ago
yesterday and today. a march
ing in the rain and had no
tents at night, wheat here
is headed out, we have plenty
of fresh mutton and pork
and some beaf there is
plenty of hogs and sheep
here. but not much of anything
else. I pitty thous who are to
be woynded in the earning battle
for the weather is so warm
I wrote a letter to Mary
Price yesterday.
Well I cant think of any
thing more to write so I will giut
My best respects to all
      from your son
            Fred Kellogg
      Co H 15 Ill vol.
      Hurlberts Division Tenn
            Via Cairo.

Army of Tennessee
Camp near Corinth, Miss
May 14th 1862

Dear Mother

As I have time this after noon I will write you a few lines and let you know that I am a live and well. We are now very near Corinth. not over 4 or 5 miles. The picketts have been constantly fireing ever science yesterday morning. our Co. was out this forenoon as skirmshers. there was only 5 shots fired by our Co. the balls were all the time flying and some of them came as close as I wished to have them. the fireing now seams to have stoped. we are only 2 miles from the rebles entrenchments. The weather is very warm and pleasant. I have not seen Rome nor Lyme sience I last wrote you. I suppose Frank is here with General Pope.[52] We have advanced very slow but sure. We have camped as many as ten times sience we left the landing. as soon as we get in a new camp we throw up entrenchments so if the rebles should make an attack on us we would have some protection.[53] I have no idea when the general engagement will commence but I suppose soon. I hear the firing now and it is pretty brisk too. Rome let me have some money to send to you sometime a go but I have not had a chance to yet. Our reg. is in very good health now. We are camped in the woods where the wood ticks are very plenty so that we have to pull off our shirts and pick the devils off from us 3 or 4 times a day. I have rescieved a good many letters latly. Charley Champlin is doing well or was when I last heard from him. Well I cant think of any thing more to write and so I will quit but I will write a gain soon if any thing happens. Give my best respects to all

From your Obedient Son
Frederic
Co H 15th Ill Reg. Hurlberts Division Tennessee

P.S. I want to know if Theron has recieved any letters or heard from me within 8 weaks.
I think if the picketts aint careful they will rais a fuss before morning.

---

[52] Brigadier General John Pope.
[53] Halleck had combined Grant's Army of the Tennessee, Buell's Army of the Ohio and Pope's Army of the Mississippi, taking command of this "Grand Army." His over-cautious move to Corinth drew severe criticism from President Lincoln, Secretary of War Stanton and many of Halleck's own generals.

Army of Tennessee
Camp near Corinth Miss
May 14th 1862

Dear Mother

As I have time
this afternoon I will write you
a few lines and let you know
that I am alive and well.
we are now very near Corinth.
not over 4 or 5 miles the picketts
have been constantly firing ever
science yesterday morning our Co.
was out this forenoon as skirmishers
there was only 5 shots fired
by our Co. the balls were all this time
flying and some of them came
as close as I wished to have
them the firing now seams
to have stoped we are only a
mile from the rebles entrenchments
the weather is very warm and
pleasant

Corinth Miss   May 30th, 1862

Dear Mother, I send you 30 dollars. Corinth is evackuated. I have not got time to write you a letter but will in a day or two. 20 of this Rome sends you and ten I send.

from your Son Frederic Kellogg

Army of Tenn Camp near Corinth Miss
on the Memphis and Charleston R.R.
            have you got that 30 dollars   June 9th 1862
Dear Mother
        You will excuse me for not writing before for I have not had time before. We are 7 miles from Corinth. tomorror or day after we start for Memphis (Shermans and Hurlberts Divisions) I have not seen Rome sience we were near the landing nor Lyme either. I see that some of the papers blame General Halleck for leting the rebles leave Corinth. they are dambed fools and so are the rebles for leaving for they could have mowed us down like grass before the scythe.[54] you have read in the papers about the hills and swamps here a bout Corinth. it is all a lie. it is a very nice county a bout as rolling as it is from Norwalk to the burg. [bay?] it takes but little rain to make it awfull mudy. Wheat here is ripe and [so] are blackberries. the health of our regiment is good.
I will write to [you] as often as I can while on the road from here to Memphis.
I dont know as you can read [this] for I cant.

From your son F. H. Kellogg.
Co H 15 reg. Ill. Vol. Hurlberts Division Tenn Via Cairo, Ill.

---

[54] Beauregard waited at Corinth, his ranks depleted by battle injuries, dysentery, measles and typhoid fever. As the days of May dwindled on, the Rebel leader realized he was outnumbered and ill prepared for a battle at Corinth. Beauregard put into effect a masterful withdrawal plan, the greatest hoax of the war. Troops, equipment and supplies, sick and injured soldiers, even civilians, were covertly moved out of the city by rail. When Halleck finally ended his slow march from Shiloh, he opened fire on straw stuffed uniforms manning dummy guns. Corinth was, indeed, evacuated.

Map 11

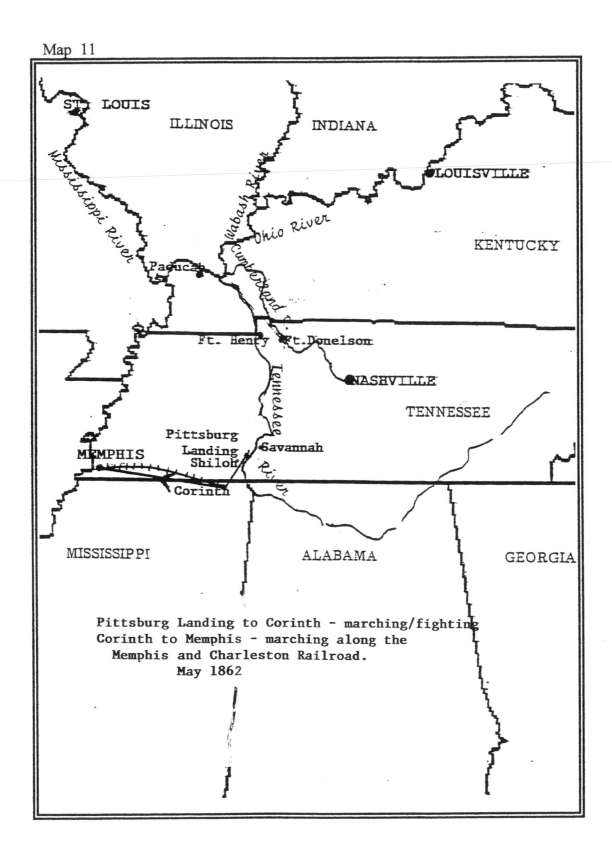

Pittsburg Landing to Corinth - marching/fighting
Corinth to Memphis - marching along the
Memphis and Charleston Railroad.
May 1862

[This letter was dictated to the Chaplin at the hospital]

States Hospital
Memphis, Tenn.
July 31, 1862

Dear Mother,

Received your last letter about the 20th. Should have written you before now but for sickness. Was taken ill the 8th of July at Holly Springs with something like billious fever.[55] Arrived at this place the 19th and am still very weak - though I can safely say that I am improving. I have a cough -quite troublesome - but with an increase of strength I think it will pass away. I am as pleasantly situated as I could wish in my absence from home. No little attention needed that I do not receive. room - large - airy. ground around the buildings shady and nurses kind and thoughtful. So do not think of me as neglected. On the contrary few sick soldiers are as well provided for as I am.

I have not heard from either of my brothers for sometime. I know not where Frank is - not heard from him since last Spring.

The weather of late pleasant and for this climate quite healthful.

I will write you again soon and thus keep you advised of my condition.

Write on the reception of this please and let me know how you all are at home.

Direct to care of the Regiment - Memphis, Tenn. via Cairo
Affectionately Your Son
F. H. Kellogg
F. A. Griswold
Chaplain 34th Ind. Vol.
Scribe.

---

[55] Later diagnosed as typhoid fever and pneumonia. Fred was taken to his father's home in Illinois to recuperate and was discharged. All the brothers suffered through numerous illnesses. Rome was recovering from measles when he began the march from Munfordville to Shiloh. Lyme's diarrhea, caused by drinking polluted water on way to Corinth, plagued him all his life. Frank contracted mumps at Vicksburg in the summer of 1863. So severe were the complications that Fred left Illinois to accompany Frank to their mother's home in Ohio to recover.

State Hospital
Memphis - Tenn - July 31. 1862

Dear Mother:

Received your last letter about
the 20th - Should have written you before
now but for Sickness. Was taken ill
the 6th of July - at Holly Springs with something like billious fevers arrived at this place
the 19th - and am still very weak - though
I can safely say that I am improving.
I have a cough - quite troublesome - but with
an increase of Strength think it will
pass away - I am as pleasantly Situated as I could wish in my absence
from home - No little attention needed that
I do not receive - Room large - airy - ground
around the building Shady - and nurses
Kind and thoughtful - So do not think
of me as neglected. On the contrary few
Sick Soldiers are as well provided for
as I am.

I have not heard from either of my broth-
ers for Some time - I know not where
Frank is - not heard from him Since last
Spring -

The weather of late pleasant - and for

[*Fred was discharged for disability. His father, Moses, found him and escorted him to Illinois to recuperate. Apparently he spent time with his father and step-mother near Genoa and with his sister Mary and her husband, Ebenezer Price and children, Lyman and Baby Bessie near Rockton.*]

Genoa [Illinois]
Oct 6th 1862

Dear Mother

I rescieved your kind and welcome letter Saturday night. the reasons that I cant come are this I have not got the money nor I have not got clothes either. I have $65.00 due me from the service witch I shall get when I get my dischage witch was made out and sent to headquarters to be signed before I left Memphis. General Hurlbert told Father that it would take 3 or 4 weaks for it to return there and advised him to dress me in citizens clothes and not wait for the discharge and when it returned he would send it to me. I am looking every mail for it to come but when it comes I want the money to buy me a horse. I have one and if I get a mate I will work a farm another year if I get well and I think that I shall be sound by spring. I am a gaining very fast now. I have laid my cane a side and walk without one. I walk to the post office and back and go all a round town and can get on my horse and ride him.

Whos doings was a telegraph asking to have him go for me. It has cost me for Fathers and my own exspences over $90.00 and [I] owe him 17.00 yet. I would like very well to come home and make you a visit but it will cost 30 or 40.00. If you are a coming out another year cant you wait until then to see me. I shall be fat then and now I am as poor as the devil. I dont weigh 100. but I eat as much as a man weighing 300. I dont get my bounty until the war is over.

The mail goes soon so I have not got time to write more

from your Son
F. H. Kellogg

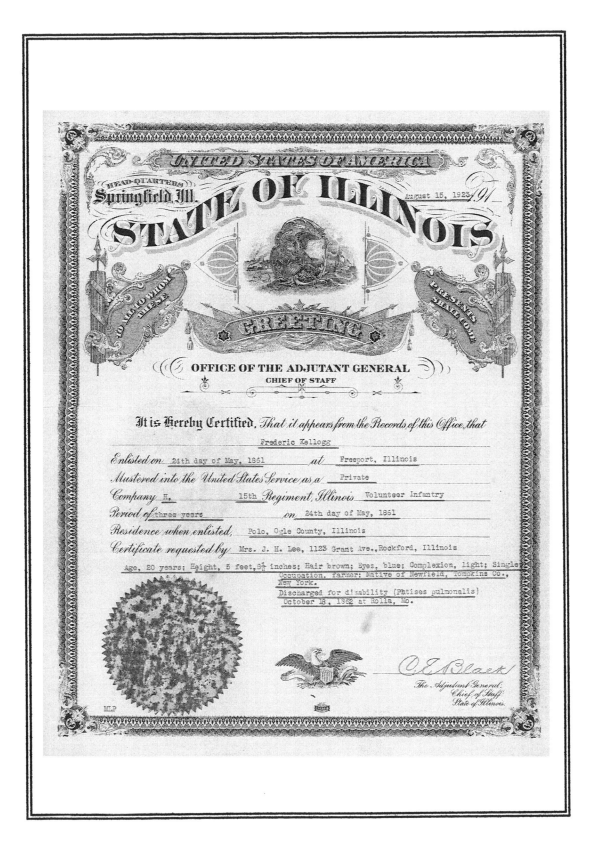

Rockton [Illinois] Jan 25th 1863

Dear Mother

I got back here last Thursday. I was gone from here 4 weaks.
I went from here two days before Christmas. I went from here to Charley
Champlains and Charley, Kate, his sister and Lydia Mack and I went out
to Mt. Morris. We had a very good visit there and then I went down to
Genoa and there I found a letter from Rome. it was wrote the 1th of Nov.
I was there a bout a weak and then I went to Millford 8 niles below
Rockford and now I am a going to go to work for someone or go to the
army. I am well now. I weigh 154 1/2 pounds, 5 pounds more than I
ever weighed before. I have wrote to Frank and I have wrote him a good
long letter. a sheat of foolscap crambed full. Mary thinks that he will
laugh some. Well hope so. I know it used to do me good to get a good
long jolly old letataer. Mary says you will worrie yourself to death if I
think of going to the army. I can go and get a team to drive if I dont
enlist. but Moher I dont like the name of being a dischard soldier and its
no worse for me to go now than in the first place. for driving team I can
get 30.00 a month and rations. and I shall have to go to work soon at
some thing for a more lonesome fellow you never saw than I am. if I was
at work I could be contented. There is no young folks here in Rockton
that I care anything a bout. I think Rome has forgotten his friends or else
he thinks he has not got many.

Young Lyme has just tied me fast to my chair. he is a grate deal
like Rome used to be. when he gets hold of a book he dont know nothing
but what he is a reading. he is a very good boy. But Bessie is a raising
the old harry all of the time. we are a having avery mild winter. there
has been no sleighing yet and no very cold weather. it has been very
pleasant to day. I am geting nearly wrote out. I have been writing to
Frank and am tired of writing. If I go South I shall not go yet for awhile.
I shall wait until I get a letter from Frank. I am geting awful patriotic not
all at once though.

Fred Kellogg

Genoa
Feb 27th 1863

Dear Mother

I rescieved your letter (the one you sent to Rockton) a weak a go
last tuesday. last week I was at Belvedier a witness on a murder trial so
I did not have time then to answer and this week I have been to work.
But now I will try and write you a few lines. I had a letter last night from
Rome. he is well. he said he would send me some money soon or as soon
as he was paid a gain. you said if you got his pay for the time he was in
the volunteer service you would send me one hundred dollars if I wanted
[it]. if you get it soon I wish you would do so. I want to work some land
and I shall want some money to get seed grain and feed with. I have
money enough to buy a harness and a plough with. I can get land here to
work on shares. But I would rather hire. I have heard of some land that
can be hired for one dollar an acre. if so I would rather hire land. I shall
go and see as soon as the roads get passable. If you do not get the money
soon you need not send it without writing me first for if I should get some
from Rome I might not want it.
        You want to [know] where Frank is. he was at Memphis a few
days a go. Bill Mcquairria wrote home. he said Frank is well. they got
the letter last night.
he is in Logans division.
        Co. G Shirrestume Batterrie
        Logans[56] division 17th army corps
        Memphis,Tenn

        I shall not go south a gain. Give my best regards to Ock and family
                                                        Fred

---

[56] John A. Logan

Genoa
March 22d 1863

Dear Mother

I rescieved a letter some time a go from you and I will answer it. I had a letter from Frank. I got it a week a go last friday. it was sent to Rockton. I was out there. Mary and the children are well. Father had a letter from Frank last night. he was well and says he likes it better there (lake providence)[57] than any place that he has seen south. he says that Rome will do darned well in the army if he dont get pluged. last monday morning as I came through Rockford I had my photograph taken. it was not finished then. When he finished it he sent it to me. it is a good one if it wasnt for two or three blots. I have wrote to Rome and Frank to day. It has rained and snowed for 3 or 4 days and the mud has no botom here now.

Your son
Frederic

[57] Lake Providence, Louisiana is on the west bank of the Mississippi River between Vicksburg and the Arkansas border.

Genoa
May 13th 1863

Dear Mother

I have not answered your letters yet and have not time now to.
that money has not got here yet.   I have been bothered some about it.
I have been to Sycamore twice to Cortland once and to Belvedier twice.
I have wrote twice to Ock a bout it. I wrote to him because I thought he
would get it sooner than you would but I get no news of the money and
no answer from him. I dont see why Rome did not send it to me instead
of sending there. If he had of sent it to me it would have made a grate
deal of difference with [me] for I would not have lost so much time as I
have for ten dollars. besides Mr. Wood made calculations on haveing his
money and as I did not get it I had to go and help him haul off some of
his grain to rais the money. I have not got any of my corn planted yet. If
Ock has not done anything about the money I wish you to demand it and
send it to Sycamore for I must have it soon. If I had thought that Rome
was a going to send it all over the world and I was to be bothered so
a bout it I would not have undertook to farm. If I dont get the money
soon Wood will think I [am] a liar and now he thinks that I am a pretty
good fellow. he says I am the best man to work he ever see. I had a letter
yesterday from Brad Champlin, Charleys brother. he is in Rosecrans
army near Rome. he said he had just been to see Rome. he said Rome
was well and that he was a fine fellow. When I got his letter I thought it
was from Rome until I commenced reading it. his writing and

[*page missing*]58

---

58 This is the last letter from Illinois. Fred learned his brother, Frank, was hospitalized with
severe complications of the mumps. He went to St. Louis and accompanied Frank to their
mother's home in North Fairfield, Ohio. Fred apparently stayed there until he enlisted in the
Ohio Cavalry. His letters in 1864 indicate Mary Price and her children were now living in Ohio,
probably with their mother. Since no mention of Mary's husband, Ebenezer is made, perhaps he
had gone to war.

Camp Smith   Nashville,Tennessee
Jan 23d, 1864

Dear Mother

I wrote you a few lines from Columbus and now I will let you know where I am and that I am all right. I have not time to write but a little tonight. I have been here five days and have enjoyed myself first rate. I found Tipp Ells[59] here. he is acting Sargent Major. I stop with Tipp and Capt. Smith from Newfield, N.Y. and a Sargent so I have been lucky for once for when we came here it was awful mudy and cold at night. But I was with Tip where there is a good stove and we had plenty blankets. We had a hard time a coming here from Columbus. We were 5 days on the road. I have not the time to give you a full account of it but when you go down to Ocks you can get it for I wrote it all to Clara.[60] I am a fraid that I shall not see Rome for we go to Huntsvill Alabama. We go tomorrow. You need not answer this until you here from me again. Give my love to Mary and Lyme and kiss little Bessie for me. I suppose Frank has gone to Vicksburg before this. When I get to our destination I will write a good long letter. I suppose you will think that I am good at promising. But I did not agree to write to any one but you. So there is no one eles to find fault and I know that you wont. Tip sends his regards to you and all his friends. When you write to Rome you can tell him that I am down here and will give him a call as soon as I can. We are camped 2 miles from the City on Lebenon Pike. The weather here is fine now but there is some mud but it cant commence with the mud at Fort donelson yet. there is a grate deal of fighting here between the conscripted men and the volunteers.[61]

From your loving Son
Fred

---

[59] Apparently a hometown boy known to Fred and to his mother.

[60] Clara is Fred's niece, daughter of Oscar and Mary Elizabeth Kellogg. She was twelve or fourteen.

[61] Those who volunteered had little respect for those who waited to be drafted or conscripted. Problems between the "green" men and the veterans were prevalent, also.

Map 12

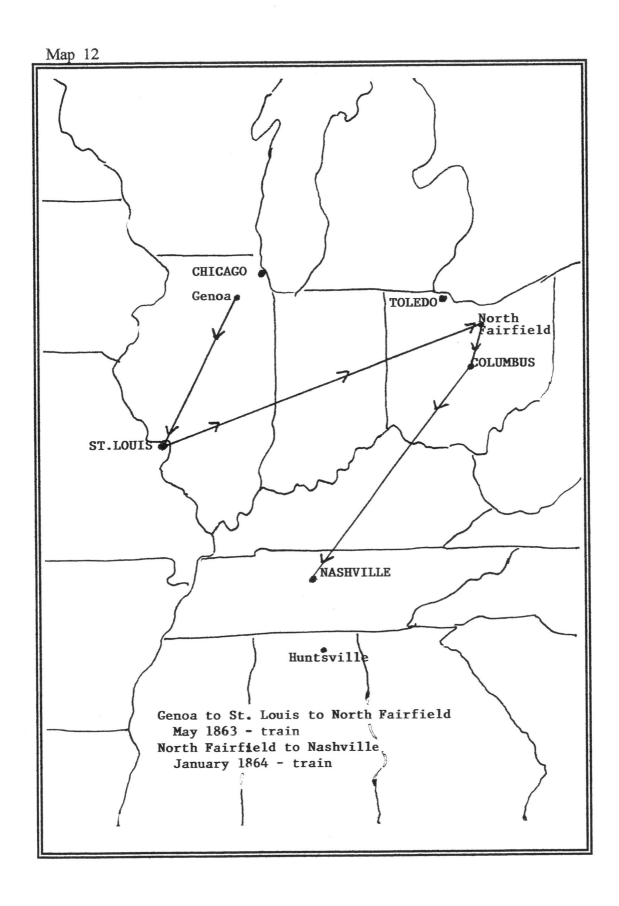

CHICAGO

Genoa

TOLEDO

North
Fairfield

COLUMBUS

ST.LOUIS

NASHVILLE

Huntsville

Genoa to St. Louis to North Fairfield
   May 1863 - train
North Fairfield to Nashville
   January 1864 - train

Hd Q
Camp Smith, Nashvill, Tenn

Jan 31st, 1864

Dear Mother

As I have not left Nashvill yet I will write and let you know the reason. We were ordered a way some two weeks a go but could not get transportation. And now I dont believe we shall get a way from here for some time to come. I see in the papers that Logans division is at Huntsvill if so I will see Frank when he gets with [them] a gain. We are a having good times here and I dont care how long we stay here. I am contented. We have all kinds of men here, drafted and new recruits and old veterans and substitutes. the offscourings of all Gods creation. Mother I will only write a little so that you will know that I [am] all right. if you dont hear from me a gain soon you will know that I have not left here for I will write you as soon as we leave. There is nothing to write about here only that there is from 50 to 2000 men coming in here everyday and as many a leaving.
Tip Ells is well and sends his regards to you. I have seen two men from Wisconsin that I knew but I have seen no one from Ills. yet.
Give my love to Mary and her babies.

From your son
Fred Kellogg.

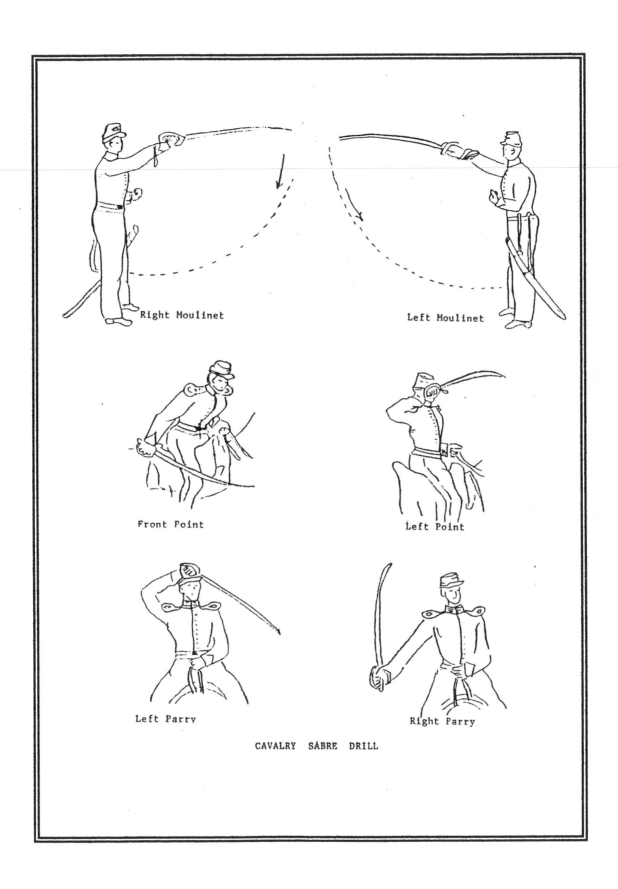

Right Moulinet

Left Moulinet

Front Point

Left Point

Left Parry

Right Parry

CAVALRY SABRE DRILL

Camp Smith
Feb 9th 1864

Dear Mother

I am still at Nashvill and having a good time generally. We exspect to leave here this weak. But I dont know how it will be. but I hope it will turn out as it did before for I like this kind of soldiering. I dont have anything to do here. It is talked here that we are go to the front and guard some railroad bridge until our reg. gets back from home but how true it is I dont know but when we get there I will write and let you know all a bout it. I have not heard any thing from home sience I left. but I have told everyone not to answer my letter for I dont know where I shall be when their letters get here. But I suppose you all are all right but if you aint I cant help you anyway so I will content my self by saying its only for three years. What boys of the 3d O.C. [Ohio Cavalry] that I have seen yet I dont think much of with one exception and that was the one who came with me. he was from bronson. he is avery good fellow. I would give 100 dollars if I was in an Illinois regiment or Ind. either. When we get with the reg. if I dont find the boys better than what are here I shall try and get with some other regiment if I can. Tip is well and send his respects to you. he has been awriting home. I have his pen now and it does a little better than the one I have been using.

Give my love to all and kiss my little girl Bessie Price. tell Lyme to be a good boy.

From your loving son
Fred Kellogg

election and that was the one who came with me. he was from bronson he is a very good fellow. I would give 100 dollars if I was in an Illinois regiment or Ind either. When we get with the reg—if I dont find the boys better than what are here I shall try and get with some other regiment if I can tife is well and send his respects to you he has been awriting home I have his pen now and it does a little better than the one I have been using. Give my love to all and kiss my little girl Bessie Pue tell Hymie to be a good boy

From your loving son

Fred Kellogg

Camp Smith, Nashvill, Tennessee
Tuesday, Feb 23d, 1864

Dear Mother

I am still here at Camp Smith yet and thinking that you would like to hear from me a gain I take the presant oppertunity to write you. So here goes. I am well and have enjoyed better health sience I left Ohio than I have before for nearly two years. I have meet anumber of Fairfield boys here. Sunday I meet Arsie Mackentere, but he did not know me untill I told him who I was. Yesterday Rob Parks came here in camp. to day I was down town and meet Lester Elster. Arsie can tell as big lies as ever. Rob Parks told me a bout James Penfields death.[62] At first I could hardly believe it, but the next thought told me it was nothing for one to die now days. Tip is all right and he has given me his photograph. I will send it to you in this. Mother you may answer this and tell me if you got letter I wrote you from Columbus. I have a tropical rose that I got out of a green[house] here at the State Aslyum. I sent one to Clara some time a go. I have not wrote to Nanie yet but shall soon. I want you to put Tips picture where it will be seen but not hurt for I think a good deal of him.

Direct Fred Kellogg, Camp Smith, Nashvill, Tenn. Care of Delos Ells

Write soon to your Son

F. H. Kellogg

---

[62] James Penfield was a brother of Theron's wife, Frances Ann Esther Penfield.

Camp Smith. Nashvill. Tennessee.
Tuesday. Feb 23th 1864,
Dear Mother
I am still here at
camp Smith yet. And thinking
that you would like to hear from
me a gain. I take the presant opperk-
unty. to write you. So here goes
I am well. and have enjoyed
better health since I left Ohio
than I have before for nearly
Two years. I have meet a number.
of Fairfield boys here. Sunday I meet
Arsie Mackentere. But he did not
know me untill I told him who
I was. Yesterday Rob Parks came
here in camp. to day I was down
town and meet Lester. Lester.
Arsie can tell as big lies as ever
Rob Parks told me about James
Penfields death. At first I could
hardly believe it. but the next thing
told me. it was nothing for one
to die now days. Tip is all right
and he has given me his photograph
I will send it to you in this

Camp Smith, Nashville, Tenn
March 10th, 1864

Dear Mother

I rescieved your first letter a bout a week a go. Yours of the 2d
I got same day and was right glad to get them too. They are the only
letters I have rescieved sience I left Ohio. We had a little war here his
morning. I will tell you how it happened. there was some greenhorns got
a shell (32 pounder). they had taken out the cap and some of the powder
then set it on a stump. one of them lit a match and droped it in the shell.
The shell exsploded and raised the devil generaly killing two men. Well
one of them is not dead yet. he might better be for his body is cut half
into. one of his arms is all tore to pieces. There was six others wounded.
the one that was killed dead was over one hundred rods from where the
shell was. a piece struck him in the back of his head and nearly tore it off.

The weather here now is like May in Ohio. Only it rains here a
bout half of the time. There was 20 men deserted from a company of
Tenn. Sunday night. We had an awful storm here last week. it rained
and the rain froze to the trees so that it broke the trees down. the limbs
from the trees came down as though they were sent from a bove,
smashing down tents. the limbs commenced falling a bout midnight.
There was no more sleep that night. The boys got up and every time
a limb would fall the boys would yell. Tip got up and said there was a
limb a going [to] smash our tent. then Farley got up. but Knap and I was
too lazy to get up. But the limb came down with a crash just before
morning without doing any damage. There was one man killed several
hurt and a number of horses killed and cripeled. Mother when you write
a gain I want you to give me Romes and Franks directions. I wrote to
Rome when I first came here but have rescieved no answer. I would
write a gain if I thought he would get my letter. I will write to Genoa
and find out about my trunk for I dont want to loose it. I shall go out to
the asylum a gain if I can and if I do I will get what flowers I can. I have
heard of some nice gardens here in Nashville and if I get a chance I shall
go and see them and it may be I can get you some flowers there. if so I
will.

Camp Smith. Nashville. Tenn.

March 10th 1864.

Dear Mother

I received your first letter a bout a week a go. yours of the 9th & got tuesday. and was right glad to get them too. they are the only letters I have received since I left Ohio. We had a little war here this morning. I will tell you how it happened. There was some greenhorns got a shell (32 pounder) they had taken out the cap and some of the powder then set it on a stump. one of them lit a match and droped it in the shell. The shell exploded and raised the devil generaly. killing two men. well one of them is not dead yet. he might better be. for his body is cut half into one of his arms is all tore to pieces. there was six others wounded. the one that was killed dead. was over one hundred roods from where the shell was. a piece struck him in

When you go down to Ocks find out if they have had any more of my photographs struck off. if they have send me one. I wrote for them to have some more taken and to send me one but now I want two. I shall send you another soon of a friend of mine who I got acquainted with here. his name is John Applegate 3d Ind. Cav. There is a rumer here in camp that the 3d [Ohio] are to go back to Ohio and organize with the reg. at Cleavland but I have seen to much soldiering to believe it. I dont believe anything that I dont no is so.

I had to stop writing and it is evening a gain and a raining as usual. Tip has been detailed to do other buisness. he will leave this battalion within 3 or 4 days. he will not leave camp though. I think I shall fare as well as I do now for I am prety well acquainted with the Officer that commands this battalion now. I think I am all right. Well Mother I have wrote out so I will close. Give my love to Mary Price and Lyme and kiss little Bessie for me. Tell Lyme to write to me and I will answer him and tell him all a bout the war. the 55th regiment[63] was in Nashville last week. I went down town to see them but could not get in the barracks where they were and I told them more than a dozen lies. I told them I had a Father and Brother and friends to numerous to mention. So I did not get to see them.

From your hopeful Son

Fred Kellogg

---

[63] Fred must have had reason to believe his father was with this unit at the time.

I would write a gain if I thought
he would get my letter. I will
write to Genoa and find out a
bout my trunk. I dont want
to loose it. I shall go out to the
asylum a gain if I can. and if I
do I will get what flowers I can
I have heard of some nice garden
here in Nashville. and if I get
a chance I shall go and see then
and it may be I can get you som
flowers there if so I will.

When you go down to Pete
find out if they have had any
more of my photographs I struc,
off if they have send me one. I
wrote for them to have some
more taken and to send me one
but now I want two. I shall
send you another soon of a frien
of mine who I got acquainted
with here. his name is John Apple
3d Ind. cav. There is a rumer here
in camp that the 3d are to go
back to Ohio. and organdize
with the reg— at Cleavland
but I have seen to much soldierin
to belive it. I dont believe anything
that I dont no is so

Direct Fred Kellogg 3d O.V.C. Camp McClellen, Nashville, Tenn
                                    Camp McClellain 3d O.V.C.[64] camp
                                    Nashville, Tenn. March 26th 1864

Dear Mother
        I rescieved your kind and welcome letter yesterday. I was
disappointed when I got it for I had made up my mind I was never
a going to get any more letters. I have wrote 49 and have rescieved 5.
I got a letter from Charley Champlin a bout 3 weeks a go. he has inlisted
in the 12th Ill. Cav. they are at St. louis now. He said that Kate was
married. a part of the reg. came here last week (from home) so we had to
leave Camp Smith and join them. We are now in camp about 9 miles west
of Nashville. There is a bout 800 of us. We have cavalry tents.
My Partner says tell you that the rebles are scarce but gary [gray] back lice
are plenty. We just took a seaveh [survey] and I found one that will
weigh less than an ounce. he is the first one that I have seen or felt a bout
me. Now I will tell you what our tents are. Each man draws one half of a
tent witch is a bout as large as a sheet. two men go together. they take
and button them together and then they are very comfortable for two
men. We have to get down on our knees to get in them. When it storms
we take our rubber blankets and put them at the ends. If you dont
understand how they are, just take two sticks and drive them in the
ground and have them 3 1/2 feet high and 6 1/2 feet a part, and a pole
on them.   then put two sheets over them and pull the lower edge out as
far as you can and have it to the ground. My partner and I cook for
28 men. We have soft bread all the time now We are to have 95 cents
a month from each man for cooking. We have our water fetched and
wood choped for us. It rained all yesterday but today is is very pleasnt.
Mother I am getting fat enough to kill. I only weight 20 pounds more
than I did when I left O. I now weigh 150 1/2 pounds. We have not got
our horses nor equipments yet. I dont think we will leave here for two
months yet. We have a good lot of rye straw in our tent to lie on. We
went out in the country 3 miles to get it and we milked two canteens of
milk from a cow at the same place.

---

[64] Ohio Volunteer Cavalry

Direct Fred Kellogg 2d O. C. camp
Mc clellin Nashvill Tenn

Camp McClellain 2d o.s.c. camp
Nashville Tenn March 26th 1864
Dear Mother

I recieved your kind
and welcom letter yesterday
I was disappointed when I got it
for I had made up my mind I
was never going to get any more
letters. I have wrote 9 and have
only recieved 5. I got a letter
from Charley Champlin about
3 weeks ago. he has enlisted in
the 12th Ill. cav. they are at St
Louis now. He said that Kate
was Married. A part of the reg-
came here last week (from rome).
So we had to leave camp Smith
and join them. We are now in
camp about 4 miles west of
Nashville. There is about 8,00
of us. we have cavalry tents

Now I will go to my dinner. Mother I want you to send me 6 pearl buttons with eyes to them such as are used on vests. I want them to put on my shirts. I have shirt buttons but I have no neadle small enough to sow them with. You can send them in a letter. I must tell you a bout my partner. he is one of the livlyest fellows in camp. his name is John Miller, but the boys all call him crzy. he makes more fun than all the rest of reg. I will tell you the position I am in now while awriting this. laying on my belly and the paper laying on the ground so you need not exspect it be wrote very nice. Mother I have nearly played out.
I wrote to Ock for to send me a hat [and] a pair of boots. I suppose he will send them by some of the boys when they come back. if you can, get me a rubber to put on my pocket book. There has been a fight[65] just now.

Give my love to Mary and Lyme and dont forget to kiss Bessie for

Fred.

---

[65] There was no major battle at this time. There might have been a small skirmish, or perhaps he is referring to a brawl among his camp mates.

Now I will go to my din
ner. Mother I want you to
send me 6 pearl buttons with
eyes to them such as are used
on vests. I want them to put
on my shirts. I have shirt buttons
but I have no needle small enough
to sew them on. You can send them
in a letter. I must tell you about
my partner. he is one of the liveliest fellows
in camp. his name is John Miller. but
the boys all call him Crzy. he makes
more fun than all the rest of the reg.
I will tell you the position I am
in now while writing this. I am laying
on my belly and the paper laying
on the ground so you need not
expect it to be wrote very
nice. Mother I have nearly played
out. I wrote to Eck for to send me
a hat. a pair of boots. I suppose he will
send them by some of the boys when
they come back. if you can get me a
rubber to put on my pocket
book. There has been a fight
just now. Give my love
to mary and Lynne and dont
forget to kiss Bessie
for Fred

Camp 3d OhioVol Cav
Nashville, Tennessee
April 9th 1864

Dear Mother

      I have just rescieved and read your letter and was dispointed too for I did not look for it so soon. I am very much oblidge to you for sending me the buttons and rubber. they are just what I want. Our regiment is now all here. I am a member of Co B. We are the 2d Co and in the 1st Battalion. I think it is the best Co. in the reg. Our Capts name is Livermore.   I think that he is a very fine man. Tip Ells was here yesterday. he was not feeling very well and looked very bad.
I should not be surprised if he is sick. There is a grate deal of small pox here. there is anumber here in surgery. There is a good many a having the measles too. I had a letter from Mary Ock and Clara 2 days a go.
I answered them the same day that I got their letters. We have been having rain all most all the time for a week. to day it is very pleasant only the wind blowes very hard. Ock did not sent the boots or hat with the boys when they came. I dont care anything about them now. At least I dont want them sent now for fear that I shall never get them. We have not got our horses nor arms yet. And our Officers say that we wont get them for some [time] yet. But I dont care I am content to stay here as long as I can. Your letter was the 7th one that I have rescieved and this is 40th one that I have sent. We have a very good dinner. We had boiled potatoes, sour crout and onions, fryed pork and fryed bread. Coffee too.
I have some twigs of misseltoe that I will send you in this. it grows on the trees here. I never have had a chance to go out to the assylum a gain.
I mean to go if I can. I shall have to go and drill soon. there is nothing to write a bout. I wrote to Frank some time a go. I think I shall have answer from him soon. Give my love to all and dont forget to kiss my little girl.
We are a having good times. We have no duty to do except to drill twice a day when it is fair weather. My partner has a very sore arm. he has been ....for all that he just came a long and took me by the feet and pulled me out of the tent.
I will try and write a longer letter next time.

                                             [scrawled signature]

Camp 3d Ohio vol cav
Nashville Tennessee
April 9th 1864.

Dear Mother
                    I have just recieved
and read of your letter. And was
dispointed too. far I did not look
for it so soon. I am very much
Oblidge to you for sending me the
buttons and rubber they are just what
I want. Our regiment is now all here
I am a member of Co. B. we are the
2d Co. and in the 1st Battalion. I
think it is the best Co. in the regt
Our Capts name is Livermore.
I think that he is a very fine man
Kip Ells was here yesterday he was
not feeling very well and looked very
bad. I should not be surprised if he
is sick. There is a grate deal of small
pox here there is a number here in every

Columbia, Tennessee Camp 3d Ohio Cav.
Dear Mother   April 16th 1864
        We left Nashville the 13th. the first day we marched 22 miles. the
next day we only went 13 miles and yesterday we got here after a 15 mile
march. We got carbines before we left Nashville and that was all we did
get in the cavalry line. We marched here on foot. I dont know yet what
we are to do here. It is rumered here in camp that we are to guard the
town so as to keep bushwackers away from here. There is some of them
around here. They fired on the cars night before last. I stood the march
first rate. I only had two of my toes pealed on my left foot. You know
that that boot was all ways to small. I have just been out this morning
and got me a bundle of hay for a bed. I sleepted cold last night and
I thought it would go better with some hay or straw to ly on.
I exspressed one blanket and my over coat to Ock from Nash.
The blanket is a good one. I bought it for one dollar. when you go there,
to Ocks, get them and take care of them. I have had no letters sience
I wrote you last but thinking you would like to hear from me and feeling
as if I wanted to write to someone and knowing of no one who I had
ought to write before I wrote to you I set myself on the ground and with
the paper in my hand I'll do it. We are camped on the best campground
that I was ever camped on. We are on a hill a bout 50 rods from duck
river. We had a good time to come here in. the weather was butiful and
the roads good. A good many of the boys had the toothache in their legs
and feet and some gum boils on their heals. Mother I wish you to send
me a half a dozen stamps when you write a gain. They have just put on a
camp guard to stop the boys from getting hay for beds. I guess the old
farmer where I got my hay has not got as much more than would fill a
straw tick. We lived good on the way here. I shot a hog one night and
the Colonel put an other man a carring a rail for it. So I went to the
Colonel and told him that I killed the hog. He wanted to know what I did
it for and I told him that we had no meat to eat and so I killed the hog. so
he told the fellow to lay down the rail and go to his quarters and told me
to come and ask him the next time before I killed any more. I lied to him
a little for we did have some meat, but I wanted some fresh and I got it
too. and the next time I want any I shall have it if I can get it and I dont
think I shall bother much to ask the colonel either. Give my love to all.
                                                    from your son Fred

Map 13

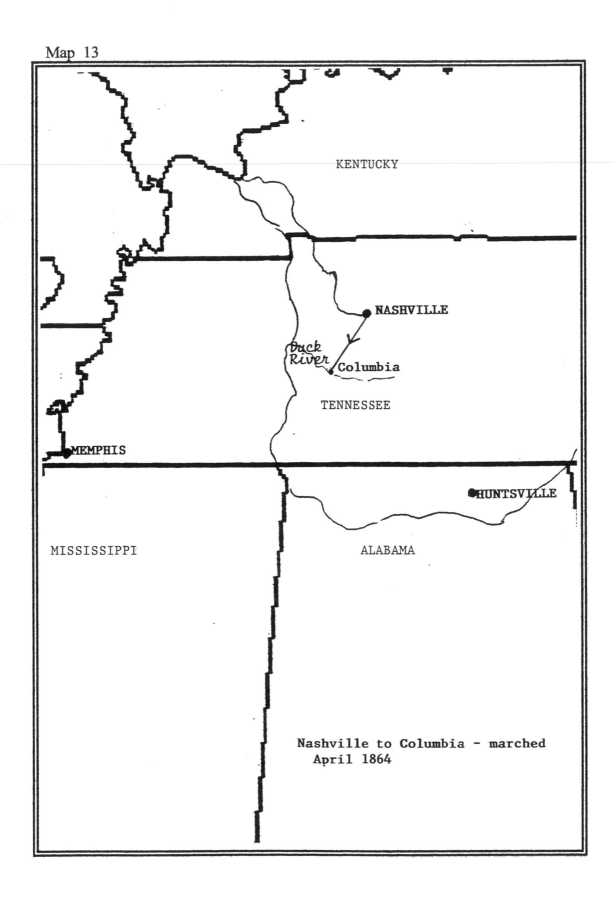

Nashville to Columbia - marched
April 1864

Camp 3d Ohio Cav   Columbia, Tennessee
April 21th 1864

Dear Mother

I rescieved your last yesterday and was very glad to get it too. I have had five letters within 3 days with yours, and I cant answer but one of them. So here goes. The reason is that I have no stamps. But thinking that it is my duty to look at home first and thinking it is about all the comfort you have is areading and knowing that you are all ways antious to hear from us boys. I had made up my mind that you would worrie about Frank. Yet I hardly think but what he is all right and if he is not, you nor I can not help him. so I think we had better take the world as it comes and be gay and happy still. I wrote to him sometime a go and have not had any answer yet. I wrote to Father a few days a go. when I hear from him I shall find out where Frank is for they will be likely to know there at Genoa.

We have not got our horses yet but exspect to get them soon. Some boys of our reg. was out last night on a scout and took rebles. one of them was a Capt. They belong to Forest's[66] command. We have taken 6 or 7 a round here sience we came here. There is some talk that Forest will come and try this place but I dont think he had better undertake the job. We have quite a force here now. there is some talk here to day that we are to leave here soon. I should not be surprised if it was so and I dont care how soon we do go. Well Mother I think it is strange that Rome does not write to me. I have wrote him twice sience I left Ohio. Well I have played awriting to him untill I get one from him. We are a having good times here now. not much duity to do and plenty to eat. I wrote you the next day after getting here. Columbia is quite a prety place nearly as large as Norwalk. I have just heard that one of the 4th regulars Cav was killed this morning just before daybreak while on picket and another shot at. The bushwackers are plenty about here. they did not get the devil. he was to smart for them. The sittizens here say that there is a lot of them up the river from here about 5 miles. It is strange that there is not more of our boys killed for they are all over the country every day. Well I shall have to close. I wrote you to send me some stamps in my last letter. If you did not get it I will say here please send me some.   Fred

---

[66] Confederate Cavalry leader, Nathan Bedford Forrest.

This popular song title became a catch phrase used by soldiers of both armies as well as their loved ones at home. Verses were composed on the spot to fit the current situation. The Yankee chorus version was "Let the world wag as it will."

In contrast to the cheerful lilt of "Be Gay and Happy Still," the mournful tune and sorrowful lyrics of "Sad and Lonely" expressed emotions of somber times.

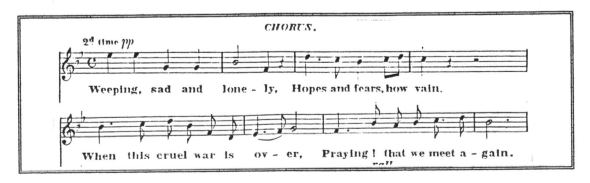

[Written vertically across the writing on the first page of this letter]

If we leave here I will let you no. I will write to you as often as I can for if it does you as much good to get letters as it does me I think I ought to write you as often as possible. I wrote to Ock yesterday to have him send me my old discharge.

Give my respects to all the folks.   I have had four letters from you latly.

I never injoyed my self better than I do now.

From your Aff. Son
Fred Kellogg

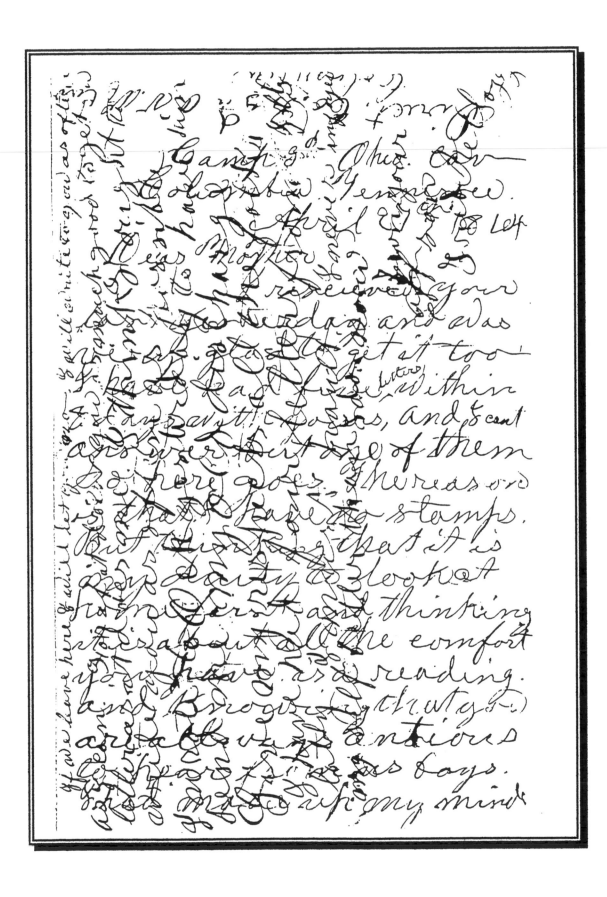

Camp 9th Ohio Cav
Columbia Tennessee.
April 23 1864

Dear Mother

I received your
letter yesterday and was
very glad to get it too
I have had three letters within
a few days or three or four, And I cant
answer but one of them
and here goes. The reason
that I have no stamps.
But I think that it is
my duty to look at
your first and thinking
it is about all the comfort
you have is a reading.
and I know that you
are all very anxious
to hear from me as boys.
has made up my mind

Columbia, Tennessee May 3d, 1864
In the woods on Duck River on pickett.

Dear Mother

      I just rescieved yours of the 4th and was darned glad to get it to for I have been a writing a letter and I had no stamp to put on it. Our Co is on pickett and have been for 4 days and do not exspect to be relieved for some time. there is only 1000 men here now. Wilders and Mintas[67] Brigades left here last week so there is only two regs here - 3d and 4th Ohio and half of each reg has gone to Nash. after horses and the burshwhackers are a trying to rais a little hell here now. One Co of our reg. and one Co of the 4th Ohio was drove in last night by them. I have not heard a bout the causalities yet. They were the other side of town. we could hear the firing where we was. I am on the night relief and on at the ford at the river where the bushwhackers could easy pick one off in day light. it is the place where one of the 4th regular was killed last week. Our Co has 5 picket posts, 6 men at a post at a time. the rest of Co stay back in the rear as reserve. The Capt has just had two of the boys arrested for shooting. They were a killing a hog. It was not for killing the hog, but for shooting while on picket. Those Brigades that left here last week took 30 days rations with them. Where they are bound for I dont know.
I would sooner be on picket than be in camp. Yesterday afternoon 6 of us went over the river with a boat and went out in the county 4 or 5 miles. We got a lot of eggs, some butter and our canteens filed with milk and the joke of it was to hear the women haw [howl] when we marched off without paying them anything. there is some talk here that Forest will give this place a call, but I dont believe anything of it, but if he should he could easy take it now. We are exspecting the 1st Ohio Cav here today. they are mounted. We shall be mounted soon and I suppose that we will leave here soon. Well Mother this is a hard looking letter but you can tell who it is from weather you can read it or not. Why dont Mary Ock send me thoes photographs. tell her I will pull her ears the first chance I get. Well I have played out. Give my regards to all.

                        From your Son
                        Fred Kellogg.

---

[67] Commanders of two of the three Brigades in Fred's Regiment. Fred was in the third, commanded by Colonel Eli Long. General Kenner Garrard was regiment commander.

[*Though Fred enlisted in The Third Regiment Ohio Volunteer Cavalry in January, 1864, he was not mounted until mid-May. Information regarding the service of the regiment was taken from Ohio Regimental Histories, found in "A Compendium of the War of the Rebellion" by Frederick H. Dyer, housed in the U.S. Army Military History Institute, Carlisle Barracks, Pennsylvania. Names are spelled as they appear there.*]

Unit flag of the 3rd Cavalry
Army of the Cumberland.
Blue design on white background.

3rd REGIMENT CAVALRY SERVICE.   Atlanta (Ga.) Campaign May 1 - September 8. Courtland Road, Ala., May 26. Pond Springs, near Courtland, May 27. Moulton May 28-29. Operations about Marietta and against Kennesaw Mountain June 10 - July 1. Roswell June 10. McAffee's Cross Roads June 11. Noonday Creek June 15 - 19 and 27. Powder Springs June 20. Near Marietta June 23. Assault on Kennesaw June 27. Nickajack Creek July 2 - 5. Big Shanty July 3. Rottenwood Creek July 4. On line of the Chattahoochie River July 5-17. Garrard's Raid to Covington July 22 - 24. Covington July 22. Siege of Atlanta July 24 - August 15. Garrard's Raid to South River July 27 - 31. Flat Rock Bridge July 28. Peach Tree Road August 15. Kilpatrick's Raid around Atlanta August 18-22. Red Oak, Flint River and Jonesborough August 19. Lovejoy Station August 20. Jonesborough August 22. Operations at Chattahoochie River Bridge August 26 - September 2. Occupation of Atlanta September 2. Florence September 17. Operations against Hood and Forest in North Georgia and North Alabama September 29 - November 3. Near Lost Mountain October 4 - 7. New Hope Church October 5. Dallas October 7. Rome October 10 - 11. Narrows October 11. Coosaville Road, near Rome, October 13. Near Summerville Road, near Rome, October 13. Near Summerville October 18. Little River, Ala., October 20. Leesburg and Blue Pond October 21. King's Hill, near Gadsden, Ala., October 23. Ladiga, Terrapin Creek, October 28. Ordered to Louisville, Ky., and duty there till December. Ordered to Gravelly Springs, Ala, December 28, and duty there till March, 1865. Wilson's Raid to Macon, Ga., March 22 - April 24. Selma April 2. Montgomery April 12. Pleasant Hill April 18. Double Bridges, Flint River, April 18. Macon, Ga., April 20. Duty at Macon and in Dept. of Georgia till August. Mustered out August 14, 1865.

Regiment lost during service 1 officer and 58 enlisted men killed and mortally wounded and 6 officers and 229 enlisted men by disease. Total 294.

Columbia, Tennessee Camp 3d OVC   Monday, May 16th 1864

Dear Mother

I have just rescieved a letter from you and one from Nannie and now I am agoing to answer them. I got one from Ock and one from Mary yesterday. I got my Discharge[68] just in time to get my pay. Our reg was paid on Saturday but yesterday when my papers came the Captain said he thought I could get my pay yet so he and I went downtown where the paymaster was and he fixed it all right and I got my pay. I have sent 65.00 to Ock. I sent it by the State agent. I have answered Ock and Mary. I told Ock to let you have what money you want and the rest take care of for me. I was agoing to write to you this afternoon anyway for I may not have a chance a gain very soon for we expect to leave here within 4 or 5 days, I suppose for the front.

I was downtown this forenoon and got my boots fixed up so I think they will stand me until winter. I am glad that Ock did not send me any boots. I have just wrote to Tip Ells and I am agoing to write to Nannie. I am in good health and enjoying myself first rate. I have been on picket over half of the time for 3 weeks. I had a grate deal rather be on picket than not for it is not half so hard as it is in camp and one can live a grate deal better. One of Co L was killed to day and another taken prisoner by some bushwhackers. they were with a train acoming from Nashville and stoped at a house to get a drink. The one that was a prisoner got a way at night and lucky for him to for they was agoing to kill him and would but for the Capt who was with them. Well I must go and water my horse and then finish.

Well I have my horse watered and fed. Mother the more I see of this country about here the better I like it. I do certainly think that this is the nicest part of the world I ever saw. It is realy butifull to go in some of the groves here. We have moved camp 3 times sience we came here. Oh I all most forgot to tell you about my horse. I think a very good one. But you know the old saying that every man has the best horse. We have not got saddles yet but expect to get them tomorrow. Then we will be all ready for fun. that is if it is our lot to have any fun. Well Mother I will write you as often as I can but if you do not hear from me quite as often as you want to do not think but what Fred's all right. From your loving Son

---

[68] It took nearly two years for Fred to get his Infantry discharge and pay owed him.

THE HORSES OF THE CAVALRY

A new Cavalier quickly learned his life revolved around a four-legged beast. This beast was his transportation, his partner in battle, his best friend. Therefore, the needs of his horse came above all else. He searched for clean water for her to drink, often a hopeless task when hundreds of horses needed water from the same small stream. If the army could not provide food, he foraged grain or hay from a near-by farm -- or fed her his own supper. When there was no stable, the soldier's own blanket warmed her, his rubber sheet kept her dry. He might neglect his own health, but he regularly examined his horse for glanders or rotting hooves. No effort was too much, for without a horse, a Cavalier was back in the walking army!

Training a horse for cavalry duty brought physical exertion and emotional ruination. Many of the horses had not yet been broken to the saddle. They kicked and reared, leaped skywards and jumped sideways. They backed away when urged forward. They whirled madly when ordered to stand still and stopped dead while the rest of the troop galloped away. The men begged and pleaded, yelled and screamed, threatened and swore. Slowly and painfully men and animals came to understand each other. At last the day came when they could answer the trumpet calls -- wheeling, marching and countermarching. They became a beauty to behold.

The horse's steady pace on long marches was so smooth a soldier could sleep in the saddle, one leg hooked around the pommel, his head resting on his chest. At night, each man tethered his horse to his wrist. She would keep watch all night, walk to and fro, but never would she step on her sleeping trooper.

In battle, the horses seemed to share the fears of defeat and the glories of victory. When the firing began, the horse was unmindful of the bullets singing past. She would lower her head to charge an infantry man and knock him to the ground. In meeting a mounted enemy, she would rear and strike out with her forefeet. When the Brigade drew sabres, the horse would shift her weight from side to side, helping her mount maintain his balance while wielding his blade. If the rider fell, the horse often waited to be mounted again, gently nudging the Cavalier who could no longer rise. Horses have been known to drag their dying companions from the battlefield, shielding them until help arrived.

True heroes were the horses of the Cavalry!

On the march near Athens, Ala
May 25th 1864

Dear Mother

I rescieved a letter from you the day before we left Columbia but I have not had a chance to answer it before this. We left Columbia last Sunday the 22d. Sunday and Monday it was very dusty amarching, but yesterday it was far from being dusty. Yesterday morning just as we got up it commenced raining (two oclock in the morning) and we marched nearly all day in the rain. We are now one mile and half from Athens. I excpect we will lay over here to day for to draw rations. We had no feed for our horses last night nor this morning yet, excepting some of us that went out and got corn from cittizens. I have just got back to camp. I have been 2 miles from camp and brought corn for two horses. We exspect to go from here to Decater [*Ala.*] and there join a force of infantry and go to Roam [*Rome,Ga.*] You will know by the papers where we are before we do ourselves. I would not wonder if I saw Rome soon. if we go near him I shall try and see him. Mother you did not tell me where Frank was in your letter. I wish you to give me his Directions so I can write to him. We have marched our horses hard and I have heard some of the boys say that we will stay here two or three days and let them rest, but I hardly believe it. I should not wonder if we did not stay here all day for it is only a bout 14 miles from here to Decater. We got mail last night. I got a letter from Annie. She writes a good letter. We only came through 3 towns from Columbia here. Limville. Palaski and a little place on Elk river. the first two days we came through a butiful country but yesterday it was not so nice. it put me in mind of the country betweene Pittsburg landing and Corrinth. Mother you had ought to have seen us last night when we got in camp. We were the dirtyest set of men I ever saw I think. The mud on my back was nearly one inch thick and just so with all it rained nearly all the time and whenever we started our horses on a trot then the mud would fly. Mother I dont believe you can read this but I guess you will know who it is from any way. I will try and write to Nan and Annie today. I shall write to you and Nan every chance I can for you two never complain and answer me. Remember me to all who cares for me.

From your son

Fred Kellogg

Direct Co B 3d O.V.C. 2d Brigade. 2d division of Cav. Nashville, Tenn.

Map 14

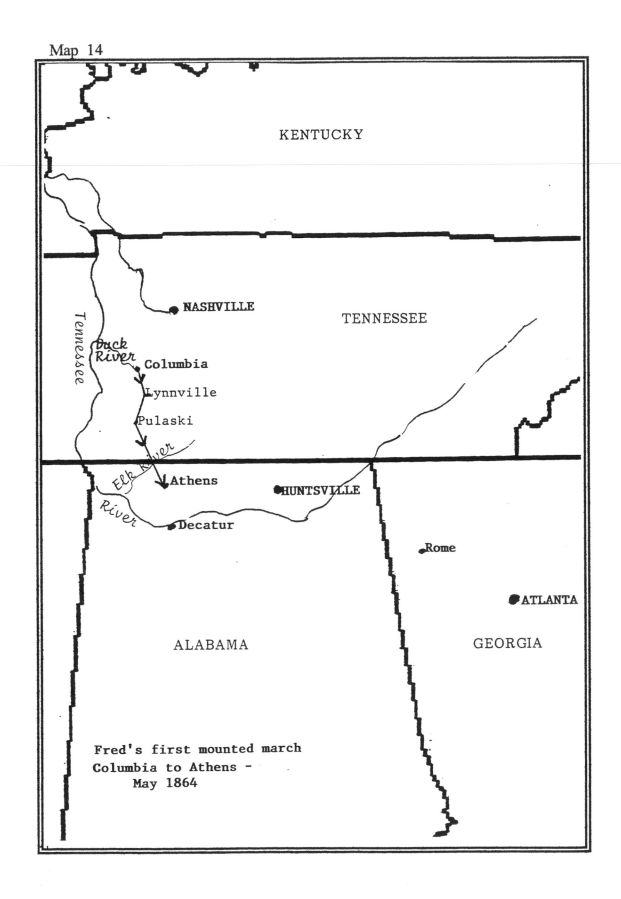

KENTUCKY

TENNESSEE

Tennessee

Duck River

NASHVILLE

Columbia

Lynnville

Pulaski

Elk River

Athens

HUNTSVILLE

River

Decatur

Rome

ATLANTA

ALABAMA

GEORGIA

Fred's first mounted march
Columbia to Athens -
        May 1864

In front of the rebles on the Kinnessaha Mountain[69]

Monday June 20th, 1864

Dear Mother,

I rescieved a letter from you some time a go but have had no chance to answer before for we have not been still long enough at any one time sience I wrote before to night. We have not unsaddled our horses but twice at night and we have had (4) four prety sharp fights with the rebles. We have been very lucky so far for we have had only 20 killed and wounded out of our regiment yet, and only one of our company and he but slitely wounded in the left shoulder. A week a go Saturday 5 Cos of our reg had a very rough time. Our battalion was dismounted and one Co come over the crick mounted to help us and they had 6 men wounded 7 horses killed and 6 wounded. Our Lieut Colonel Howland had his horse killed and got a wound in his thigh. There buglar, dito. 1 wounded - Co A. 1- Co b. 4- Co G. 2- Co H. Yesterday our Division fought all day and all I can learn of it is 1 killed, 10 wounded. We have to fight here dismounted altogether last week we had two engagements. The rebles are on the mountain and intrenched. I have witnessed two days of the artilery duel. I was where I could see the shells from both sides strik our guns rather beat them.

Logans division[70] was near us two days or we were near them. I have not seen any of the infantry yet. We are on the exstream left of our army. there has been no stop to the fighting out on the right of us with the infantry for 3 days and nights. I have heard it nearly all the while myself for I have been on guard every night, last night on picket and we have not been relieved yet but will be soon. we have all drawed 60 rounds of cartridge today so I would not be surprised if we had fun a gain tomorrow. the rebs are in sight of our posts and we are all the time fireing at one another but they are off so far there is not much danger.

---

[69] Kennesaw Mountain. Confederate General Joseph E. Johnston had taken a stand on the mountain, firmly entrenching his troops. When several days of concentrated shelling could not dislodge him, Sherman decided on a frontal attack against the strongest part of the Confederate line. The action was without hope; by 11:00 am the Union was repulsed with 3,000 casualties. This letter tells a good deal about the battle, even though the story is interrupted by other thoughts. Garrard's reports (page 117) and map (page 119) show where Fred was during this battle.

[70] Fred knew his brother Frank was with the 2nd Illinois Light Artillery, part of Logan's Division. He also knew brothers Lyman and Romeyn were among the infantry somewhere along the eight mile wide battle front.

OFFICIAL REPORTS

The second sentence of Fred's letter, "We have not unsaddled our horses but twice at night..." only hints at the furious action that took place almost the instant he was assigned a horse -- four months after enlisting! Reports of his Division Commander, Brigadier-General Kenner Garrard, found in "A Compendium of the War of the Rebellion" compiled by Frederick H. Dyer, relay much of that action. Fred's Brigade Commander was Colonel Eli Long.

Information taken from a report to Brigadier General W. L. Elliott, Chief of Cavalry, Department of the Cumberland.

> On the 6th [June] Colonel Long with his brigade joined the
> division, via Decatur and Rome, and enroute met, engaged,
> defeated and pursued Roddey. On the 9th, we engaged and
> drove three brigades of cavalry and one of infantry in front of
> Big Shanty.

A report of June 10, to Major-General James B. McPherson, Commanding Army of the Tennessee, reads in part:

> This morning I sent Long's brigade down on the Marietta
> and Lovegood's bridge road, and secured the intersection of
> that road with the Big Shanty and Roswell Factory road. I sent
> Minty's brigade across the Noonday [Creek] on the old Alabama
> road toward Roswell Factory and four miles from here he became
> engaged and has been fighting all the afternoon. To relieve him
> I sent part of Long's brigade, 900 men, down the Big Shanty Road
> to come in on the flank of the enemy, but neither Minty nor Long
> could make any headway although they both charged and took
> a line of rail breast-works.

Garrard also stated:

> On the 10th my division took post on the old Alabama road
> near where it crosses Noonday Creek and until the enemy
> abandoned his works on Kennesaw Mountain remained on the left,
> conforming to the advance of the army and guarding the left flank.
> My orders were to protect that flank and keep the cavalry of the
> enemy so engaged that he could not detach any large force to
> intercept our communications. This was effectually accomplished,
> but not without much exertion and activity, resulting in six
> engagements with Wheeler's force, on the 12th, 15th, 19th, 20th,
> 23d, and 27th of June.

What corps is Rome in.[71] It rains here nearly all the time, blackberries are getting ripe. Wheat is ripe and our reg has harvested a good many acres. You said something a bout our men destroying reble proporty. you ought to have been in the rear of the 17th army corps as we were two days. they left nothing in the houses and burnt nearly all outbuildings and all the fences. We are not half so bad for we only take their corn and bacon and let our horses eat their wheat and oats, sometimes drive off their cattle and kill a pig occassionly.
I never was in better health than now.

Fred.

---

[71] Rome was in General George Thomas' Army of the Cumberland. He was a first lieutenant and probably a company commander. Lyman was also under Thomas. He was a captain at this time and was aide to General David S. Stanley. Stanley earned the Congressional Medal of Honor in November, 1864 for meritorious service in the area south of Nashville.

Map 15

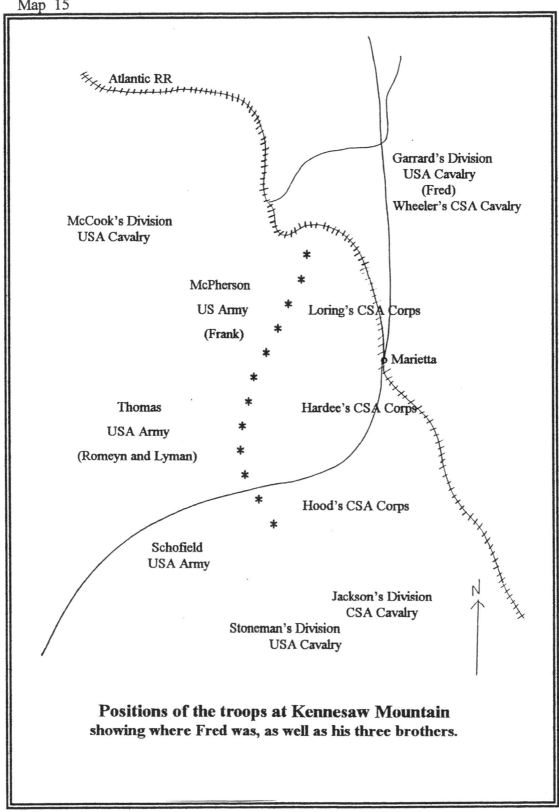

Positions of the troops at Kennesaw Mountain
showing where Fred was, as well as his three brothers.

Camp near Roswell, Ga[72]
July 11th 1864

Dear Mother

Thinking that you would like to hear from me and having a few leisure moments I will try and write you a few lines. We have not had a days rest sience I wrote you last. We have either been afighting or scouting or on picket or out aforageing and an other thing. it is so hot that I dont like to write but I have wrote you twice and Nan once and Ock once sience I have rescieved any from any of you but it dont make a darned bit of difference. I shall write when I feel like it and when I dont I shant. I travaled all one day to find Rome and could not, but sience then we were only 2 miles from his division one night but the next morning we left there before day light. We are afighting nearly every day. the 4th we had the best man of our Co killed and an other wounded. We were afighting all day. the rebs charged us 3 times. it was then you had ought to have heard our Spencers rattle. Our Co has got Spencer carbines. 7 shooters. We drove them out of their breast works (stone ones) and then held them until night. there was only 6 Co.s of us on the skirmish line, the rest of the division was back in line by the batterie.

They call for the letters

So good night

From Fred

---

72 Roswell, Georgia was a manufacturing center. Garrard's troops destroyed several factories and a cotton mill that was making gray cloth for rebel uniforms.

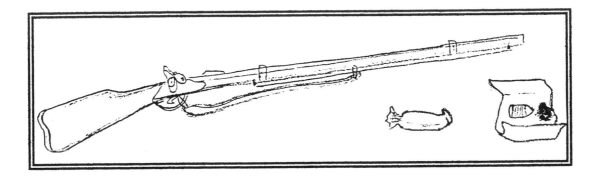

The ENFIELD RIFLE issued to Fred in Missouri, was a smooth bore, .577 caliber muzzle loader firing a cone-shaped bullet known as the "Minie Ball"   A complicated series of tasks prepared the rifle to fire.   A soldier must first tear open a paper packet with his teeth.   The black gun powder inside, surrounding the minie ball, smeared his face, burned his eyes and left a lingering bitter taste. The powder was poured down the muzzle, bullet inserted and rammed solidly down the barrel with a ramrod which the soldier then placed back in its holder mounted beneath the rifle barrel.   A percussion cap was placed in the firing pan, just under the hammer. The minutes it took to reload must have seemed endless to a man under fire, yet the Enfield Rifle was a marked improvement over the old muzzle-loader and powder horn many soldiers brought from home.

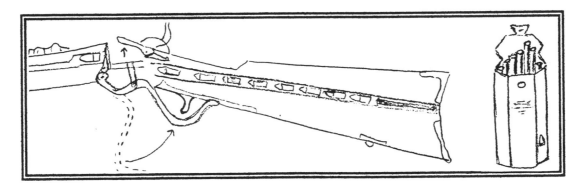

The Cavalry used the SPENCER REPEATING CARBINE, the barrel shortened to 22 inches, .54 caliber and using a single piece cartridge containing the percussion cap, powder and bullet. A tin tube, containing seven cartridges, was loaded through the butt plate of the gunstock. The cartridges fed from the breech toward the firing chamber of the barrel, providing seven-shot repeating action. A Blakeslee Patented leather case, carried by each Cavalier, held ten addition cartridge tubes.   Such a revolution was this gun that the Rebels claimed the Yanks could load up on Monday and shoot all week!

Camp 3d O.V.C.

July 19th 1864

Camp near Mcafees bridge[73] 2 miles south of the Chattahoochee river Ga.

Dear Mother

As there is a chance to send mail this morning I will write you a few lines so you will know that I am all right. We are a having very good times now and plenty to eat. Our regiment went out on a scout the other day. We went east of here 20 miles to a place called Coumings. Our company done first rate. We captured 7 mules 2 horses and all the tobaco that we could carrie. I made over $75.00 on the tobaco I got. I wish I was where I could send it to you. I will try 20 dollars in this and run the risk. I have not had a letter in so long I dont believe I could read one now if I should get it. some of the boys got letters last night and judging from what they wrote I think that the folks at home are a finding fault with Sherman because he dont move faster. I wish to God I could kill every one of the fault finding Sons of bitches. They will surport Old Abe Lincoln who dont want anything done and find fault with thouse who are adoing all that can be done. We are afightin nearly all the time and it is awfull hot weather to do such work. Breakfast is ready and it is time this was mailed so I shall have to close. There is more blackberries here in country than any other place I ever saw. I think I eat a bushle every day. Our battallion was out 5 miles day before yesterday. Co A had one man captured and D had one [and] had a horse killed and when we were a coming back Co K went down on some honey. We took up 4 hives. it did not eat bad. and our mess got a lot of meal and some flour.

Write when you get ready to your Son

Fred

3d O.V.C. 2d Brig 2d Cav Division Army of the Tenn.

---

[73] Mentioned several times in Garrard's reports as McAfee's bridge or Dr. McAfee's place. Our research has failed to discover the exact location.

Camp 3d C. v. v. c. July 19th 1864
Camp near Mc afees bridge 2 miles
south of the Chattahoochee River
G a.

Dear mother
        As there is a chance
to send mail this morning &
will write you a few
lines. so you will know
that I am all right. we
are a having very good
times now and plenty to
eat. our regiment went
out on a scout the other
day. we went east of here
20 miles to a place called
coumings. our company
done first rate. we cap-
tured 7 mules 2 horses and
all the tobaco that we
could carrie & made

Camp 3d O.V.C. near Atlanta, Ga
Aug 2d 1864

Dear Mother

      I have just rescieved yours of the 25th. I rescieved one from Nan two days a go and   I got one from you week or more a go in witch you said you had wrote to me a bout the deth of Lyme's children, but I never rescieved your letter so I dont know any thing a bout them only that some or all of them are dead.[74] You seam to feel uneasy about us boys concerning the fight near Atlanta some time a go. I dont think Rome nor Lime was in it from what I have heard and I know I was not for we were 40 miles east of Atlanta a destroying the Atlanta and Charleston R.R. But you need not worry if you dont hear from me as often as you would like to for it is seldom that we are in one place long enough to write a letter. There has been a hard fight sience the one you speak of. Our Division was a way then too. We were then 40 miles south of Atlanta. We went within 4 miles of the Macon R.R. when the rebs surrounded us but they got badly whiped but we could not cross the river for there was too many rebs on the other side. So we came back by the way of Covington. I have not seen Rome nor Lime yet. Charley Champlin has been wounded a gain at Batton Rouse. his brother Brad was killed the 27th of June near Kensaw mountain. if we dont leave here tomorrow morning I shall try and find Rome. I understand that the 16th Army Corps is only 4 miles from here. but I make no calculations on seeing him tomorrow for I hear the boys hollowing another raid and I should not be surprised if it were so. I sent you 20 dollars in a letter a short time ago. I shall send what money I have to you by George Cole next month when he is discharged and if I dont sell a couple of Gold penholders before he goes I shall send them too and the big one I want you to have. I have a little silver cup too. I have not time to write more. I have got to go for corn.

[no signature]

3d O.V.C. 2d Division Army Cumberland.

---

[74] Lyman and Caroline had four children. The three youngest, Edward Cargill, Robert Swartwout and Roberta, ages seven, five and three died at this time, leaving only the oldest, Harry Sturges Kellogg, surviving. Family records do not reveal the cause of death. At this time, Lyman (as a Captain) was commanding the 18th Infantry Regiment on a temporary basis (from June 14 to September) as all his superior officers had been killed or wounded. He was unable to get a furlough to go home to bury his children nor to console his wife.

A portion of a report from General Kenner Garrard to General Sherman.

Headquarters Second Cavalry Division
Decatur, July 24, 1864

General: I have the honor to report that your instructions have been carried out. My dispositions were such as to enable me to take every point by surprise and insure my safe return, with a loss of only 2 killed. Results: Three road bridges and one railroad bridge (555 feet in length) over the Yellow River, and one road and one railroad bridge (250 feet in length) over the Ulcofauhachee, were burned. Six miles of railroad track between the rivers were well destroyed. The depot and considerable quantity of quartermaster and commissary stores at Covington were burnt. One train and locomotive captured at Conyers and burnt. One train (platform) was burnt at Covington, and a small train (baggage) at station near the Ulcofauhachee captured and burnt. The engine to the last train was detached across the river. Citizens report a passenger train and a construction train, both with engines, cut off between Stone Mountain and Yellow River. Over 2,000 bales of cotton were burnt. A large new hospital at Covington, composed of over 30 buildings, just finished, were burnt, together with a very large lot of fine carpenters' tools used in their erection. Those in hospital at Oxford (two miles north of Covington) along with their surgeons, were not disturbed. I have received 140 prisoners and 11 officers and about 200 Negroes, who have been sent to the provost marshal, Army of the Tennessee. I cannot mention too highly the zeal and promptness of my whole command, and to their good conduct and earnestness I am indebted for this success. Since leaving Marietta this division has been so constantly in motion it is now very much out of condition, and I would be pleased to have a few days quiet to shoe horses and repair equipments. I was absent from Decatur less than three days, and as a division marched over ninety miles, and at the time of the receipt of the order, twelve hours before starting, was scattered from McAfee's Bridge to Decatur, guarding all the roads to the east and south of this flank of the army.

Very respectfully, your obedient servant,

K. Garrard, Brigadier-General.

Camp 3d O V C
near Atlanta, Ga
Aug 7th 1864

Dear Mother,

I rescieved your last yesterday and very glad hearing from you and from the 20 dollars that I sent and am glad that it came in good time for you. I dont know what is agoing to happen. We have not had a fight nor moved camp for four days.[75] Our company had a little excitement yesterday. We went out in the country some 8 miles in search of some coal. We had one six mule team with us. after we had got out where we thought we would find it the advance guard went on a head to see if they could find any and others were sent in other directions. I was one of the advance guards. We went about one mile, found some coal and what we wanted. We sent one back to report. Others had found some so he came back and had us join the Co. We met them on their way back. We were sent on the advance again to go where we had found the coal.
We wheeled our horses and troted them back for we had found some plums and peaches and we were in a hurry to get back. When we had got within 20 rods of the house we heard some firing in the rear. We haulted and I went back to see what was up but before I got back everything was quite a gain. But I found that the boys had got a Mr. Reb and that Holley, one of our boys had got 4, four revolver balls in his face. There was five rebs came right out of the woods in front of 3 of the boys who were back a bout 15 rods in the rear of the wagon and rear guard, and ordered them to sirrender. the boys did not like going South so they would not surrinder. Holley got 4 balls in the face and today is a round camp.
Tell Nan I will write to her as soon as I can but she need not wait for me to write. I have not seen Rome nor Lyme yet. We go on picket tomorrow. We got one of the rebs and the rest of them went out of the way.

from your Affectionate Son
Fred.

---

[75] Sherman apparently granted Garrard's request for a few days rest.

five rebs came right
out of the woods in
front of 3 of the boys
who were back a
bout 15 rods in the
rear of the wagon
rear guard; and ordered
them to surrender
the boys did not like
going south, so they
would not surrender
Holley got 2 balls
in the face and to
day is a round camp
tell nan & will write
to her as soon as &
can, but she need not
wait for me to write
& have not seen Rome
nor & im yet, we got on picket,

Camp 3d O.V.C.
near Atlanta Ga
Aug 15th 1864

Dear Mother
     I wrote you a sheet some time a go but have not had time to finish before. We have been in this camp some time now. I see by the papers that Longs brigade was captured with Stoneman but that was a misstake.[76] I went one day where the 14th Army Corps was and they were not there so I did not see Rome. they are now on the exstream right of the army and we are on the left and in the rear. I dont know as you can [read] this old sheet. I want you to send me a pair of galissis[77]
     [no signature]

---

[76] General George Stoneman, another Union Cavalry officer, often operated with General Garrard. On this occasion, Long's troops (including Fred) were ordered back to Decatur. Stoneman rode on in an attempt to get to Andersonville to relieve the Union soldiers being held in prison there. On being surrounded by Confederates, Stoneman and 700 of his men were captured. Stoneman and his officers were held in Macon, his other troopers taken to join the unfortunate prisoners they had hoped to free.

[77] He meant "galluses", an old term for suspenders. The meaning becomes more clear in the next letter.

Camp 8^d O.V.c.
Near Atlanta Ga
Aug 15th 1864
Dear Mother
I wrote you
a sheet some time
a go but have not
had time to finish
before. we have been
in this camp
some time now
I see by the paper
that Jones brigade
was captured with
Stoneman, but that
was a misstake.
I went one day where
the 14th army corps
was, and they was
not there so I did
not see Home, they

Camp O.V.C. Near Atlanta, Ga
Aug 16th 1864

Dear Mother

As I have time I will write you a few lines. I sent you a letter yesterday. One of our boys was killed yesterday while we were out a forageing. He was killed by some bushwhackers who were lying in the bushes. two of the boys were back in the rear of the company. they had been to a house and bought some butter and milk. the rest of Co was in the cornfield getting green corn. When they had got within 20 rods of the Co 5 rebs came out of the woods and fired on them. they were not over 20 feet a part. Willson was shot through the body. he lived until dark. his time was out the 3d of next month. Our Division went out on a scout yesterday. they were gone when our Co got back but we followed them up. We went to Decater. We found a few rebs there who we made skidaddle through town in a hurry. We got back in camp at a rather later hour. 12 1/2 O clock.

I shall send home a blanket and some money by Sargent Cole when he goes. he will be discharged sometime next month. he will call and see you. I want you to send me a pair of suspenders for mine are nearly played and I wish you would have two good dark colored casimere shirts made and send one at a time by mail. if you cant get casimire get something eles. have a pocket on the inside of each on the left side. I want good long tails to them. There is nothing new here. The firing is kept up night and day. there is nothing but a continual roar of heavy artilary all the time. there is just enough musketry to make it musical. At Decater last night the rebs charged us 3 times but our Spencers soon dischouraged them. there was to much music for them to digest. Well we have plenty of green corn now so that we live first rate. I think that Cav. has a better chance to live then infantry for we have a better chance to forage. We can shoot a hog and fetch him right a long or take what ever we want where we find it. the reason I did not finish my letter yesterday, the orderlie called for the letters before I was ready. Write when you can to your loving son. Tell Nan she need not wait for me to write but to write to me just when she has a mind to.

Fred Kellogg

pair of suspenders for
mine are nearly played
and I wish you would have
two good dark colored
cassimere shirts made
and send one at a time by
mail if you cant get cassimere
get somthing eles have a pocket
on the inside of each on the
left side I want good long
tails to them there is
nothing new here
The firing is keeping
night and day there is nothing
but a continual roar of
heavy artelary all the time
there is just enough
muskettry to make it
musical. at Deeters last
night the rebs charged
us 8 times but our spincer
soon discouraged them
there was to much music

Camp 3d OVC Between Atlanta and Roswell, Ga.   Sept 11th 1864
Dear Mother

I just rescieved the suspenders all right was a little dispointed because there was no letter for me. I suppose you have heard before this, that Rome and Lime both are wounded. Lime through the right arm and Rome through the right hip. I did not see them. I went to their regiments to see them but was to late for they were on their [way] north. Neither of them bad.[78] We have had a hard time ever science we started out with Killpartrick[79] on the raid. When I get time I will write you all a bout it. I saw Clarance the night before we started for the rear of Atlanta. But there is one thing sure the rebs went out of Atlanta in a hurry.[80] there was some prety hard fighting near and at Jonesboro. there is where Rome and Lime were wounded. their Division charged the rebs in brestworks. We have had no hard fighting sience we were on the raid but we are on picket nearly all the time and we have plenty picket firing. Now we are back in the rear of the army but there is enough for us to do here for the woods is full of bushwackers. they fired into our reg yesterday while we were agoing a long and to day there was a good many shots fired at the forageers. Well I must tell you how I got it to day. While out a forageing Adams and I went for a hive of honey. Well Adams got the honey and Kellogg got the bees. Well I will tell the truth the bees got me. some in my hair some in my bosoms and some [blacked out] and they give me perfict hell. When I get some new cloths I will write again.

                                                        Fred.

---

[78] In his "Recollections of Civil War Service", Romeyn gives this account: "The ground in our immediate front was open, sloping down to a creek and up to the timber where the enemy waited for us. I had command of two companies of the 16th. The 18th was the first to reach the enemy. The Captain commanding the 18th [brother Lyman] was shot down as he leaped his horse over the parapet, while leading his regiment. I went on with my two companies and drove the Confederates from the trench in my front. A dozen Confederates began to enfilade my men. One of the bunch sent a ball through my right hip. I fell and realized I was severely wounded. I was able, however, to retain command of my men until the rest of the brigade came forward and added another laurel to its wreath of victories."
Both Romeyn and Lyman were sent to Ohio, both recuperated and rejoined their units within a few months. The enlistment period for Frank's unit expired. Discharged, Frank went home to Ohio.
[79] Garrard's brigades rode with those of General Judson Kilpatrick.
[80] For one hundred and twenty days the Union pounded away at the Rebel defenses ringing the outskirts of Atlanta and hurled thousands of shells into the city itself. During the night of September 2, 1864 Confederate General Hood ordered the destruction of anything the Union might use, including eighty-one carloads of ammunition, and then abandoned the city. On September 3 Sherman wired General Halleck, "Atlanta is ours, and fairly won."

Map 16

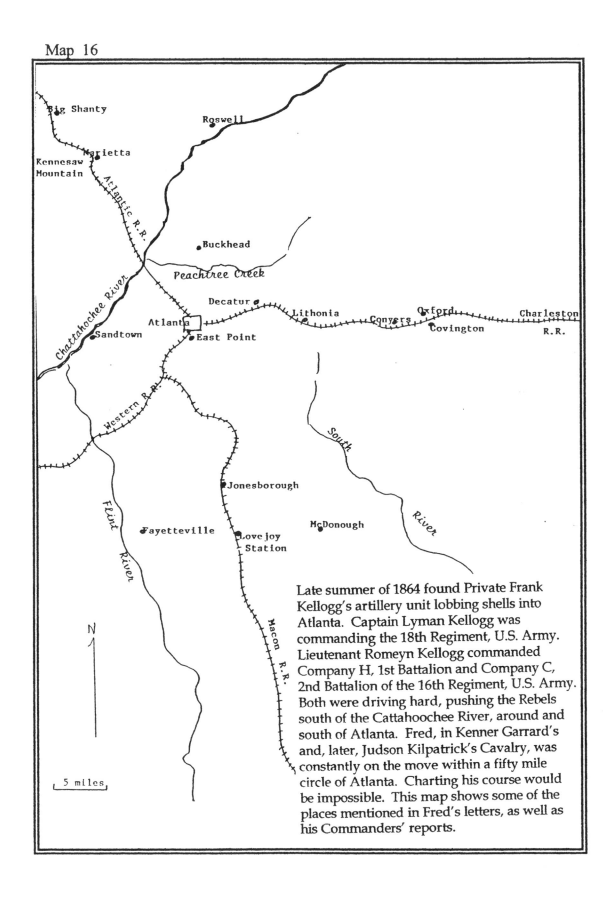

Late summer of 1864 found Private Frank Kellogg's artillery unit lobbing shells into Atlanta. Captain Lyman Kellogg was commanding the 18th Regiment, U.S. Army. Lieutenant Romeyn Kellogg commanded Company H, 1st Battalion and Company C, 2nd Battalion of the 16th Regiment, U.S. Army. Both were driving hard, pushing the Rebels south of the Cattahoochee River, around and south of Atlanta. Fred, in Kenner Garrard's and, later, Judson Kilpatrick's Cavalry, was constantly on the move within a fifty mile circle of Atlanta. Charting his course would be impossible. This map shows some of the places mentioned in Fred's letters, as well as his Commanders' reports.

Camp 3d O.V.C. Cav.
Sept 20th 1864

Dear Mother
        I rescieved yours of the 29th and 31th of Aug yesterday and as
I have time now I will write you. If you have not sent those shirts when
you rescieve this you need not send them until you hear from me a gain.
We now exspect to go to Nashville within a week. the Officers say that
we are to turn over our horses tomorrow and that our reg will start for
Nashville next Monday. The non veterans start for home to morrow.
Geo. Cole will be up and see you after he gets home.
        Now I will tell you a little a bout the Killpatrick raid. We left our
camp at Buckhead 8 miles northeast of Atlanta the night of 17th of Aug
at ten Oclock. the next morning at ten we joined Killpatrick at Sandtown
witch [is] 15 miles northwest of Atlanta. We lay there until ten o clock
that night (the 18) when we all started after having orders read to us that
we were to cut the enemies communications or die atrying. then we
started, Kills division and two brigades of ours, Minties and Longs.
We did not go over four miles before we run on the rebs. [We] captured
5 of them and made the rest skedaddle and day light the next morning
19th we crossed the Mount Gurnsey R.R. Kills division was a head,
Minies brigade in the rear. just as Minties brig came to the RR the rebs
came on them from Atlanta. Rosses brigade of six regiments, they opened
on Mintie with artilery and all their men was dismounted. Mintie
dismounted his men and went for them. the spencers soon made them
get out of the way. We were ordered back to help him with our brigade
but before we got back he had them whiped. We had 20 men wounded
here and two ambelances distroyed by their shell. Killpatrick then sent
our brigade a head. We did not go over two miles after we passed Kills
division before we came on the rebs. Co A and our Co were advance
guard. There was 8 or ten of Co A in advance when the rebs fired on
them. they fell back and we formed a line with our two companies. We
then advanced 8 men from our Co to try them on. We advanced up the
hill to the woods and there we found them forming a line for us. We fired
on them. they were not over 8 rods from us when we fired on them. they
charged us in return. We went back as if the devil was after us. As they
came over the hill the boys who were in line opened on them and they
went back in a hurry. But they soon came a gain and this time there was

to many of them for us and we had to fall back. Co A had 3 men wounded and 8 horses wounded. Our regiment all dismounted then and went for them and drove them and kept driving all day until 4 o clock when they came to a crick where they tore up the bridge. here the rest of brigade dismounted and then we charged them and got to the crick and our regiment kept them back with our Spencers until the 1st and 4th crossed the crick. We soon found them most to strong for us and then Minties brigade dismounted and came to help us. We then started them and kept them agoing until we came to the Macon RR at Jonesboro. When we got there it was dark and I was what I call tired. Then we went to work a distroying the R.R. We worked until 12 Oclock. then we were ordered to mount our horses. We went where they was but they warnt there. We had to go over two miles before we found them. I guess there was mad men that night. We then traveled east for a long time and then south and then southwest and struck the RR at daylight, the 20th. here one half of our Co were sent to work at the RR and the rest of us commenced getting something to eat. But before we were through we were ordered to mount. We did not go over 20 rods before we formed a line with our battalion and we did not have long to wait before the rebs were in sight. they soon made us get out [of] there. Co C had two men wounded. Co D, 2 and Co A, 1. Our Co was luckey. C had 2 horses wounded and A, one. the rest of the regiment went farther back and dismounted and got behind the fence and let them come very close and then let them have it. the rebs fell back but only for to take a new start. Here we discovered we were fighting infantry. they soon were on both flanks and in front and we had to get out of the way. the 1st Ohio lost a good many men here. Kill found out he could not hurt the RR here so he lit out going east and then south and left our brigade in the rear to keep off the rebs and put Minties brigade a head. We had hardly got rid of them in the rear when Mintie came on them. then we were ordered foward to help him. here we fought them until afternoon but those in the rear came up so Kills men had to fight. It was not long before they had us completly surrounded and then sent in a flag of truce for us to surrender. Kill sent word back to General Ross to go to Hell. he was a going out of there. He then formed us in a field and ordered us to draw sabers and to charge, Mintie on one side of the road and Long on the other a head. it was fun to hear Long yell. he went at the head of our reg. here I was unlucky and I don [know] but [what] I was lucky for being unlucky for we only went a few rods when my horse fell in a ditch and Kellogg a long with him. I got him as soon as I could and mounted and let him have the spurs as well as I knew how, but it was of no use. he had hurt himself and soon fell a gain. this time I thought more of Kellogg than I did of my horse so I left him. the rebs then were not over 25 rods from me. If you had seen me run then I guess you would think I was good on foot. I was not the only one a foot. I soon had company, some who had had their horses killed and some had fell in the ditch. I went about a half mile and found a reb ammunition wagon. 5 of the mules had been shot and the other was half scarts to deth but I finaly got his harness off and mounted him. he was an ugly cuss and I then thought of Balam.[81] I would not now blame him if he had of pounded his ass until this time. there was 2 of our Co wounded in the charge. after we had got out of the scrape I got a saddle so I was a little better off. We had just got together when the rebs came on us a gain. this time our brigade lost a grate many and Long got wounded twice through the right arm and through the groin. finaly we got away from them and marched nearly all night and I never saw it rain harder in my life than it did that night. in the charge we lost our pack mule and all of our eatables so all we had after that until we got back to our old camp was green [corn]. We got back the night of 23d. the 21st we had to ford a river. here I came near loosing my mule. he swame a gainst a stick of timber and got badly hurt but he carried me to camp so I dont find any fault. We burnt all the briges we came to so that the rebs could not follow us. after that nothing happened until we got near camp then such cheering and yelling I never heard before excepting the day of the charge.

If we go to Nashville I will write as soon as I get there and if we dont go I will write a gain soon, but you can write and direct to Nashville. I will get it any way. Weather we go there or not some thinks our brigade is a going to another department. I hope so. I have seen enough of Ga. No I have not either for I have not seen Atlanta yet. I shall go there day after tomorrow. When you write let me know where Rome and Lime are and how they are and all a bout it if you know. I suppose Frank is at home if so tell him to write Fred.   Give my love to all.   Fred.

---

[81] He is referring to the Bible, Numbers 22: 21 - 35. Balaam struck his ass to keep him on the road, not knowing the ass could see the Angel of the Lord whereas Balaam could not.

Fred's account of "Kilpatrick's Great Raid" is verified by General Kilpatrick's report to Captain J. E. Jacobs, Assistant Adjutant-General: [Only a portion of report given here.]

Headquarters Third Cavalry Division,
Department of the Cumberland,
Camp Crooks, Ga., September 13, 1864

Captain: I have the honor to submit the following report of the operations of my command during the recent campaign, commencing with the advance across Taylor's Ridge and the battle of Resaca, and ending with the defeat of the rebel army and fall of Atlanta:

I left my camp at Sandtown on the evening of the 18th instant with the Third Cavalry Division, and two brigades of the Second and two batteries of artillery, numbering 4,500 men, to attack and destroy the enemy's communications.   Pickets from the Sixth Texas were met and driven across Camp Creek, and the regiment routed from its camp a mile beyond at 10 o'clock in the evening, and at 12:30 a.m., General Ross' brigade, 1,100 strong, was driven from my front in the direction of East Point, and held from the road by the Second Brigade, Third Division (Lieutenant-Colonel Jones), while the entire command passed.   The West Point railroad was reached, and a portion of the track destroyed at daylight.   Here General Ross attacked my rear.   He was repulsed, and I moved on the Fayetteville road, where I again found him in my front.   He slowly retired in the direction of Jonesborough, and crossed Flint River at 2 p.m., destroying the bridge.   Under cover of my artillery, Colonels Minty and Long, commanding detachments from their brigades, crossed the river and drove the enemy from his rifle pits.   The bridge was repaired, and the entire command crossed and occupied Jonesborough at 5 p.m., driving the enemy's cavalry in confusion from the town.   I now learned that the telegraph and railroad had been destroyed at Bear Creek Station at 11 a.m. by a portion of my command, under Lieutenant-Colonel Klein, and that General Armstrong had passed through Jonesborough in that direction at 1 pm.   For six hours my entire command was engaged destroying the road.   At 11 o'clock in the evening Colonel Murray's division was attacked one mile below the town and driven back.   I now suspended operation upon the road and attacked the enemy and drove him one mile and a half.   Fearing an attack from the direction of Atlanta, I moved before daylight, in direction of Covington, five miles, and halted and allowed the enemy to come up; left one brigade to engage his attention, and moved rapidly in direction of McDonough, six miles, thence across the country to the Fayetteville road, and reached the railroad one mile above Lovejoy's Station at 11 a.m. on the 20th instant. On attempting to move on the station I encountered a brigade of infantry -- was repulsed; I and my command only saved by the prompt and daring [bravery] of Colonels Minty and Long, and Captain Estes[82], my assistant adjunct-general.

The enemy were finally checked and driven back with heavy loss. We captured 1 battle-flag. At this moment a staff officer from Colonel Murray informed me that a large force of cavalry, with artillery, had attacked his rear. In twenty minutes I found that I was completely enveloped by cavalry and infantry, with artillery. I decided at once to ride over the enemy's cavalry and retire on McDonough road. A large number of my people were dismounted, fighting on foot, and it took some time to mount them and form my command for the charge. During the delay the enemy constructed long lines of barricades on every side. Those in front of his cavalry were very formidable. Colonel Minty, with his command in three columns, charged, broke, and rode over the enemy's left. Colonel Murray, with regiments, broke his center, and in a moment General Jackson's division, 4,000 strong, was running in great confusion. It was the most perfect rout any cavalry has sustained during the war. We captured 4 guns (3 were destroyed and 1 brought off); 3 battle-flags were taken; his ambulances, wagons, and ordnance trains captured, and destroyed as far as possible; many prisoners were taken, and his killed and wounded is known to be large. My command was quickly reformed, thrown into position, fought successfully the enemy's infantry for one hour and forty minutes, and only retired when it was found that we had left only sufficient ammunition to make sure our retreat. We swam Cotton Indian Creek and crossed South River on the morning of the 21st, and reached our lines near Decatur, by way of Lithonia, without molestation, at 2 p.m. August 22. We effectively destroyed four miles of the Macon road, from Jonesborough to Bear Creek Station, a distance of ten miles. One train of cars was fully, and a second partially, destroyed. We brought into camp 1 gun, 3 battle-flags, and a large number of fresh horses and mules and about 50 prisoners. My entire loss in killed, wounded, and missing will not exceed 300 men. Two

---

82 Twenty-one year old Llewellyn G. Estes led a charge across a burning bridge, driving the foe away from the Flint River. For this heroism, Estes was awarded the Congressional Medal of Honor.

hundred of this number were killed and wounded. Only the dangerously wounded were left with the enemy.

While it is most difficult to single out instances of gallantry, I cannot close this report without mentioning to the favorable consideration of the major-general commanding, the following named officers whose gallant conduct attracted my attention on so many occasions: Colonel Minty, commanding two brigades from the Second Cavalry Division, for his untiring energy throughout the march, and the consummate skill displayed at the moment when we were repulsed at Lovejoy's Station, and the subsequent gallant ride of his command over the enemy's barricades, deserves immediate promotion. Colonel Long was equally distinguished, and well deserves the promotion he has received. He was twice wounded, and yet remained on the field. Officers were never more gallant, and skillful; men were never more brave. They well deserve a success so great.

Before closing my report, I desire to assure the chief of cavalry that the officers and men of my command have endeavored to zealously and faithfully discharge every duty assigned then, and I only hope that he and those my seniors in rank are as well satisfied with my conduct and operations as I am with the efforts of my command.

Respectfully submitted.   J. Kilpartick

Brigadier-General, U. S. Vols., Commanding

Report of prisoners of war captured and rebel government property captured and destroyed by Third Cavalry Division, Department of the Cumberland, during the campaign of Atlanta.

Prisoners of war captured at different times and various

places......220

Captured during the month of July and August:

Horses...52

Mules...92

Cannon captured near Lovejoy's Station..............1

Cannon spiked near Lovejoy's Station..................3

Caissons destroyed near Lovejoy's Station...........2

Miles Macon and Atlanta Railroad destroyed.....3

Chattanooga, Tennessee
Nov 8th 1864

Dear Mother

I will write you a few lines and let you know that I am a live and a mong the living.   I have had 3 letters from you sience I have wrote you. there has been no time that I could write before. We have been a going night and day ever sience I saw Rome and Lime. In the month of Oct. our Div had 12 fights with the rebs and only one but what we drove them, then we fell back and the next day took two Divisions of infantry and some artilery and went for them a gain, our regiment in advance. We drove them in their brest works where they used their artilery. Our Colonel had his horse killed. We had 4 or 5 men wounded and 8 or 10 horses killed.   then the infantry came up and brought up two batteries, one on each road. it was a grand sight to see the infantry march in line across the open field and the rebs throwing shells right a mong them and not one of them flinch. they soon routed the rebs. Our Colonel wanted to charge them, but Gen.Osterhought[83] would not let him. Our Division turned our horses over to Killpatrick at Rome a week ago yesterday. We are now on our way to Nashville for horses. When I have time and a place to write I will let you have a full account of our doings for the last two months. I have had good health all the time, never better. I weigh 148 pounds fat enough to kill. I exspect there is some back luck a head for me for I was made 4th Corperal a bout two months a go. But for godsake dont direct my letters Corp. Kellogg, but Fred Kellogg is enough. What is Frank a going to do.   tell him not to enlist a gain nor go for a substitute. Our regiment is a voting today. I am sory to say that I cant vote. I would not vote for Mcclellen[84] for I think him a traitor and I'll be dambed if I would vote for Lincoln. let me know if Rome has sent me a hat or anything else. if he has not tell him he need not unless I write for them. I got the shirt all right. I hear some talk that we will go to Louisville, Ky. for horses. Write as soon as you get this and Direct Nashville.

Give my compliments to all who inquire after   Fred

---

[83] General Peter J. Osterhaus
[84] General George McClellen, assigned by Lincoln to attack Richmond from the coastal area south of the city, constantly delayed his movements, requesting more and more of the troops and guns protecting Washington. Many people felt he was deliberately trying to weaken the Capitol's defenses and dubbed him a traitor. As the war dragged on and on many soldiers, as well as civilians, lost confidence in Lincoln as a leader.

Portions of a report, dated October 26, 1864, from Brevet Maj. Gen. J. H. Wilson to Chief of Staff, Brig. Gen. J. A. Rawlins, regarding the status of the cavalry.

I wish I could write you as fully as I wish, but there is some danger of letters falling into other hands than those intended. This is for you and General Grant, that you may be correctly informed of the condition of the cavalry question out west.

The last returns show a cavalry force of nearly 60,000 men, but in reality there are not over 14,000 mounted. There are three divisions here in the field commanded by Kilpatrick, McCook, and Garrard, mounting about 1,500 men each, 4,500 in all. They have about twice as many dismounted, guarding railroads and block-houses. Colonel Garrard commands a division formerly attached to the Army of the Ohio; five regiments are at the remount camp at Louisville preparing for the field, leaving only parts of two regiments in the field near Atlanta. There are five new Indiana regiments, averaging 750 men, now at Nashville, never mounted. They are splendid material, in for three years, and should be brought out at once. In all there are six divisions actually organized. These divisions average about ten regiments each, 500 men, or an aggregate of 30,000.

But what are the facts now? We cannot raise 6,000 because horses, arms, and equipments have not been furnished. General Sherman estimates that Forrest (now commanding all the cavalry of Beauregard's military division) has 26,000 men mounted. From this hasty sketch you may readily perceive how vastly superior the enemy is to us.

My main efforts are now directed to mounting McCook, Garrard, and Kilpatrick, and I am doing all in my power to urge that forward. You will see the absolute necessity of my having good officers. At present I have but one brigade commander who is a general officer. Garrard, Elliot and Knipe are to be assigned to infantry, for which they are better suited. I have already asked General Grant for General Upton and Colonel Mackenzie, Custer, Pennington, and Reno. The cavalry of the Army of the Potomac has already achieved an acknowledged superiority over that of the enemy, and officers detached from it will not disable it, but will carry a prestige with them highly advantageous to us out west. I don't think, either, it will discourage our own officers, for we shall have a large field for promotion. I would like, therefore, to have the officers I have designated and the horses, arms, and equipments sufficient to put my troops in the field so that, finally, I may be able to exceed Forrest in numbers.

Camp 3d OVC near Louisville, Ky
Nov 20th 1864

Dear Mother

I wrote you from Chattanooga a short time a go, but then we did not know where we were a going. We are now in Louisville. We will be here probly 2 weeks and maybe longer, but I think not. We will be paid tomorrow. I shall send you $200.00. I did not send any blanket by Cole. I lost it on the Killpatrick raid. You can send that other shirt now if you have it ready. I have a nice pair of boots that I think I shall send home before we leave here. They are most too light for winter. they did not cost me anything. one of the boys captured them. (He got whole box from a sutler) When you write let me know how much if any did Ock keep of that $65.00 I sent from Columbia so I will know how much money he has of mine. We have had a harder time sience we turned our horses over than we ever did before. I wish we had of staid down there and went with Sherman. I dred the going from here to Ala. a gain. It has rained nearly all the time sience we turned over our horses. I have not had a letter from any one but you for over two months. Well I am glad of it for I have not got any to answer. We dont fare half as well here as we did when we were in Ala.and I shall be glad when we leave here. the 4th OVC Cav has been taken from the 1st brig. and the rest of the 1st and 2d have been put together so we are now in the 1st brig. Long is a going to command our division and Mintie our brig.[85] When we turned over horses there was 21 men of us in our Co. Now there [are] 60 and they are not all here yet. I cant think of anything eles to write. Give me all the news when you write. when I feel like writing I will write again and try to do better. If any one wants to know anything a bout Fred tell them he is all right.

From your loving son
Fred Kellogg

---

[85] Eli Long was Fred's brigade commander. He has now replaced Kenner Garrard as division commander while Colonel Minty is now brigade commander.

Map 17

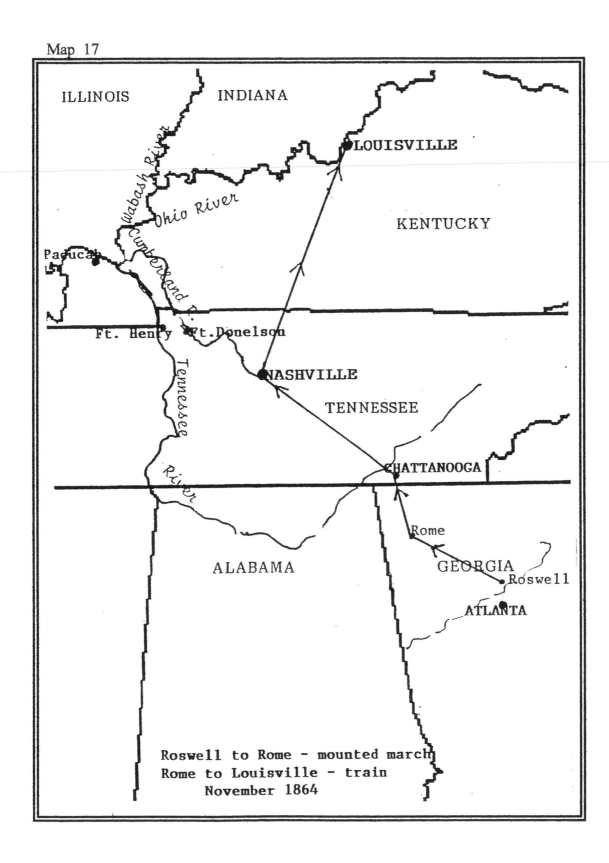

ILLINOIS   INDIANA

Wabash River

Ohio River

LOUISVILLE

KENTUCKY

Cumberland R.

Paducah

Ft. Henry   Ft. Donelson

Tennessee

NASHVILLE

TENNESSEE

River

CHATTANOOGA

Rome

ALABAMA   GEORGIA

Roswell

ATLANTA

Roswell to Rome - mounted march
Rome to Louisville - train
November 1864

Louisville
Nov 28th 1864

Dear Mother

I send you two hundred dollars by Sam Bassett. You can keep it [where] it draws interest. I have not time to write much now. I have been sick but am all right now. I send a pair of boots to you. [You] can take care of them and dont let the mice or rats eat them up.

Fred

Camp 3d OVC Louisville, Ky.
Dec 6th 1864

Dear Mother

I have been looking for a letter from you for some time but have not got it yet. I have been sick but I am now well a gain. We are a going to draw horses to day so I think we will not stay here long. The 4th has gone. Mother I did not get all of my money that I had lent so I want you to send me 10.00 in letter. I have spent all of my money and so I have to go down on my banker. When I sent that 200.00 I did not think we would stay here as long as we have or I should not have sent as much as I did.

Fred

Camp, 8 A. V. C. Lovisville, Ky,
Dec, 6th 1864

Dear Mother

I have been
looking for a letter from
you for sometime but
have not got it yet. I have
been sick but I am now
well again, we are a
going to draw horses
today. So I think we will
not stay here long, the
4th has gone. Mother
I did not get all of my
money that I had lent
So I want you to send
me 10,00 in letter. I have
spent all of my money
and so I have to go
down on my banker
when I want that I owe

Camp 3d O.V.C. Louisville, Ky
Dec 15th 1864

Brother Rome[86]

I recieved your kind and welcome letter yesterday and am much olidge to [you] for it. I had nearly made up my mind that I had no friends or else they were all on a spree for I have not had only one letter before yesterday for over a month. yesterday I got four. I have just answered one of them. I am nearly froze so I dont think I shall write much in this. We have got our horses and good ones too. We pressed them here in the City. I have got the best horse I ever rode. Last monday night at eleven Oclock we were ordered out to saddle and be ready with one days ration in 20 minutes. 3 companies of us went out on the Shelbyville road 20 miles, got there a little before daylight, fed our horses and 7 of us went to a house and got a good warm breakfast and at 7 Oclock we started back for camp with orders to take all horses fit for Cav. work. I was sent in charge of one lot off from the main road. We had a very cold ride of it during the night, but on tuesday I had lots of fun and plenty to eat and drink. I got 4 horses. At every place we went they would ask us in to have something to eat and drink. We had all the wine, wiskey, pies, cake, apple cider that we wanted and I had 3 good warm dinners. We got back in camp just at dark. We expect to leave here soon and I hope so for we have it a grate deal easier when we are out in the field then we do here. I got a letter from Mother mailed at the same time yours was. I wrote to Mother sometime a go to send me some money but I have not it yet. but I suppose she did not get my letter as soon as I thought she would. tell her I will write when it gets warmer. I will write to Frank tomorrow and to Nannie, too. Rome you dont want to advise Frank a bout anything. if you do, do it in such a way that he wont think you are advising him. I think he will listen to me. I will write him any day. I was prety sick for a few days but I [am] all right now. I weigh 146 pounds.
this will have to do for this time and I will try and do better next time

From your brother
Frederic.

---

[86] Romeyn is at home, recuperating. Lyman is recuperating in a Columbus, Ohio hospital. Frank is home, also, having been discharged when his enlistment time had expired.

Camp 8th ove. Louisville K.G.
Dec 15th 1864

Brother Rome

I recieved your
kind and welcome letter
yesterday and am much
obidge to for it. I had
nearly made up my mind
that I had no friend or else
they were all on a spree for
I have not had only one
letter before yesterday
for over a month yesterday
I got four I have just
answered one of them
am nearly froze so I
dont think I shall write
much in this We have
got over horses and good
ones too we pressed them
here in the City, I have got the

Louisville, Ky.   Dec 17th,1864

Dear Mother

I have just rescieved two letters from you. one wrote the 2d and the other the 11th and both sent from the post office on the 13th. So there is one letter I ought to have had a good while a go. I got the shirt all right some time a go and I got the money to night and am much oblidge for it. I shall have to have some more if we stay here long but I dont think we will. We are all ready to go as soon as the weather will permit. there is 80 of us from our battalion, 20 from a company downtown to patroll the city mounted. We have our horses in stable when we are not a patrolling. There is four releaves so we are a having a very good time. that train of cars you spoke of was the next train behind ours. the 7th Pa. Cav. was on that. but we had a gay ride between Cleaveland and Chattanooga: one truck jumped the track from the hind car. I was on the next car and we were all on top of the cars. there was a grate deal of excitement   all but one man jumped off and he was not hurt. You want to know what was the trouble with me when I was sick. I will tell you. first Father came here and I went downtown and stayed with him 2 days and sleeping in a warm room I caught cold. the day that Father went to Nashville he said he was a fraid I was agoing to be sick and sure enough   I was. the next day before night I was alying in my tent as sick as a cuss. one of the boys went for the doctor. he came and the first thing he put two dambed plasters on me one on each lung and said I had got the lung feavor. I was prity sick for only a day or two and sience then I have enjoyed good health. I am writing on two half sheats of paper from your letters I had in my pocket. I am in the office of the livery stable where we have our horses. I see that Thomas is raising a little Hell with Hood.[87]   I wish our division was there to help him. I am getting tired of laying still and then we live a grate deal better when we are out after them than we do here. I did intend to write to Frank today and I should if we had not come home. I wrote to Rome a day or two a go. in one of your letters you seam to be troubled a bout your wood. all I have to say is I think you are foolish for money will buy wood and as long as you have any of mine I dont want you to want or worry for anything. have Rome or Frank buy a good lot of it and have it hauled right to the door. Does Annie work for Ock yet. last spring I had letters from Annie, Clara and Mary. I answered all of their letters but I have not heard from either sience June or July.   From your son   Frederic

---

[87] Confederate General John Bell Hood made a move toward Atlanta, but was repulsed by General George Thomas, the man Rome (and thousands of others) so revered.

Louisville K. Y. Dec 17th/1864

Dear Mother

       I have just received two letters from you one wrote the 2nd and the other the 11th and both sent from the post office on the 15th. So there is one letter I ought to have had a good while a go. I got the shirt all right some time a go and I got the money to night and am much oblidge for it. I shall have to have some more if we stay here long but I dont think we will We are all ready to go as soon as the weather will permit. There is 80 of us from our battalian & 8 from a company down town to patroll the city mounted we have our horses in stable when these photographs I want mother to take and keep them for me.

Camp 3d O.V.C. Louisville Ky   Dec 20th 1864

Brother Frank   I am agoing to try and write you a few lines but it is so damb cold I can hardly hold the pen. first I have some questions to ask you. what are you adoing and what do you intend to do. as the Old man told his son there's one thing you should do but I know you will do as you please and you are a fool if you dont, that is, dont go to the army a gain nor have anything to do with it. I will tell you what I would do if I were in your place. I would put on a silver plated harness and go to school. And I think I should make my self prety plenty with the young ladies, but I would not let them rub there __ on me very much either and if I did not do that I would go to Illinois and hire some land and try my luck and see what I could do. Frank I dont want you to think that I want to advise you for I dont, for I know damb well I know enough to know my own buisness and I think you know yours but Frank if you should think of doing anything so you need a team I want you to let me know and I will let you have money to get it with. I will let you have all the money I have Frank. I think there is some of the family that thinks you and I are damb fools and never will a mount to much and I am willing they shall think as they damb please. Frank if you think you can and want to use $500.00 I will let you have it. I dont want you to think you might have bad luck as I did for every body is liable to have bad as well as good luck and having back luck think I would be troubled a bout the money for Frank I should not for I know you would do as well as you could and that is as much as any one can do. And you might do well and then I allways would be glad to think I let you have the money and if I should happen to leave my bones down here to whitter then I want you to have what money I have that Mother dont want any way. I wish this damb war was ended. I would be with you sure. Frank I have got a splendid gray pelfy and he can put on as much stile as any horse in the regiment. to day the ground is froze so it is very comfortable underfoot, but the mud has been nearly to ones boot tops. you can imagine how it was on the horse line. there has 8 men deserted from our company sience we came here. 4 of them I hope they will be caught and have to suffer the consequisences and the other 4 I dont blame. I would have deserted had I been fooled as they were. they enlisted for the unexspired turm of the regiment witch was about one year and they were a going to keep them 3 years. Well I must close for I have got to cleane my sabre and gun for inspection. So good by   From your brother Fred.

Camp 3d. O.V.C. Louisville Ky.
Dec 20th, 1864.

Brother Frank

I am a going to
try and write you a few
lines. but it is so damb
cold I can hardly hold the
pen. First I have some questions
to ask you. What are you a doing
and what do you intend to
do. As the Old man told his
son the riddle thing, you shall
do out & know you will do
as you please and you are a
fool if you dont, that is) dont
go to the army a gain nor have
any thing to do with it. I will
tell you what I would do if
I were in your place. I would
put on a silver plated harness
and go to school. And I think I

Camp of Co B 3d O.V.C.
Bardstown K.Y.
Dec. 27, 1864

Dear Mother

We left Louisville a week a go, our battallion. Co A stoped at Mt. Washington. Our Co stoped here and C and D went on. E stoped at New Havan and G went on and were captured and Christmas C fell back here, but we are all safe now for the rest of our regiment and the 98th Illinois came here yesterday. Well Mother I had a little good luck Christmas. that is my kind of good luck. There was 4 of us went out a mile and half from camp to see an old reb and get a Christmas dinner. he invited us the day before. We left our horses hitched in front of the house at the fence and thinking no harm, went in and all of us [sat] down in the dinning room and we found as good a dinner as I ever set down to. We had just got nicely at work at the turkey when we heard the report of firearms in front of the house. I grabed my gun and [went] out as quick [as] I could, the other boys close behind but I was to late to save my horse. Mizs Sue Monday had mounted him and sailed out after mounting my horse. they shot the others to prevent us from following them. I got sight of them as they went under the hill out of sight. There was 4 of them. Mizs Sue Monday, Capt. Davidson, a deserter from our army, and Capt Branford, one of Morgans men who tunneled out of prison at Chicago. I have not learned who the other was. they did not kill either of the horses. shot ones eye out, one through the neck and the other in the head. I lost every thing I had but what I had on. I lost 2 blankets, an over coat, a rubber [blanket], a half tent and a new pair of pants that I had paid a dollar to have the pockets fixed and I never had put them on and the new shirt you sent me, two pair of drawers and two pair of stockings and worst of all, two dollars worth of navy tobaco.[88] But I was a little lucky after all for when they shot the horses my horse tailed out and Mizs Sue had to let her horse go so I got him. She left a gun on the saddle so I got that. it was a splendid gun. the horse I traded off and have a very good one now but he cant shine with the one Miss Monday got. I never will get

---

[88] Navy tobacco was chewing tobacco.

"I was to late to save my horse. Mizs Sue Monday had mounted him and sailed out."

as good one as he was a gain. I traded the saddle off that was on the horse I got and have a good goverment one now so all I am out is my own private property. All I have to say is that Mizs Sue Monday need have no fears of being cought while she rides my little gray.

Well Mother I will have to have ten dollars more so please send it in your next. Mother you must not exspect to hear from me as often as you have for I can not write. I would write this sheet full if I had time but I have not. We were out to Fairfield, ten miles from here last night on a scout, our Co. We got back in camp a little after 12. We had a dark and mudy time of it. the dambed guerrillas are very troublesome here, and Gen. Lyons[89] is only 18 miles from here with his whole command. the rest of our division will be here in 3 days and then Mr. Lyons had better make peace with God or get out of the way for old Long[90] will go for him rough.

From your affectionate son
Fred Kellogg

[89] Hylan Lyon, a Confederate Cavalry commander.
[90] Referring to his own Division Commander, Eli Long.

Map 18

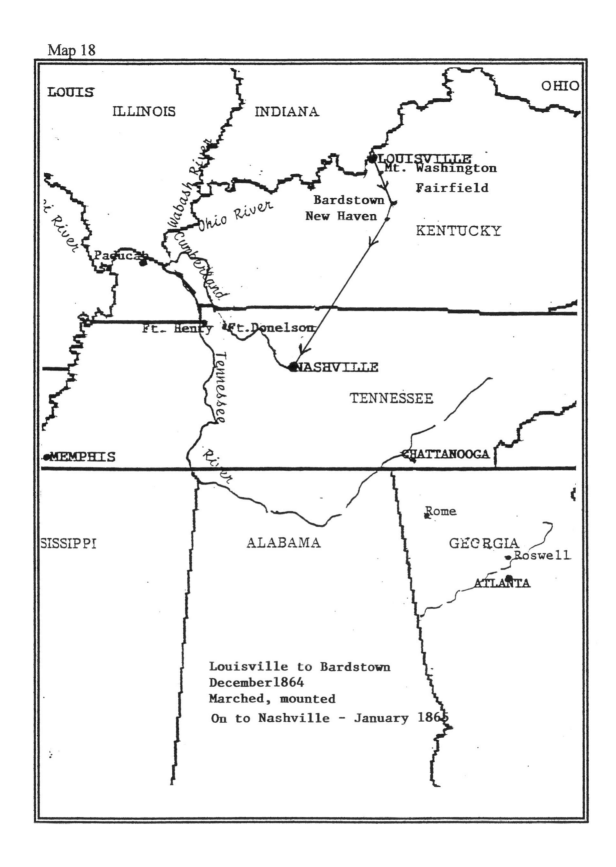

Louisville to Bardstown
December 1864
Marched, mounted

On to Nashville - January 1865

On board of the Hunstville Paducah K.Y. Jan 14th 1865

Dear Mother

It is with pleasure I seat my self to inform you where I am and how I came to be here. I suppose you will wonder that I am here, but sutch are the fortunes of war. One knows where he is to day but God only know where one may be on the morrow. My horse got lame and played out. So I am with the dismounted men of our division. We left Nashville the 12th. I saw Father there. our division has gone to Eastport where we will land. We got here last night. We dont know when we will go up the Tennessee but I dont think we will go for a day or two for I dont think the fleat will be ready. there is about 250 of us from our division. I am afraid that we wont be mounted a gain very soon. When we see the reg a gain I shall try and buy one of the boys to trade places with me if I can for I dont like this kind of cavalry service, but I suppose I shall have to stand it anyway. We had a good time from Louisville to Nashville. One night we were on picket. It rained and snowed and was very cold in the morning. but for all that we had the best time I ever had while on picket. there was 12 of us on one road and the rest of the company was on an other. We put our horses in the stable and one man stood dismounted at a time and we had a good place to sleep in. but the fun of it was, we undertook to play a sharp game over the Old Cittizen. We sent 2 of the boys in the house to talk and keep his attention while Hawley and I was to go and take up a hive of honey. We done our part all right but the boys let the old devil out and never let us know anything a bout it. We took out about 20 pounds of the nicest honey I saw. I had it in a bowl and went down where the boys were by the fire thinking all was right. I went right up to the fire and the old devil was right there himself. I thought the cheapest way was the best way so I asked the old gentleman to help us eat it. he done so and never complained but looked a little down in the mouth. he allowed it was very good honey and reckoned it was the first stollen honey he ever eat. after we had eat what we wanted I told the old gentleman that he might go and see that the bees were all right for it was a sin to let them freze. I dont suppose I shall get an other letter for a long time for my letters will go to the regiment. I wrote you from Bardstown, K.Y. and told you a bout my Christmas dinner and also to send me an other ten dollar note. the last letter I got from you was wrote Dec. 19th. I wrote Rome and Frank both some time a go but I have not rescieved a letter from either as yet.   Fred

The United States Christian Commission

Sends this sheet as the Soldier's messenger to his home.

Let it hasten to those who wait for tidings.

On board of the Hunter
Paducah Ky. Jan 14/[6]6

Dear Mother

It is with pleasure
I seat my self to inform you
where I am. and how I came to
be here. I suppose you will
wonder that I am here. but
such are the fortunes of war
one knows where he is to
day. but God only knows
where one may be on the morrow
My horse got lame and played
out. So I am with the dismounted
one of our division we left
Nashville the 12th. I saw
Father there. our division
has gone to east port where

158

Camp 3d O.V.C. Gravelly Springs, Ala
Jan 29th, 1865

Dear Mother

  I rescieved yours with the ten dollar note 2 days a go. it came to the Company at Nashville the14th. We had a very good time on the boat. We were on it 9 days. We landed here the 21st and we have not seen any hard tack, coffee nor sugar sience and the most we have had we have had to forage. While we lay at the landing one day ten of us went over the river in a small boat to see what we could find there to eat. We went two miles to a house where we found a pleanty. We each got a ham and we got all the meal the old cock had, a half a bushle. We got a jar of honey, a pail of molasses and some dried apples. We put our stuff on two mules and made the niger go a long so to fetch back the mules. part of the boys were agoing back to the boat with him and the rest of us were agoing on farther to see if we could not get some flour, but just then up came a Sargent and six men who come over on a detail and the Sargent said he should take what we had got and divide it out to the detatchment but I did not see it and I told him so and then he said he would take it when we got to camp. that made me mad and I told him if he undertook it I would drum his bugle for him. he then said he would report me when he got back to camp. But here is the joke. We left the poor devil and went to camp and he has not got a round yet. after we got back to camp some of the boys were not satisfied and went back bound for flour but when they had got where we were in the morning some of Forest Cavalry came down on them. the boys fought them as long as they dared to. Shankle killed one of them sure. they took to the woods and got back to the boat all right. The rebs charged down the road to cut them off from their boat and run on the Sargent and 3 of his men and took them in out of the wet. We are on the east side of the river, ten mile above East Port. When I came two days a go to the Company I found 4 letters. one from you and one from Nan and two from Illinois. We are now in the sunny South a gain and the worst place I ever saw, cold enough to freeze one all the time. I exspect we will all be fat enough to kill soon for we are a living on corn mostly. today we got a little flour and some salt pork. I will write you a gain soon when it is more pleasant. Give my love to all.

  Direct Co B, 3d O.V.C. East Port, Miss 2d brig 2d div.

    Fred

Map 19

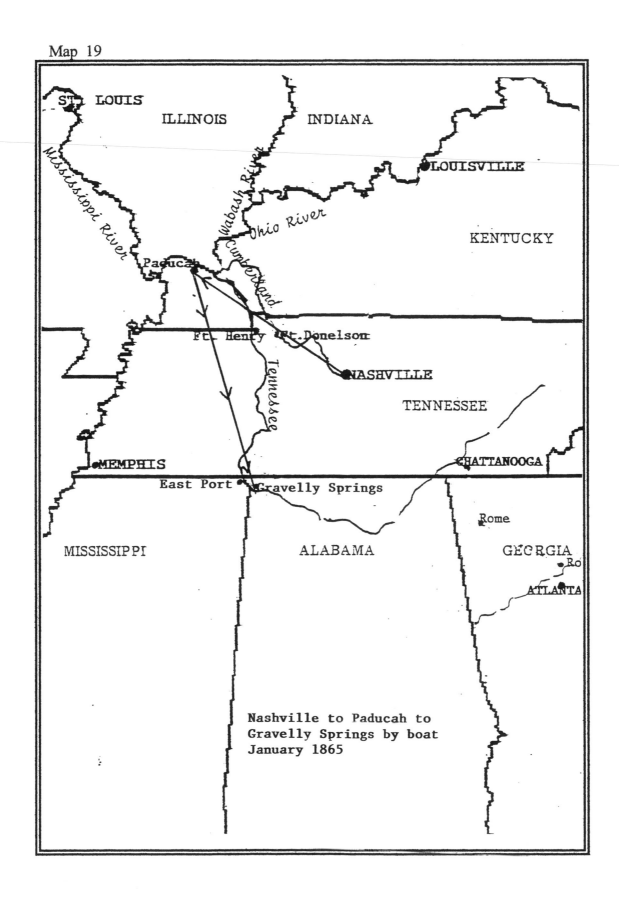

Nashville to Paducah to
Gravelly Springs by boat
January 1865

Camp of Starvation near Gravelly Springs, Ala.
Feb 4th 1865

Dear Mother

This is a very warm and pleasant day and it is most darned lonesome. there is nothing to read and nothing for one to do. So I will write a few lines to you. I have only 2 stamps left. I have wrote a good many letters latley so I wish you to send me an other half dollars worth and I will make it all right with you next fall (providing). there is talk here in camp now that there is an armistice of 60 days. I can hardly believe it. Yet there looks as if something was up. If not I would like to know why all this cavalry are lying here idle. Sience I wrote you we have drawed meal and flour and a very little meat. No sugar, coffee nor soap nor candles and only 5 hard tack a piece. We get mail nearly every day here. I have not got any that came to this camp but reckon I will have some in a bout 2 weeks for I have wrote to nearly every body I know. The weather here to day is like April in Ohio. I hear the boys telling that we are a going to get hard tack and coffee to day. I wish you would send me a paper once in a while. the last I have was the chicago Tribune of 13th of Jan. this place seams a little natural. it is like Pittsburg landing, water no better. I dont want you to think because I have headed this as I have that any of us are a starving for we are not. But I have nearly made up my mind that a soldier could live on faith if nessessary. Mother I dont feel much like writing and the fact is I dont feel much like doing any thing. I am rather inclined to be a little lazy today I think. Nan says I can console myself by saying I am not the first one fooled by a woman, if I was. I dont hardly believe that Sue Monday is a woman. I think this is the most lonesome camp I ever was in. There is not a deck of cards in the Company. When you answer this let me know what Frank is adoing and where he is. I have wrote him twice and have had no answer and I dont think I shall write to him a gain until I get a letter from him. I wrote to Ebb and Mary while at Louisville but have had no answer. I will write to Mary a gain soon. It seams strange that my trunk should get lost agoing from Belvedeer to Beloit 20 miles. Well, I have my own thoughts about it. I will not write a gain until I feel more like it.

From your loving son,
Frederic.

Camp of Starvation.
Near Gravle Springs. Ala -
Feb 4th 1865
Dear Mother
            This is a very
warm and pleasant day as it
is most darned lonesome.
There is nothing to read and
nothing for me to do, So I
will write a few lines to
you. I have only 3 stamps
left I have wrote a good
many letters lately So I
wish you to send me an other
half dollars worth and I will
make it all right with you
next fall. (Providing) There
is talk here in camp now
that there is an armistice
of 90 days I can hardly
believe it. Yet there looks as

Camp 3d OVC,
Chickasaw, Ala.
March 20th, 1865

Dear Mother

I have rescieved 3 letters from you sience I have wrote you and now I am not prepaired to write much of a letter. We got drownded out one night while we were up the river at the landing. We had to wade nearly a half mile and the water up a round our waists. I was in the water 5 hours. when I got out I was nearly chilled through and to pay me I was sick and have just got all right a gain. the river raised over 20 feet in two days.

I have got a horse and a very good one. All the boys of our Company are mounted now. the 4th Ohio has gone and our wagon train has gone and the whole thing goes tomorrow. We take 60 days rations of coffe, 40 days sugar, 11 days salt and we drawed 16 days rations yesterday of everything and they say that this is the last hardtack for some time.

We have got to live off from the country.

So you need not look for any more letters from me for some time.

I got your letter with the stamps yesterday and they came in a good time for mine all got drowned. Tell Clara I have not had time to write to her but I will when I get down a monge the rebs.

Fred.

Camp 5th Iowa 1865
Chickasaw, Ala, March 20th

Dear Mother
          I have recieved
3 letters from you since
I have write you. and now
I am not prepared to write
much of a letter. We got
drounded out one night
while we were up the
river at the landing. we
had to wade nearly a half mile
and the water up a round
our waists. I was in the
water 5 hours. when I
got out I was nearly chilled
through. and to pay me
I was sick. and have just
got all right again. The
river raised over 20
feet in two days —

Camp 3d O.V.C.
Macon, Ga
May 17th, 1865

Dear Mother

        This is the first time I have had a chance to write you sience leaving Chickasaw. I suppose you know by this time what we have done so I will say nothing a bout it only this, our brigade was sent after Old Jeff. one reg. on a road and the 4th Mich. caught him. he is on his way to Washington.
there is talk of our being at home on the 4th of July. I hope it may be true. I am well and have been all of the time. You need not answer this for the devil only knows where we will be when you get it. If I had time I would give you a full account of what we have done sience the 22d of March[91] but I have not so I wont say anything about it.
We left here a week a go after Jeff and just got back tonight. there was some old mail came yesterday. I got your letter dated March 27th. My bed fellow got 11 letters and I got two. Well Old lady it is agrowing late and I have not had much sleep lately so I will bid you good night.

                                    From your loving Son
                                    Fred.

---

[91] During this period, General Robert E. Lee surrendered to General U. S. Grant at Appomattax Courthouse on April 9. On April 14, General Robert Anderson returned to Ft. Sumter where he had been forced to surrender exactly four years ago. With a military salute and many cheers, he raised again the flag he had carried away with him. That same evening, President Lincoln was assassinated. Confederate General Joseph Johnston surrendered to General Sheridan at Raleigh, April 26. On May 10, President Andrew Johnson pronounced the war was over. Skirmishing went on, however, in remote areas for several weeks.

Map 20

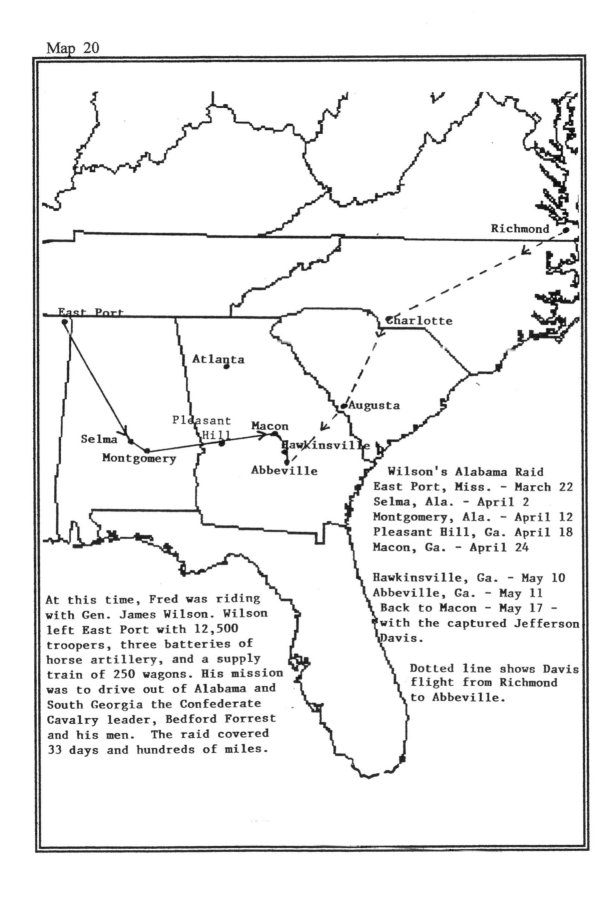

Richmond

East Port

Atlanta

Charlotte

Augusta

Pleasant
Hill

Selma   Macon
Montgomery   Hawkinsville
                Abbeville

Wilson's Alabama Raid
East Port, Miss. - March 22
Selma, Ala. - April 2
Montgomery, Ala. - April 12
Pleasant Hill, Ga. April 18
Macon, Ga. - April 24

Hawkinsville, Ga. - May 10
Abbeville, Ga. - May 11
Back to Macon - May 17 -
with the captured Jefferson
Davis.

Dotted line shows Davis
flight from Richmond
to Abbeville.

At this time, Fred was riding
with Gen. James Wilson. Wilson
left East Port with 12,500
troopers, three batteries of
horse artillery, and a supply
train of 250 wagons. His mission
was to drive out of Alabama and
South Georgia the Confederate
Cavalry leader, Bedford Forrest
and his men. The raid covered
33 days and hundreds of miles.

Macon City, Ga.
July 19th, 1865

Brother Lyme

I rescieved your kind and welcome letter some four days ago and was very glad to hear from you. Yours was the first letter that I have rescieved from a brother for nearly a year. You wished me to write and tell you everything. But I wont do it. Well Lyme there is good news for our regiment. We have orders to be mustered out. There is talk that we will start for Nashville this week. I hardly think we will before next, but everything looks favorable. our regiment was all scattered a round the country. they have all been relieved except our batt. We have been adoing duty here in town for over two months. We are to be relieved today. Lyme I never wrote Father I was sick or had been. I wrote him that my lungs were very bad. I have not missed a days duty for 3 months and we have been on duty every other day sience we have been here in Macon.

Lyme there is no news. Everything is quite.   I have not heard of a negroe being killed for 3 days.

Capt. Sam Clock of Monroeville was killed a short time a go by one of the 4th regulars. he was shot 3 times. If we have to lay over any time at Chattanooga[92] I will try and see you. the weather has been very warm here. to day it is quite pleasant. There has been a grate deal of sickness. at one time there was 15 of our company sick. two of them died. Six have gone north.

We have enjoyed ourselves very well here. there has been plenty of fruit of all kinds and there is plenty of peaches and apples now. I have no news from home. I have not heard from Mother for some time. I think your advice is good and I shall try for the farm as soon as I am discharged. remember me to Carrie and Harry. You need not answer this for I dont know where we will be. Seneca Ronk sends his regards.

From your brother
Fred Kellogg[93]

---

92 Lyman and Romeyn had rejoined their units, the 18th Regular U.S. Army and the 16th Regular U.S. Army. Both men were now in Chattanooga.
93 Though Fred does not mention it, he was promoted to Sergeant on June 16, 1865.

Macon City Ga July 15th
1865

Brother Tyne

I recieved your
Kind and welcome letter some
four days ago and was
very glad to hear from you
Yours was the first letter
that I have recieved from
a brother for nearly a year
You wished me to write and
tell you everything But I
wont do it. Well Tyne there is
good news for our regiment we
have Orders to be mustered
out. there is talk that we will
start for Nashville this week
I hardly think we will before
next. but everything looks
favorable our regiment was
all scattered around the

Edgefield, Tenn.
July 21st, 1865

Dear Mother

I rescieved a letter yesterday from you and you seamed to be very much troubled a bout me and because you had heard a lie. I have not been sick. I never missed a days duty while at Macon and we were on duty every other day. My lungs were very bad and I wrote to Father to send me a receipt for cough medicine and money to get it with and he sent it and thats all there is a bout my being sick. We are here in Edgefield across the river from Nashville. We exspect to be mustered out of the service this week, but we will have to go to Ohio to get pay. We left Macon a week a go last Sunday. We may be home next week but you need not look for me until I come. I shall stay in Ohio only a few days. You ask a bout Frank. I dont know any thing a bout him and if I did I should keep it to my self. I think Father was a dambed fool for writing to Theron anything a bout Frank and I shall tell him so. Our Officers have our papers nearly all made out. there is talk that we will be mustered out Wednesday. You need not answer this. I wrote you a few days a go from Macon. I suppose you dont get my letters from what you wrote in yours for I have wrote you every week and some twice all the time while at Macon and I have only rescieved two letters from you wrote sience the 17th of March.
Well I wont write any more on this lovely little message.

From Fred.

This is Fred's last letter. The Third Ohio Volunteer Cavalry was mustered out August 14, 1865.

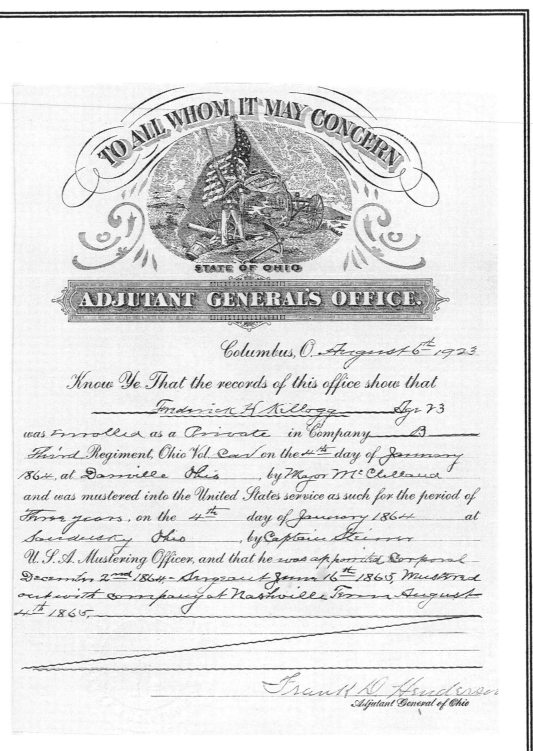

FREDERIC HENRY KELLOGG'S FAMILY
1900
Standing -- Jess, Kate and Fredrick Hudson Kellogg
Jane Hudson Kellogg and Frederic Henry Kellogg

EPILOGUE

After being discharged, Fred returned to De Kalb County, Illinois. He bought two pieces of farmland and in the fall of 1867 he rented one of them to Canadian immigrants, John and Mary Hudson. Fred first saw their young daughter, Jane, when a sweeping prairie fire threatened the entire community. Love flared in the blaze of that fire. The couple were married in Sycamore, Illinois, January 16, 1868.

Fred relocated his family to Kansas in early 1872. John and Mary Hudson accompanied them. The two men homesteaded adjoining parcels, building a stone house on the property line, thus satisfying the home building requirement for both families. They broke the virgin sod, replacing prairie grasses with corn, wheat and gardens. The Hudsons stayed in the original home, but Fred proved and sold several farms in Marion and McPherson Counties. In 1883 he moved his family from the farm to Sedgwick, Kansas to provide better schooling for his children. He took advantage of the lack of fuel on the treeless prairie and started a business selling coal shipped by train from other areas.

Fred and Jane had four children: Fredrick Hudson, Charlie, Jess and Kate.

As he grew older, Fred suffered from lung damage caused by the typhoid fever contracted during the war, but he lived to see his children grown and to cherish the first two of his five grandchildren, Katherine Cosette and Jesse Allen Kellogg.

Being a veteran of the Grand Army of the Republic was a great source of pride for Fred. His GAR button was ever present in his lapel. He recalled with fondness his comrades, the pranks they played, they songs they sang, the hardships they endured. He remembered, too, the long days in the saddle and the sabre clashing charges that helped overcome the enemy and preserve the Union founded by his forefathers.

He died on June 21, 1912, aged seventy-two, and was laid to rest with military honors in the Maple Grove Cemetery, Wichita, Kansas.

BIBLIOGRAPHY OF RESEARCH REFERENCES

Beyer, W. F. & Keydel, O.F., Editors, *Deeds of Valor*, Longmeadow Press, Stamford, CT., 1994

Carter, Samuel III. *The Last Cavaliers.* St. Martins Press, N.Y. 1979

Catton, Bruce. *A Picture History of the Civil War.* American Heritage Pub. Co., Inc., N.Y. 1960.

Chamberlain, Dick and Judy. *Civil War Letters of an Ohio Soldier.* Authors, Flournoy, CA., 1990.

Collins, Alan C. *Story of America.* Doubleday & Co. Inc., N.Y. 1953.

Crane, Stephen. *The Red Badge of Courage.* A.. Appleton & Co., 1895.

Crary, Catherine S. ed. *Dear Belle.* Wesleyan University, 1965.

Davis, William C. *Commanders of the Civil War.* Gallery Books, 1990.

Donald, David Herbert, ed. *Gone for a Soldier.* Little, Brown & Co., Boston, 1975.

Downey, Fairfax Davis. *Clash of Cavalry.* McKay, 1959.

Dyer, Frederick H. *A Compendium of the War of the Rebellion.* Press of Morningside Bookshop, Dayton, Ohio, 1979.

Eddy, T. M., D.D. *The Patriotism of Illinois.* Clarke & Co. Publishers, 1866

Esposito, Vincent J. *West Point Atlas of American Wars.* F.A. Praeger, Pub., 1959.

Foote, Shelby. *The Civil War.* 3 vols. Random House, N.Y. 1963.

Freeman, Douglas Southall. *R. E. Lee - A Biography.* Charles Scribner's Sons, N.Y., 1935.

Glass, Paul. *Singing Soldiers.* Grosset & Dunlap, Publishers, 1964.

Greenleaf, Edith Margery, ed. *Letters to Eliza.* Follett Publishing Co., 1970

Griess, Thomas E., series ed. *Atlas for the American Civil War.* Avery Publishing Group, Inc., 1986.

Hammond, Harold Earl, ed. *Diary of a Union Lady.* Funk & Wagnalls Inc., 1962.

Haskin, William L. and Rodenbaugh, Theo. F., ed. *The Army of the United States.* Maynard, Merrill & Co., N.Y. 1896.

Heaps, Willard Allison. *The Singing Sixties.* Univ. of Oklahoma Press, 1960.

Hoehling, Adolf A. *Last Train From Atlanta.* Yoseloff, 1958.

Kellogg, Edgar Romeyn. *Memoirs of the Civil War.* By the author, 1905.

Monaghan, James. *Civil War on the Western Border.* Little, Brown & Co., Boston, 1955.

Rodenbaugh, Theo. F. and Haskin, William L. , ed. *The Army of the United States.* Maynard, Merrill & Co., N.Y. 1896.

Sandburg, Carl. *Abraham Lincoln.* Charles Scribner's Sons, N.Y. 1936.

Serven, James E. *200 years of American Firearms.* Follett Publishing Co.

Shaara, Michael. *Killer Angels.* Ballantine, N.Y. 1974.

Smith, Gene. *Lee and Grant.* McGraw-Hill, N.Y. 1984.

Turner, George Edgar. *Victory Rode the Rails.* Bobbs-Merrill Co. Inc., 1953.

Ward, Evelyn D. *Children of Bladensfeld* Viking Press 1978

Watson, William. *Letters of a Civil War Surgeon.* Purdue Univ. Studies, 1961.

Wiley, Bell Irvin. *Life of Billy Yank.* Babs-Merrill Co., Inc., 1952.

Wiley, Bell Irvin. *Life of Johnny Reb.* Babs-Merrill Co., Inc., 1952.

War of the Rebellion. Government Printing Office, 1891.

100 Years of Famous Pages from the New York Times. Simon & Schuster, 1951.

INDEX

Dry Suit Diving:
A Guide to Diving Dry
4th Edition
by
Steven M. Barsky
Dick Long
&
Bob Stinton

Hammerhead Press
Ventura, California
www.hammerheadpress.com

Original photography and illustrations by Steven M. Barsky unless otherwise noted.

In most cases, product photography has been supplied by the manufacturer of their respective products, including Diving Concepts, Diving Unlimited International, Trelleborg-Viking, and Whites Manufacturing.

Design and typography by Hammerhead Press.

Printing history: First printing 2006

Printed in the United States of America by Ojai Printing, Ojai, California.

ISBN Number: 0-9674305-6-9

Library of Congress Control Number: 2006926288

Other Books by Steven M. Barsky

Published by Best Publishing
Careers in Diving (with Kristine Barsky and Ronnie Damico)
The Simple Guide to Rebreather Diving
    (with Mark Thurlow and Mike Ward)
The Simple Guide to Snorkeling Fun
Small Boat Diving
Spearfishing for Skin and Scuba Divers

Published by Hammerhead Press
Diving in High-Risk Environments, Third Edition
California Lobster Diving (with Kristine Barsky)
Investigating Recreational and Commercial Diving Accidents
    (with Tom Neuman, M.D.)
The Simple Guide to Commercial Diving (with Robert W. Christensen)
Underwater Digital Video Made Easy
    (with Lance Milbrand and Mark Thurlow)

Published by International Training, Inc.
Deeper Sport Diving with Dive Computers
Easy Nitrox Diving
Underwater Navigation, Night, and Limited Visibility Diving
Wreck, Boat, and Drift Diving

Published by Scuba Schools International
The Dry Suit Diving Manual

DVDs from Hammerhead Video
California Lobster Diving, the video
Dry Suit Diving in Depth
The Simple Guide to Boat and Wreck Diving
California Marine Life Identification

Contents

Foreword by Sir John Rawlins

In the winter of 1956, I was trained as a Royal Navy Shallow Water Diver in Great Britain. We used closed-circuit oxygen and semi-closed circuit nitrox breathing apparatus and wore neck entry dry suits. The dry suits then were made of rubber-coated nylon over a cotton undersuit. Wetsuits were unavailable to us at that time.

The dry suit system we used seemed to work well, provided the dives we made were relatively short and shallow. Aside from the chill we experienced from diving in cold water, almost all of our operations were conducted from inflatable boats. If you didn't get cold during the dive, the chill you experienced during the ride back to shore was enough to make most divers hypothermic. However, in those days, the training was tough and divers were expected to be tough, too. If you complained about the cold you could be expected to be dropped from the course, so nobody mentioned their discomfort.

Diving below 60 feet with these dry suits was very uncomfortable. The pressure caused the suit to compress around the diver in tight folds that pinched the skin and caused welts. One suit in particular, that always fit loosely in the crotch, could be suddenly and startlingly painful if the diver went below 70 feet!

Long before suit inflation systems became common, my dive team and I experimented with a suit inflation system. We used a small high-pressure cylinder carried in a pouch on the thigh, and used various gases including air, carbon dioxide and freon. We vented the gas from our suits during ascent by slipping a finger under the flexible seals at the neck or wrists. There were occasional problems such as rapid uncontrolled ascents due to accidental over-inflation and occasional partial flooding. Fortunately, due to the extensive training our Royal Navy divers received, no casualties resulted from these potentially disastrous incidents.

This same dry suit system I had used back in 1956 was still in service in 1965, when we conducted a detailed physiological study of thermal effects of diving in cold water. Oral temperatures were recorded on 15 trainee divers when the water temperature was 40 degrees F. After 30-40 minute long dives, when temperatures were taken 5 minutes after exiting the water, the divers' temperatures ranged from 96.5 to 88.6 degrees F. In 8 of the trainees the temperatures were below 93 degrees F and in 5 it was 91 degrees F or less.

The colder men exhibited symptoms of nausea, lightheadedness, and headache. One of them had signs of early cold injury in one hand. He collapsed and had to be pulled from the water. Another trainee also collapsed and lost consciousness.

These observations highlighted the dangers of hypothermia in diving, the rapidity of its onset, and its unpredictability resulting from individual diver's reactions in response to cold. It was obvious that if hypothermic collapse took place outside of a training situation the outlook FOR THE DIVER WASN'T GOOD.

The introduction of the foam neoprene wetsuit was received enthusiastically by the Royal Navy divers. The suits were easy to get into, they were comfortable, and they looked good. The story that they worked by preserving a layer of warm water around the diver was accepted without question. It quickly became obvious, though, that this warm layer inside the suit represented heat loss from the surface of the diver's skin. It also became apparent that the diver would remain warm only as long as the diver's metabolism could enable a heat gradient to be maintained across the warm layer and the suit material to the surrounding water.

It didn't take us too long to learn that for long or deep dives, wetsuits were very inferior to dry suits. By that time, dry suits were available with standard suit inflation systems and valves.

In 1967, I rode in a wet sub at 3 knots during a test dive wearing a dry suit with a proper suit inflation system. The designer of the vehicle wore a wetsuit, and exhausted his semi-closed circuit nitrox breathing apparatus in 30 minutes. The speed of the sub forced cold water through his suit, increasing his breathing rate, causing him to run through his breathing supply rapidly. He was forced to surface while I had the fun of driving the sub back to base underwater, quite warm and with breathing gas to spare. It was a valuable lesson.

In 1968, I joined the U.S. Navy's Sea Lab III project as part of the thermal protection division. The scientist who had worked on the project before me had shown that even when divers wore 4 layers of 1/4 inch foam neoprene they could not maintain thermal balance in 40 degree F water. Some form of heat replacement for the diver was essential. A dry suit with an undersuit heating system was the obvious solution, but U.S. Navy policy did not allow dry suits to be used at that time.

Wetsuits had several major disadvantages for the Sea Lab habitat that was scheduled to be placed at 600 feet. First, a foam neoprene suit would compress to about half of its original thickness when taken to 600 feet. It took 120 hours for the suit to expand back to 65% of its original thickness, as the helium in the underwater habitat diffused into the cells of the material. In addition, since the thermal conductivity of helium is six times that of air, the insulation value of the suit at depth was about half the normal value. Finally, when the diver entered the water, the helium rapidly diffused out of the neoprene and the suit collapsed again.

The most significant disadvantage of the wetsuits, however, was the flushing of cold water in and out of the suit with the diver's movements. Even breathing caused this effect. We observed that when divers worked hard, heat loss almost doubled!

The decision to use wetsuits in Sea Lab III proved disastrous. When the habitat was placed on the bottom at 600 feet it leaked heavily, and two divers were sent down to try to stop the leaks. With an air temperature of 56 degrees F and water temperature of 47 degrees F it took the divers two hours to transfer from normal atmospheric breathing air to an atmosphere of 98% helium and 2% oxygen via the diving bell to the bottom. The divers became so chilled that they reported that entering the water felt "like stepping into a hot bath." Within minutes they were shivering uncontrollably and felt they were not getting enough gas to breathe. The dive was aborted.

Seven hours later they were prepared to try again, although there was no means of knowing to what extent they had managed to rewarm. The procedure was as before, but after only 4 minutes in the water one of the divers collapsed and lost consciousness. By the time he was recovered into the bell he was dead.

The Board of Inquiry attributed his death to improperly prepared breathing gear. I examined the set myself and I am not convinced. As we have seen above, hypothermia alone could have accounted for his collapse; certainly it must have played a major part.

Hypothermia is a killer. Divers have been shown to be incapable of accurately judging their own thermal state. There is no reason for a diver to expose himself to these dangers today now that we have dry suits that do not leak and that are fitted with reliable valves. Insulation materials are available with properties that were unobtainable in 1960.

For the serious sport diver today, the dry suit offers the best protection against cold and significantly reduces the chances of suffering from decompression sickness. Safe and efficient use of a dry suit, as with all diving equipment, requires good training, good discipline, and good practice. That is what this unique book is all about.

Sir John Rawlins, Surgeon Vice-Admiral, Royal Navy, Retired

Introduction

Back in 1987, I sat down to write the first book on dry suit diving, entitled, *The Dry Suit Diving Manual*. At the time, I was working for Viking, one of the largest manufacturers of dry suits in the world. In those days, dry suits were not widely accepted by sport divers, but the era of the modern dry suit had begun.

During the two years that I worked full-time for Viking I had the opportunity to work with Dick Long of Diving Unlimited International (DUI), to form the Dry Suit Manufacturer's Group. Our goal was to promote dry suit diving safety, and we received the endorsement of other manufacturers in the industry. We developed a list of dry suit diving guidelines that were widely adopted.

In 1989, I started my own company, Marine Marketing and Consulting. I was hired by Diving Unlimited to assist with their marketing, write their user manuals, and consult on the diving industry. Although I already knew Dick, we got to know each other well and became much better friends. I also had the opportunity to become friends with Bob Stinton, chief engineer for DUI, and learn from his vast knowledge of thermal protection systems. Working with DUI expanded my knowledge to other types of dry suits, underwear, and accessories.

In 1991, Dick, Bob, and I collaborated to write the first edition of *Dry Suit Diving, A Guide to Diving Dry*. The original version was published by Watersport Publishing. The book was a far more comprehensive guide than the *Dry Suit Diving Manual*, and reflected the changes and sophistication that had come to dry suit diving.

Over the years, I've had the chance to work with other manufacturers to develop dry suit manuals for their products, including Gates (now Hunter) and Mares. I've also presented dry suit diving seminars, and programs on polluted water diving for the National Oceanographic and Atmospheric Administration (NOAA), the Environmental Protection Agency (EPA), and the Canadian Defense Ministry.

Today, we have better dry suits than were available in the past, better insulating undergarments, and improved methods of teaching dry suit diving. We also have new diving technology, such as rebreathers and dive computers, that can't be fully exploited without the use of a dry suit.

Since it was initially released, *Dry Suit Diving, a Guide to Diving Dry,* has become recognized as the source for the most detailed information on dry suit diving. Numerous diving instructors have used this book with their classes. Many divers have used the book as a guide to selecting their first dry suit and to go beyond the basics offered in training agency manuals.

In this fourth edtion of this book, we have kept the best of the past editions and added more new material, including many new photographs, technical information, and a new layout.

If you have never used a dry suit before, you're in for a treat. It's truly the best way for the recreational diver to dive in cold water, and will give you the opportunity to make many fascinating dives.

I hope you enjoy this fourth edition of *Dry Suit Diving*, and will get as much pleasure from dry suit diving as I do.

Steven M. Barsky

Acknowledgments

Nothing is ever as easy as it sounds, and that includes producing a book. It's not just the writing, but all of the other aspects of the book that make it successful. For a book like this one, those other aspects included rounding up the equipment, working with boat operators and models, shipping the gear back to the manufacturers, verifying technical information, shooting the photos, editing, layout, and production. Without the encouragement and cooperation of many people, this book would never have happened.

Phil Joy at Hunter provided many photos of their production facilities. Sue Anne Griffin at O'Neill also furnished us with early photos of Jack O'Neill. Shirley Richards at 3M provided technical information and photographs of their Thinsulate® material. Stig Insulan of S.I. Tech assisted us with historical photos from his early days of diving. Jennifer Heine at Whites Manufacturing always came through on time and with exactly the images we needed. Jim Roberts at Diving Concepts provided both gear and photos. John Drewniak at Trelleborg-Viking has always been especially supportive and generous with both his time and equipment. The staff at Diving Unlimited International, Inc. bent over backwards to make sure we had the gear we needed for photos at the right time.

Photographers who have generously contributed their photographs include Kristine Barsky, Ronnie Damico-Cole, Pete Nawrocky, Anthony Rue at Halcyon, and Bev Morgan. Bev also took the time to read the chapter on the history of thermal protection and shared many valuable insights on the early days of diving.

Many of our friends and dive buddies appear in the book and helped us get the photos that make this book special. They include Ronnie Damico-Cole, Gary Davis, Dave Forcucci, John Heine, Stig Insulan, Jon Kushner, Dan Richards, Cliff Schmidt, Mark Thurlow, and John Trone. In particular, thanks to Bob Evans for taking us diving and giving us the opportunity to work off his boat.

Across the sea, Sir John Rawlins, retired Royal Navy doctor, and Nick Baker, secretary of the Historical Diving Society, gave us a great deal of assistance. Sir John enlightened us on historical diving practices from the Royal Navy, while Nick was able to secure photos from the Siebe Gorman archives.

Our late friend, John Wozny also reviewed the manuscript and made many valuable suggestions for improvement. We miss John sorely.

We can always count on Mark Perlstein whenever we do a project like this; and once again, he read the book and made many suggestions for improvement. We know few people who spend more time in the water than Mark.

Faith Ortins at Diving Unlimited International also reviewed the text and gave us many important ideas for changes.

The principle model for the book was Kristine Barsky, who once again sacrificed days of her personal time to assist with this project. She modeled for most of the photos in the book and made many dives to ensure we got the best photos possible. In addition, Kristine spent hours editing and verifying information for us. There is no way we could have completed this project without her cooperation and interest.

Steve Barsky
May 2006

This hard hat suit or "dress" was the earliest type of dry suit for diving.

Chapter 1
A Brief History of Diver Thermal Protection

The main limiting factor in man's ability to go underwater has always been the ability to keep the diver warm. Given an unlimited air supply and the proper facilities for decompression, a diver could, theoretically, stay underwater for many hours. But without the right thermal protection, most divers will become chilled and inefficient even in relatively warm water.

Divers have experimented with many ways to stay warm. As materials, technology, and insulation have changed, diving suits have become more rugged and warmer. However, the basic principles of human physiology, insulation, and heat loss have not changed. Each new dive suit design represents another attempt to solve these problems.

Heavy Gear

In 1837, Augustus Siebe, an Englishman, developed the closed diving "dress" that connected to the diving helmet invented by John and Charles Deane. This equipment was originally developed for commercial divers who worked on the bridges, piers, and wharfs throughout Great Britain.

The closed dress was originally developed to allow the diver to bend at the waist, without losing air out of the bottom of his helmet. The suit was made of waterproofed canvas. With the closed dress attached to the base of the helmet, the diver was completely isolated from the water, except for his hands. The side benefit to this was that the diver's body was kept dry. Long underwear, or even clothing, could be worn under the dress to keep the diver warm. Siebe's dress was the first "dry suit."

Siebe's dress was a *passive insulation system*, with no external energy supplied to keep the diver warm. The suit worked because it trapped a layer of air between the diver's body and the external water environment.

Although Siebe's first helmet was not equipped with valves, the helmets he developed later featured both inlet and exhaust valves. The valves allowed the diver to precisely control his buoyancy.

This equipment has been known as deep sea diving gear, commercial gear, or heavy gear. Over the years, many different inventors developed new heavy gear designs, but the basic principles of this type of equipment have remained unchanged. This equipment is still in use in some parts of the world today.

World War II

Just prior to World War II, in 1938, recreational diving was limited to a small but dedicated group of enthusiasts in the Mediterranean. Among these divers was Jacques Cousteau, who built an early dry suit for scuba diving from vulcanized rubber. The suit had no valves or means of pressure equalization.

During World War II, naval operations reached a scope and sophistication not previously seen. Diving became more important than ever before as a means of salvage and for combat purposes. The term "frogman" was born during this era to describe combat divers using various types of diving equipment.

Both the British and the Italians worked very hard at developing "midget" submarines that could carry one or more divers. These tiny submersibles were known as "wet subs" and were very similar in concept to some of the sport diving submarines still seen today. The main purpose of the wet subs was to carry a team of divers into an enemy harbor, undetected, so that explosives could be placed on the hulls of warships.

British Navy divers during World War II wore dry suits.

The divers who rode these subs wore closed diving suits and closed-circuit rebreathers. The suits were not much different from those worn with traditional heavy gear. They were bulky and heavy, making it difficult to swim. The closed-circuit rebreather is a type of breathing apparatus that recirculates the diver's exhaled breath, purifies it, and emits no bubbles.

Most of the work that was done to develop diving equipment during this time was performed by Sir Robert H. Davis, who worked at Siebe, Gorman & Company in Surrey, England. Davis was a famous diving inventor who wrote the classic book, *Deep Diving and Submarine Operations*.

Davis describes in detail some of the tests that were conducted to see if the divers could function in the 45 degree F water for the long sub rides into enemy waters. At that time, it was hard to find materials that would keep the divers warm, yet allow the divers to swim. Electrically heated suits were considered, but the idea was abandoned since the divers had to leave the sub to attach the explosives to the ships. In all probability, neither battery technology nor materials technology were developed to the point that this would have been possible during this period.

Photo courtesy of Siebe Gorman collection

The British Navy ultimately settled on silk underwear next to the diver's skin, woolen underwear on top of that, and kapok padded shirts and pants for the top layer. However, the major problem remained the diver's hands and no satisfactory solution was developed. Davis mentions that some divers actually went barehanded with only a thick coating of grease to protect them! The divers referred to one version of the dry suits as the "clammy death"...

In 1946, Cousteau developed the constant volume dry suit. To get air into the suit, the diver blew air past the seal of his mask into the hood of the suit. The suit was equipped with exhaust valves on the head, wrist, and ankles, so air could be vented in any position.

Dry Suits and Wetsuits in the 1950s

After World War II, sport diving became popular in the United States. Some of the elements that contributed to this growth were movies like *The Frogmen*, the Cousteau book and film of *The Silent World*, and the appearance of *Skin Diver Magazine* in 1951. Also, there was a great deal of surplus military diving equipment on the market that had not been previously available.

Dry suits were the only type of effective thermal protection available for the sport diver during this period. As with all diving suits, even today, one of the major problems has always been how to get into the suit. The method of entry, whether by zipper or other device, always affects the fit and much of the performance of the suit.

Early dry suits had three means of entry. One design was known as a tunnel entry suit, another was via a split seal at the waist, and the third was through the neck seal.

Tunnel entry suits had a large tube located on the chest or upper back of the suit. The diver stuck his legs into the lower part of the suit, then pulled the top on over his head and arms. The tube or "tunnel" was then twisted closed and sealed with a clamp or rubber tubing.

Canadian diver Frank White in an early dry suit from the 1950s.

Photo courtesy of Whites Manufacturing

Waist entry suits were equipped with a separate set of pants and jacket. They were made in Italy by Pirelli (the same people who make tires today). Both pieces came with excess material at the waist. This material was then folded together over a hard rubber cummerbund to create an effective seal. A large, heavy duty O-ring squeezed the folded layers against the cummerbund.

Neck entry suits were one piece suits similar in design to the dry suits available

Author Dick Long in an early wetsuit.

Photo courtesy of Diving Unlimited International.

today, but without a zipper. The top of the suit had an opening large enough for the diver to stretch over his entire body. The latex neck seal was a separate piece. A metal ring fit closely over the diver's head and was worn around the neck. The rubber at the suit opening overlapped the bottom of the neck seal rubber. A metal clamp was placed over this effecting a seal.

Dry suit manufacturers during this period included Aquala, So-Lo Marx Rubber Co., Healthways, Pirelli, and Bel Aqua.

There were four major drawbacks to dry suits at this time. First, none of the suit entry methods made it easy to use a dry suit. Second, the low-pressure inflator mechanism had yet to be invented. Without this device, there was no way to equalize pressure inside the suit to adjust buoyancy or prevent suit squeeze. Third, the materials available to build dry suits were not as rugged or reliable as those available today. Finally, the insulation materials available, such as wool, did not perform as well as the insulators we have today.

Dr. Hugh Bradner, a physicist, developed the first wetsuits in 1952, although he first wrote up the concept in 1951. In a memo of June 21, 1951 Bradner wrote,

"Actually, I do not think it is necessary to have a waterproof suit. It would be possible to obtain adequate warmth by use of a dead water space from a furry type of porous material. ...a two piece suit and zipper would be desirable though there is no need in this design for a waterproof zipper.

Another design might be a sponge rubber suit which would only have to be 1/4" thick."

Bradner set up two small companies to build suits for the Navy Underwater Demolition Teams (UDT) frogmen, but withdrew from the business after a short time. He also applied for a patent but never followed through on the issue.

Bev Morgan, a lifeguard and diver in Los Angeles County, developed the first commercially successful wetsuits in 1953. He sold the suits through his store, Dive 'n Surf in Redondo Beach. The suits were made from foam neoprene rubber and had no nylon lining. The wetsuit, as most divers know, traps a thin layer of water that is warmed by the diver's body. The insulation is in the gas bubbles trapped within the foam neoprene. The wetsuit is another example of passive insulation.

Wetsuits quickly became more popular than dry suits. Wetsuits have a number of advantages over dry suits for dives in moderate water temperatures. A wetsuit is a relatively inexpensive initial investment compared to a dry suit. Wetsuits also require less maintenance and less training than dry suits. However, for dives in water colder than 65 degrees F, deep dives, multiple dives at moderate temperatures, or extended dives, the wetsuit does not offer the best thermal protection.

The dry suit steadily lost popularity until new technology became available. Meanwhile divers were experimenting with other methods of keeping warm.

Diving in the 60s –
Active Insulation and the Unisuit

Manned exploration of the oceans increased at an incredible rate during the 1960s. The combined effect of scientific exploration, technological development, and industrial progress all pushed diving technology rapidly forward.

From a scientific perspective, this was the era where it was proposed that man would colonize the seas and live underwater. Many different underwater habitats were built and placed on the bottom of the ocean. The Cousteau group built Conshelf Two which sat on the bottom of the Red Sea at a depth of 33 feet in 1963.

In 1964, the U.S. Navy placed the SEALAB I habitat at 193 feet off Bermuda. Four men lived underwater for 11 days. The Navy followed this with SEALAB II at a depth of 205 feet off La Jolla, California, in 1965. Three ten-man teams spent two weeks on the bottom during this project. The water temperature ranged from 46 to 50 degrees F.

Dick Long built wetsuits for the SEALAB II divers per the Navy's orders, but the suits could not keep the divers warm at that depth. Long had been a diving instructor and inventor for many years. He had built many suits for the Navy by the time the SEALAB project took place, but none that had been required to work under such demanding conditions.

Suit compression, water temperature, and the use of helium as part of a breathing mixture all contributed to making the wetsuits very ineffective during SEALAB II. The following remark by one of the divers is typical of the reactions to the water temperature during SEALAB II.

*"I won't say it got unbearable —it wouldn't be to the point that if an emergency arose that you couldn't stay out there, but you had the feeling of wanting to get back in there and getting under that hot shower. Once you got up in the entry-way, sat down for a few minutes while the pots were being loaded, you'd start shaking uncontrollably; you weren't that cold, you weren't that uncomfortable but you just couldn't stop shaking." from Groups Under Stress: **Psychological Research in SeaLab II.***

This electrically heated suit was built for the SEALAB experiment.

The waterproof zipper was the invention that made the modern dry suit possible. This is one of the first waterproof zippers that was developed back in the 1950s.

It became obvious that the wetsuit would not be adequate for extended dives in cold water at depth. At this point, divers began to experiment with other insulation systems. Experiments were done with non-compressible suits and **active heating systems**.

In 1965, the Uniroyal Corporation designed and tested an electrically heated suit for the SEALAB III project that was scheduled for placement off San Clemente Island. Other companies produced similar suits, but all were plagued by hot spots, wire fatigue, bulk and weight. The idea was good, but the technology was not up to the task. Perhaps we'll see a return to this type of system at some date in the future, but at the time of this writing, no such system exists.

One of the most important spin-offs of the exploration of outer space was the development of the waterproof, pressure-proof zipper. These zippers were made by B.F. Goodrich. Again, Bev Morgan was the innovator who first used a waterproof zipper in a dry suit in 1956. He made the suit from foam neoprene, with latex seals and an oral inflator. The suits were advertised in *Skin Diver Magazine*.

Ingvar Elfstrom, a Swedish diver and inventor, developed the Unisuit with Peter Wide, a supervisor of diving for the Swedish Navy. Elfstrom, had been building and marketing regulators for many years through his company, Poseidon Industri AB, prior to the development of the Unisuit. The Unisuit was the first dry suit that included both a waterproof zipper, low pressure power inflator and exhaust valves. The suit was made from foam neoprene and the zipper ran though the crotch, from mid-back to mid-chest. Pile underwear by Helly Hansen provided the insulation beneath the suit.

The Unisuit quickly established itself as the most popular dry suit on the market. It was the standard by which all other dry suits were judged. Unisuits have been used around the world and were adopted by most navies during the

Unisuits were the first dry suits to include waterproof zippers and both inflator and exhaust valves.

60s and early 70s. The suit is still popular today with many divers.

Meanwhile, in Norway, two divers collaborated on the development of the Viking suit. Stig Insulan, a former Swedish Navy diver and Jorn Stubdal, a commercial diver, worked on a vulcanized rubber dry suit, similar to those manufactured by Dunlop and Avon. Their teamwork resulted in many unique concepts for dry suits that are still in use today.

One of the most important contributions of Insulan and Stubdal was the refinement of the automatic exhaust valve for dry suits. In essence, they took the exhaust valve that had been in use on heavy

Stig Insulan was one of the people who developed the Viking dry suit.

gear helmets for over a century and redesigned it to mount on a dry suit. This development, in combination with the power inflator, gave the scuba equipped dry suit diver precise buoyancy control. Today, this valve is available on many different dry suits.

Insulan and Stubdal also developed a unique set of mannequins that were used to mold the Viking suits. The suits were assembled and pulled on the mannequins. The mannequins were then placed inside a giant vulcanizing chamber where the seams of the suits were sealed at a temperature of 250 degrees F.

Dick Long of Diving Unlimited International developed the hot water suit into a commercially successful product.

The single most successful active heating system in diving has been the hot water suit. Originally, the hot water suit was developed by a French diver named Dupre. The concept is very simple. The diver wears a loose fitting wetsuit that is supplied with hot water from the surface via a hose. The hot water flushes out through the zipper as well as the wrists, ankles, and neck of the suit. A boiler unit and a series of pumps on the surface keeps the suit continuously supplied with hot water. The effect is like diving in a bath tub of warm water. It is extremely comfortable and divers have made dives up to 16 hours in water temperatures in the low 40s wearing hot water suits. Although the hot water suit is a practical answer for the commercial diver using surface supplied (umbilical) diving equipment, it is impractical for a non-tethered, free swimming sport diver.

Westinghouse (the manufacturer of home appliances) was very involved in diving during the 60s and had their own Man in the Sea program. Jerry O'Neill, an inventor and diver at Westinghouse, further developed the concept of the hot water suit and patented parts of the suit. Westinghouse built several working units for the Smith Mountain Dam Project, the first commercial saturation diving job, but those first systems scalded the divers. At the time, they were unable to see the future applications for the gear and dropped further development.

With his insights from years of wetsuit design, Dick Long immediately saw the possibilities of the hot water suit. He continued development of the suit, and made it practical by adding tubes that would distribute the hot water to all the parts of the body.

But it wasn't enough just to develop the hot water suit, because without a reliable hot water source the suit wasn't usable. The heater required many different elements to make it a success. It required a pick-up pump that wouldn't clog if it sucked up a piece of debris, a burner that could operate on diesel fuel or other power source, a thermostat to keep the water at the right temperature, a control manifold to keep the diver from getting burned, and a pump that would deliver enough water through 1,000 or more feet of hose.

During this same period, the offshore oil industry was starting to boom, and there was an urgent need for divers to work deeper and longer. With the development of saturation diving it was possible to work at depths in excess of 300 feet for periods of up to a month. The saturation chamber complex permitted the divers to rest on the surface between dives, while still under pressure, living in the chambers. When the divers went to work they were lowered to the bottom in a diving bell where they locked out for dives of up to four hours. Until the hot water suit was developed there was no efficient way to keep the diver warm and productive.

Through Dick Long's persistence, the hot water suit became an essential part of deep and cold water commercial diving as we know it today. By 1974, the hot water suit was firmly established in the commercial diving field.

Jack O'Neill developed the Supersuit.

Diving During the 1970s

During the 1970s there were very few new developments in thermal protection for divers. DUI was busily engaged in designing and building hot water systems for deeper and deeper diving. The Unisuit became popular with cold water divers around the world. New materials and insulators were being developed, but they had yet to be utilized by the diving industry.

One of the more popular dry suits that appeared during this period was the Supersuit manufactured by Jack O'Neill of Santa Cruz, California. The Supersuit had a trimmer fit than the Unisuit, with a zipper that ran across the diver's shoulder blades.

This suit was made from foam neoprene rubber. Instead of a separate inflator and exhaust valve, the Supersuit used a power inflator from a buoyancy compensator mounted at the end of a corrugated hose. Since it was cheaper to manufacture, the Supersuit could be sold at prices well below the Unisuit. Many sport divers began to use the Supersuit in the temperate waters of California and at other locations in the U.S.

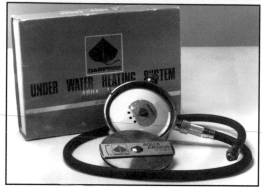

The Aqua Ardor wetsuit heater from Japan burned fuel in this canister.

Variations of the Supersuit design began to appear on the market almost immediately. It was a simple matter for even a small manufacturer to buy the waterproof zippers and inflator mechanisms to build dry suits from neoprene. Many diving equipment manufacturers marketed suits similar to the Supersuit during this period.

One active heating product that never made it to market was a fuel burning diver heater developed in Japan. The system consisted of a small canister with a metered orifice connected to a low pressure hose from the diver's regulator. The canister was O-ring sealed. Inside the can, was a wick and a fuel compartment. After the can was filled with fuel and the wick was lit, the can was sealed.

The outlet side allowed the heated air to escape. The can was designed to fit inside the diver's wetsuit. For a time, U.S. Divers considered distributing the product but ultimately rejected it.

Commercial diving operations during the 70s included the use of lock-out submersibles, designed to carry saturation divers to work at depths in excess of 400 feet. The forward compartment of the subs carried a pilot and a life support operator at one atmosphere (surface pressure). The rear compartment carried a team of divers under pressure, capable of exiting the sub to do work. The subs were equipped with breathing gas supplies and a closed-circuit diver heating system.

Tube suits provided active heating under dry suits for commercial divers.

The divers wore "tube suits" similar to those worn by the astronauts. Over the tube suits the divers would wear dry suit undergarments. Over the undergarments they wore a dry suit equipped with special inlet and outlet valves. The divers complained that it took 45 minutes to dress into this equipment.

Hot water was pumped to the diver from the sub, circulated through the tube suit, and returned to the sub for reheating. In theory, it was a very productive system, but the subs were plagued by so many operational problems they are rarely used today. One of the major drawbacks was the limited weather conditions that were acceptable for launch and recovery of the subs themselves.

Viking began to actively export its suits into the United States during this period. Robert Shrout, a commercial diver in New York, was the first distributor of Viking suits in the United States. The first Viking suits in the U.S. were designed strictly for commercial diving and it wasn't until the early 80s that Viking manufactured suits for sport diving.

The 1980s: Dry Suit Use Becomes Widespread

By the early 1980s, many manufacturers were building a variety of dry suits from new materials, especially urethane laminates. The technology that was being used to manufacture buoyancy compensators was adopted by many companies to build dry suits.

Some of the biggest changes in the dry suit market were brought about by the introduction of new materials. TLS material, a trilaminate of cloth and rubber, became available and was shown to be an excellent material for making dry suits. TLS was originally developed for use by NATO military forces in chemical warfare suits. It provides such a superior liquid barrier that it makes an excellent material for dry suits. DUI introduced its patented CF200 material, a crushed neoprene with a heavy duty nylon coating that also quickly gained a following.

Better insulation materials also became available during this time. One of the most popular was Thinsulate®, manufactured by 3M and used in ski wear and other winter sports clothing. Max Lippett of the Naval Coastal Systems Lab was the first to appreciate the properties of Thinsulate® for underwater applications. Originally, type "M" Thinsulate® was used, but for underwater use the second generation that became known as Type "B" has proven best.

Thinsulate® proved to be an excellent choice for dry suit underwear because it provides warmth without bulk. Thinsulate® fibers are hydrophobic. i.e, they will not absorb water. In the event of a dry suit leak, Thinsulate® retains much of its insulating capacity.

Thinsulate® fibers are shown here in close-up. This material provides excellent insulation even when wet.

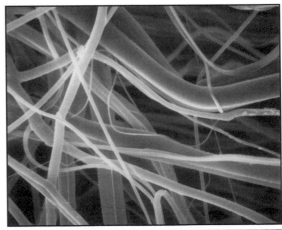

Courtesy of 3M

Viking began distributing a relatively low cost, but effective underwear made from open cell foam. The material used was actually the same material used in the headliners from Volvo cars!

A new generation of synthetic pile fibers also became available that provided good insulation at a reasonable cost. The days of woolen underwear and inefficient sweat suits for dry suit diving were over.

Another active heating method that sport divers experimented with was the Heat Wave™ reusable diver heating pack. This system consists of a heavy duty plastic pouch filled with sodium acetate. The system is known as a "latent heat" system.

A trigger mechanism causes a chemical reaction known as a "phase change" inside the pouch that generates 130 degrees F heat for 30-45 minutes. This system generates 100 BTU's per pound, not enough heat to really keep a diver warm. In fact this localized heating method confuses the human body's physiological mechanism and can create a net overall heat loss. The skin senses temperature differential, not absolute temperature. This makes the diver subjectively feel warm. But, you may actually lose more heat with this system than if the blood vessels under the skin are constricted as they would normally be in cold water.

With more reliable materials and better methods of construction, dry suit manufacturers turned their attention to making suits that were easier to use. Bob Stinton, DUI's chief engineer, came up with the idea for DUI's patented self-donning dry suit design in 1982. The idea was originally developed to allow a Special Forces diver to dress and undress himself during a mission. Simultaneously, Dick Long came up with the concept of using suspenders and a crotch strap on the suit to prevent the crotch of the suit from sagging. These combined features made it much easier for a diver to walk or run on dry land and to swim in the water.

By the mid 1980s, there were many different types of dry suits from which to choose. Seatec, Viking, DUI, Harveys, OS Systems, SAS, Parkway, Henderson, KME, Avon, Typhoon, Poseidon, U.S.I.A., and Driflex were all building dry suits. By the end of the decade some of these manufacturers no longer made dry suits.

Diver Thermal Protection Today

During the coming years we expect to see new and even better materials on the market for dry suits and insulation. The dry suits we use today will undoubtedly become lighter weight and stronger. We expect to see new methods of creating waterproof seams and the possibility of improved zippers.

With the advent of better battery systems, we may finally see dry suits that use electrically heated undergarments. This could be an extremely thin garment that would dramatically cut the weight requirements for dry suit diving.

Dry suit education has become a recognized specialty among the diver training agencies. Virtually every diver training agency today offers some type of dry suit diver specialty training.

Proper thermal protection is essential if you want to get the most enjoyment out of your diving.

Chapter 2
Why Thermal Protection is Important

What is "Cold" Water?

One of the biggest problems in explaining a diver's need for thermal protection lies in defining the concept of "cold water." Every diver has a different range of temperatures that they find comfortable. There are many factors that influence a diver's subjective feelings of comfort in the water. These factors include the water temperature, the diver's size, the diver's percentage of body fat, the diver's activity level on any given dive, how much sleep the diver gets before the dive, the type of thermal protection the diver is wearing, the duration of the dive, the number of preceding dives, and drug or alcohol use prior to diving.

From an objective standpoint, we can say that a diver has begun to be affected by cold water when he or she exhibits certain measurable physiological and/or psychological signs. Some of the more obvious signs include, but are not limited to, shivering, discomfort, loss of manual dexterity, loss of reasoning ability, lapses in memory of events that occurred during the dive, and increased air consumption. These are all signs of a decrease in body temperature. When these signs become so obvious as to be easily noticeable even to the diver's partner, it is probably long past the time when the diver should have left the water.

Divers who regularly expose themselves to cold water become somewhat acclimated to the environment, showing a reduced physiological response. However, as a diver, it is impossible to eliminate the negative effects of cold water on your body.

Subjectively, most divers who are wearing a wetsuit will usually start to make remarks about the water temperature when it drops below 60 degrees F, although a high exercise rate will generate several times the heat created by a diver at rest. Water temperatures below 55 degrees F become very uncomfortable, especially if you are making repetitive dives.

Body Size and Structure are Important

One of the most important elements in determining how cold water affects a diver involves the surface area of the diver's body relative to their body mass. Given two divers of equal height, the diver who is more slender will usually chill faster.

Male and female divers may have very different insulation requirements in the same temperature waters.

The more surface area the diver's body has, relative to their body mass, the faster that body will lose heat. Larger divers do not chill as quickly as smaller divers. Female divers usually have more surface area than males of similar height and will chill more quickly.

The old theory that females make better divers due to their extra layer of body fat is not true. Female divers will generally report subjective feelings of cold sooner than male divers.

Cold Water Effects

Divers who are cold use more air in the same period of time than divers who are warm. Scientific tests have shown that divers who are cold may increase their air consumption by up to 29% over divers who are kept warm in the same temperature water. If you want the longest possible bottom time from a scuba bottle, it is essential to ensure that you are wearing the right thermal protection for the water temperature in which you dive. Even in tropical waters, if you make multiple dives during the day, you will get longer bottom times if you wear a thin wetsuit rather than an ordinary Lycra® dive "skin." Today, there are even dry suits that are specially designed for diving in "warm" water, especially for long exposure dives.

The reason for this higher air consumption rate is very simple. The metabolism of a diver who is cold will increase as the body burns more calories in an attempt to maintain the proper internal temperature (core temperature). This process takes place inside the body without the diver being aware of it. For a diver who becomes chilled, there is a significant danger that the body will not be able to take in enough oxygen to meet both the demands of exercise and the increased metabolism to maintain the internal temperature. Without sufficient oxygen in your body you will feel fatigued.

Although you might not subjectively feel cold, after a day of diving in cold water, most divers will feel exhausted. The source of this fatigue is due to the energy requirements of diving in cold water. This "unearned fatigue" results when your cold body is unable to use fuel to replenish the energy in your muscles. If you've ever been diving in the tropics, compare how you felt after a day of diving in warm water to what you felt like after a day of similar activity in cold water. The difference is startling.

One of the ways that your body will attempt to control heat loss is through

Photo courtesy of Whites Manufacturing

"vasoconstriction." Vasoconstriction occurs when the body shuts down the circulation to the skin and extremities. If the water is cold enough, and the diver is not properly protected, the skin temperature can drop to a level close or equal to the surrounding water temperature. With extended exposures to cold water, permanent nerve damage may occur.

Other Ways You Lose Heat Underwater

Aside from the direct effect of cold water against the skin, there are other ways divers lose body heat when diving in cold water. No matter what type of suit you are wearing, if you are using scuba you will lose body heat each time you exhale through your regulator.

Some divers even use dry suits like this in the tropics.

Three factors contribute to this situation. First, the air in the scuba tank is chilled to the surrounding water temperature in a very few minutes. You can confirm this by checking your submersible pressure gauge shortly after you enter the water. When the water temperature is colder than the air temperature topside, your tank pressure will drop due to the decreased temperature.

As you inhale through the second stage of your regulator, the air supplied by the first stage experiences a pressure drop. This pressure drop causes another decrease in the air temperature. You can see a similar effect by opening the valve on a bare scuba tank topside. As the air blasts out of the tank, the tank will cool rapidly and condensation will form on the tank and valve. The cold air you inhale from your regulator is warmed to your body temperature as it enters your body. If the water temperature is 50 degrees F and the internal body temperature is 98.6 degrees F, the temperature difference is 48.6 degrees. Each time you exhale a substantial amount of heat is lost from your body.

This problem is compounded by the fact that scuba air is dry while your lungs are wet. Not only does this exhaled breath carry heat, it also carries moisture. The percentage of metabolic heat lost through breathing can exceed 20% depending upon your depth, lung volume, and exercise rate.

Heat and body fluids are also lost through urination. Divers wearing wetsuits commonly urinate in their suits in response to cold water exposure. This is caused by increased blood circulating through the kidneys as a result of vasoconstriction. As more blood volume is passed through the kidneys, more urine is produced. Each time that you urinate underwater, both heat and fluid are lost. This loss of body fluids can cause decompression problems and may contribute to bubble formation leading to decompression sickness.

Protecting Your Extremities is Essential

Since the head also has such a large surface area, it contributes to a significant loss of body heat. This makes it very important to have adequate thermal protection for your head in cold water. Estimates of the percentage of body heat lost through an unprotected head run as high as 50%. For ice diving, the use of a full-face mask is highly recommended to provide further insulation. Of course, this gear requires proper training.

For scuba divers, there is a real trade-off between adequate thermal protection for your hands and manual dexterity. The more insulation you wear on your hands, the less able you will be to operate equipment underwater. The loss in grip strength from a five-fingered neoprene glove alone has been measured at 22%. Without proper warmth, nutrients, and oxygen, the muscles of the hands will not function properly.

Minimal hand insulation, such as thin gloves, will permit greater use of your hands initially, but only until your hands become too cold to be useful.

Memory also seems to be affected by cold-water exposures and lower body temperature. Divers who are affected by cold water may have trouble concentrating on simple tasks and multiple tasks may be impossible. In water temperatures below 50 degrees F, a diver's performance capability of complex tasks may decrease by as much as 20% or more. Similarly, divers who became chilled during a dive may not remember what they were supposed to achieve underwater, or the details of the dive after it is over.

Improper Thermal Protection Exposes You to Greater Risk Underwater

Decompression sickness (bends) is just one problem that can be compounded by exposure to cold water. A diver's blood will thicken due to the loss of body fluids by urination and breathing. This loss of fluids results in poor blood circulation.

Reduced blood circulation to your extremities when you are cold in the water is just one of the factors that will make it more likely that you may suffer from the bends. Our goal is to keep the diver in thermal balance.

The ultimate result of body heat loss is "hypothermia," a condition where the diver's body core temperature drops. When your core temperature drops to approximately 97 degrees F you will begin to shiver. If this condition persists, or your core temperature drops even fractionally lower, you will shiver uncontrollably.

Proper insulation for your head and your hands is very important in cold water.

At a core temperature of 95 degrees F you will reach the point where clear thought becomes difficult. For most

Divers who become chilled may be more susceptible to decompression sickness.

people, any drop in body temperature below this is considered intolerable.

By the time your core drops to 93 degrees F you will be suffering from hallucinations. At this core temperature, up to 50% of all divers may die. Below 84 degrees F, unconsciousness is a certainty and at 81 degrees death results from heart stoppage (ventricular fibrillation).

The end result of exposing a diver to cold water without proper thermal protection is the increased risk of a diving accident. This probably occurs long before hypothermia sets in. Considering all of the possible combined negative factors, i.e., increased air consumption, increased fatigue, a loss of manual dexterity, and impaired mental capacity, it's easy to see why a diver who is chilled is a candidate for a diving accident. Any time hypothermia becomes apparent the dive should be terminated.

Why Wetsuits are Inefficient in Cold Water

If we examine the relative efficiency of wetsuits compared to dry suits, we find that wetsuits become less acceptable when you make multiple dives in a single day. Part of the problem with the wetsuit is that as you exit the water, the water inside the suit that was warmed by your body drains out. On each subsequent dive, a new quantity of water must be warmed up.

The closed cells of a wetsuit compress with each foot of descent. The deeper you dive, the less efficient your suit becomes. Water also circulates through the suit during each dive, increasing your heat loss.

Another problem that most people overlook is that as a wetsuit ages, it provides less insulation over time. The closed cell neoprene material used to make the suit breaks down when exposed to pressure. In addition, if salt water dries in the suit, salt crystals cut the individual cells, ruining their insulating capabilities.

Predicting Individual Needs for Underwater Thermal Protection

It is impossible to predict the insulation requirements for each individual diver in cold water. Two divers who are the exact same size may have very different metabolic characteristics. Their bodies produce heat and react to cold in different ways. Although we can make some general predictions regarding a diver's individual needs, it will be up to you to determine what feels best in a particular situation.

It's important to pick the dry suit that best fits your individual needs.

Chapter 3
Types of Dry Suits

Today's dry suits are very different from the dry suits first used for sport diving. New materials make the modern dry suits lighter, tougher, and more resistant to abrasion. Used properly, dry suit valves provide incredibly precise buoyancy control. Waterproof zippers make the suits easy to don and remove. Improved construction techniques give many dry suits a longer useful life than most wetsuits. Advanced features offer more comfort and improved fit. With all of the features available in dry suits today, it's possible to select a dry suit that will precisely fit your needs.

Types of Dry Suit Material

There are numerous types of dry suit material commonly available. As new fabrics are developed, we will certainly see additional new materials put to use. Any material that is waterproof and can be adequately joined together, or "seamed," could conceivably be used to create a dry suit.

The type of material your dry suit is made from will determine the characteristics of the suit more than any other single feature. For this reason, we'll discuss the materials dry suits are manufactured from first, followed by a discussion of suit features, such as zippers, valves, and other items.

The most common materials used for dry suits are foam neoprene, crushed neoprene, rubber coated fabrics, urethane coated fabrics, and vulcanized rubber. Each material has its own set of characteristics that will affect the performance of the dry suit and the way it can be used.

Hybrid suits are also available that combine Trilaminate material with crushed neoprene. Other combinations may include materials such as Cordura® with butyl rubber. Dry suits for tropical environments may be made from a combination of breathable yet waterproof materials such as certain types of Trilaminates and Cordura®.

Foam Neoprene Dry Suits

There are numerous manufacturers of foam neoprene dry suits. Many are made by wetsuit shops that specialize in custom dry suits from foam neoprene.

Foam neoprene dry suits are among the least expensive of all dry suits.

These suits are among the least expensive of all types of dry suits.

Foam neoprene dry suits are assembled from sheets of neoprene rubber, the same material used to make wetsuits. The rubber is cut to the pattern of the panels of the suit. The material is glued together using wetsuit cement.

Since wetsuit material is used, any color of neoprene material used for a wetsuit can also be used for a dry suit.

Each seam of the suit is stitched on a sewing machine with heavy duty thread. Normally, a "blind" stitch, that doesn't penetrate through the suit, is employed. To help ensure the integrity of the seams, some manufacturers coat the seams or use special sealing techniques.

Some foam neoprene dry suits are equipped with attached boots, while others are supplied with ankle seals instead. Suits that are designed this way must be used with wetsuit booties. These suits cost less, but offer less thermal protection.

Most foam neoprene suits are tailored to fit the body rather closely. In fact, in many cases, divers do not use much additional insulation underneath them. They merely rely on the inherent insulation of the neoprene itself and the layer of air trapped inside it. This arrangement will work at moderate temperatures and shallow depths, but will not be satisfactory for colder or deeper waters. In northern California, where scuba is not permitted to be used for abalone diving, foam neoprene dry suits are popular with many divers.

In situations where a foam neoprene dry suit leaks, you still have the benefit of the insulation of the neoprene material. Foam neoprene dry suits are also the only type of dry suit that are inherently buoyant. With a snug fitting foam neoprene suit, with little or no additional insulation, even if the suit floods completely you won't experience much of a change in buoyancy. Loose fitting foam neoprene suits, will experience a greater buoyancy change if the suit no longer holds air.

All foam neoprene suits suffer from a loss of buoyancy and insulation at depth, just as a wetsuit does. This drawback should be considered before purchasing a suit of this type.

Over time, the buoyancy and insulation capabilities of a foam neoprene dry suit will decrease as the cells of the suit break down. Each time you dive, a certain number of cells collapse due to the increased pressure underwater. Just the action of swimming, bending, and working with your arms will break down the neoprene cells, especially in high wear areas like the knees, shoulders, and elbows.

Once the cells of the suit begin to break down it is very difficult to keep a foam neoprene dry suit dry. This action will begin to weep water into the suit. The only way to repair a suit in this condition is to actually cut out and remove the damaged section of the suit.

Punctures in foam neoprene dry suits are difficult to locate and repair. Any puncture introduces water into the cellular material of the suit. Repairs to a foam neoprene suit can only be performed when the suit is completely dry.

The life expectancy of a foam neoprene dry suit will vary between 200 and 300 dives, depending upon your individual style of diving and the care you give your suit. Smog and ozone are particularly detrimental to all types of diving gear, especially foam neoprene.

Crushed Neoprene Dry Suits

Crushed neoprene is a very tough, yet flexible material. It is an excellent material to use to make a dry suit.

Crushed neoprene starts out as a thick sheet of foam neoprene rubber. An extremely heavy duty nylon is bonded to the neoprene. After the suit is built, it is then "crushed" in a proprietary process. The resulting material is very thin, has a great deal of stretch, and is extremely rugged. The nylon used on the exterior of crushed neoprene material is among the most abrasion resistant of all dry suit materials. The process is patented, and is very labor intensive when done properly.

Dry suits made from crushed neoprene can be tailored from start to finish. This helps give the suit an outstanding fit. Due to the tremendous stretch of crushed neoprene, the suit can be customized to be quite snug and a very supple suit results.

Properly fitted, crushed neoprene dry suits typically have a low internal volume. They also tend to have fewer folds and wrinkles than vulcanized rubber dry suits and certain other urethane coated suits. This makes this type of suit flexible and easy to use for swimming.

Crushed neoprene dry suits can be very form fitting.

Due to the nature of the crushed neoprene material, suits made from this fabric have slightly higher insulation values than dry suits made from vulcanized rubber or urethane coated fabric. This will allow you to use lighter dry suit underwear than you might normally select. Most divers find they can dive in waters three degrees cooler than the rating of their underwear when they wear a crushed neoprene suit.

One of the few drawbacks of crushed neoprene material is that to make permanent repairs, the material must be completely dry. The suits themselves are also heavier than some of the lighter weight urethane and Trilaminate suits. However, for the diver who dives aggressively, such as a wreck diver or professional diver, crushed neoprene material is probably one of the best choices for a dry suit.

Compressed neoprene material is also used to make dry suits. This is not the same material as crushed neoprene and does not have the same density, which results in a suit that is not quite as rugged as crushed neoprene.

Urethane Coated Fabric Dry Suits

Dry suits made from urethane backed nylon fabric became quite popular during the 1980s. Urethane is a synthetic material that creates a waterproof barrier when it is properly applied to nylon. Dry suits made from this material are commonly referred to as "pack cloth," or more correctly "polyurethane laminate" dry suits.

Nylon fabric is normally graded according to a rating system known as "denier." Generally speaking, the higher the denier number, the heavier the fabric. For example, 420 denier nylon is heavier than 210 denier nylon. This heavier fabric is more resistant to abrasion, but it is heavier in weight and less flexible.

This suit has a heavy duty nylon exterior with a polyurethane inner layer.

To assemble a urethane fabric dry suit, the material is cut to the pattern and stitched together. To produce a watertight seam the joint must be sealed with a heat tape machine that welds a urethane tape over the seam. This type of dry suit is common because it is relatively easy to manufacture, and less expensive.

In a more complex assembly procedure, all of the seams are folded twice and then stitched. Although this method requires more labor and is more expensive, it produces a reliable seam.

Urethane coated fabrics are used to make some of the most light weight dry suits. The material is reasonably flexible.

Most nylon fabrics have little or no stretch. This is an important consideration in the design of a dry suit made from this material. In order to provide the room a diver needs to get into or out of a suit, and freedom of movement in the water, there must be enough excess fabric to compensate for this lack of stretch. This is one of the reasons why certain dry suits fit the way they do, i.e., loose and baggy.

The estimated life span of a dry suit made from urethane coated nylon material is approximately ten years of regular diving activity. When the urethane starts to break down this will show up as cracking in the

Photo courtesy of Whites Manufacturing

Photo courtesy of Diving Unlimited International

material. When a suit delaminates early in its life it is usually because the material was overheated during the seam sealing process.

TLS Dry Suits

TLS is an abbreviation for Trilaminate suit. The layers in TLS material are tightly woven nylon with a layer of butyl rubber in between. The butyl is a superior rubber to prevent chemical penetration.

TLS suits are stitched and the seams are sealed. As with other coated nylon fabrics, good seam construction is essential.

TLS suits are among the lightest weight yet strongest types of dry suits. The material is highly resistant to deterioration from smog and ozone. The suits dry very quickly after diving or rinsing.

Trilaminate material is also available in a very thin, breathable configuration that is used for diving in the tropics. The cut of these suits tends to be a bit more snug than a typical cold water dry suit, since the warm water suit is designed to be used with less insulation. For long duration dives in warm water, this is an especially good way to keep warm.

TLS suits are quick and easy to repair. The suit is easily patched with Aquaseal® if punctured. The estimated life of a properly made and maintained TLS suit is up to ten years of active diving.

Trilaminate suits are very light weight. Note the self-donning design of this suit.

Vulcanized Rubber Dry Suits

Vulcanized rubber dry suits have been around for many years. The majority of these suits are made from a combination of natural and synthetic rubber known as EPDM.

Vulcanized rubber is an excellent dry suit material. It dries quickly and can be patched in much the same way that you repair an inner tube or inflatable boat.

Vulcanized rubber dry suits must be made from the right combination of materials. Without sufficient synthetics, the suits are prone to ozone attack and rapid deterioration.

It takes the right combination of materials to keep a vulcanized rubber suit from "ballooning" when inflated. The amount of stretch in the suit is primarily a function of the lining inside.

The inside of a vulcanized rubber dry suit is normally covered with a soft fabric. This makes it easier to dress into the suit. The fabric also provides a surface where moisture produced by your body will condense. The waterproof barrier is on the outside of the suit.

Seams on vulcanized rubber suits are sealed under heat and pressure.

Manufacturing a vulcanized rubber dry suit is different from the other suits described thus far. The seams of these suits are actually fused together under heat and pressure. In theory, the material should "cross-link," making the rubber into a one piece garment. If you look at the inside of these suits you will see that they are stitched along the seams, but this is only to hold them together prior to vulcanization.

Although vulcanized rubber suits have good stretch, they usually fit most divers rather loosely. The reason for this is that the manufacturing process for this type of suit is very expensive and most manufacturers offer no more than four or five sizes.

While vulcanized rubber suits can be "customized", all of the tailoring occurs after the suit is manufactured. A skilled technician can alter a vulcanized rubber suit to fit almost any diver.

Some suits are made from vulcanized rubber material, but the seams are not vulcanized. Instead, the vulcanized material is merely glued together.

Vulcanized rubber dry suits are available in a variety of thicknesses; from very light material through extremely heavy material designed for commercial diving. The heavier the material, the more abrasion the suit can withstand. Vulcanized rubber dry suits are normally supplied with latex seals.

Cordura®

Cordura® is an especially rugged fabric that is more durable than polyesters or nylon by themselves. It is a type of weave of material that is normally referred to as "ballistic" nylon. When it is bonded to a waterproof base material and used on the exterior surface of a dry suit, it makes an especially rugged dry suit. It is a high performance fabric.

Dry suits made from Cordura® must be cut a bit more generously than those made from material that has some stretch, since the material has no elasticity.

Cordura® dry suits.

Courtesy of Diving Unlimited International.

Essential Features for All Dry Suits

The essential features for all dry suits, besides the suit material, include the wrist and neck seals, zippers, and valves. Beyond these primary items, all other features are consider "optional."

Hybrids and Other Materials

Dry suits today are often made from a combination of materials that were not formerly used together, but when combined in particular ways, make a lot of sense. These suits are sometimes referred to as "hybrids." For example, some suits may have a crushed neoprene bottom, and a Trilaminate upper torso.

Other suits combine stretch nylon with foam neoprene, sandwiched between another layer of stretch nylon.

Dry Suit Reliability

Most dry suits today are extremely reliable, provided you follow a reasonable program of maintenance. If you purchase a good quality dry suit from a reputable manufacturer, your dry suit should provide you with many years of excellent service.

It's important to purchase the right type of suit for your particular application. A tropical dry suit is not designed for hard-core wreck diving on the east coast of the U.S. or in places like Scapa Flow in the United Kingdom. A heavy duty vulcanized rubber suit will not be the best choice if you are an underwater photographer who does lots of swimming to hunt for critters to film underwater.

Courtesy of Whites Manufacturing, Diving Concepts, and Diving Unlimited International.

Your dry suit should be designed for the particular activities you enjoy underwater.

Wrist and Neck Seals

There are two types of seal materials that are commonly used for dry suit wrist and neck seals. Latex is one popular material and foam neoprene is another. Each material has its own set of advantages and disadvantages.

Neck seals and wrist seals on most foam neoprene suits are made from thin foam neoprene. Although latex seals can be attached to a foam neoprene suit, this is not a standard procedure for the majority of manufacturers. Foam neoprene neck seals should never be cut, but they may need to be stretched before they are used the first time.

Foam neoprene neck seals may be stretched over a standard 80 cubic foot scuba cylinder and allowed to stand this way overnight. Foam neoprene wrist seals may be stretched over a tin can that is larger than the seal and allowed to remain this way for 12 hours.

Latex seals are the most common dry suit seals in use today. Latex seals have more stretch than foam neoprene and provide a very smooth fitting, comfortable seal. They create the least pressure on the diver's wrists and neck.

It is important to remember that all seals restrict blood flow somewhat. At the neck, too tight a neck seal will mean less blood going to your head, which could cause you to pass out. Restricted blood flow also means restricted heat flow to the extremities.

Dry suit seals are supplied in a cone or "bell" shape. Since most dry suits are sold as stock suits, it is not possible for the manufacturer to know the neck size of the person who buys the suit. By supplying seals that are cone shaped each diver can trim the neck seal to the size they feel is most comfortable.

Latex wrist seals can usually be supplied in different thicknesses. Thicker latex seals are not more resistant to punctures, but are less vulnerable to tears. They are much more difficult to don and remove by yourself.

Many divers like latex seals because they are very quick to repair. A puncture in a latex seal can be fixed with patches similar to those used to repair inner tubes.

New latex seals almost always need to be trimmed for use by the diver. Generally speaking, the circumference of a latex seal should be just a bit smaller than the circumference of your neck or wrist at the smallest part. The exact size will vary with the thickness of the seal material and the firmness of your

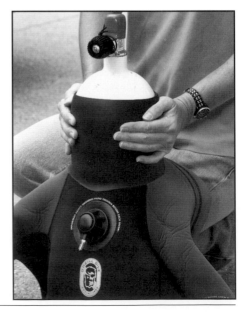

Neoprene seals will almost always need to be stretched before use. Use caution and do not leave the neck seal stretched for too long a time over too large a cylinder. The material has memory and the seal may become too large.

Take your time when you trim latex seals!

muscle tissues in your neck and wrist. The seal must be snug enough to be water-tight, but not so tight as to interfere with blood circulation. If your skin bulges over the edge of the seal, it's too tight.

To trim a latex neck seal, it's a good idea to have your buddy help you. Have your buddy hold the seal at opposite ends so that the neck opening is pinched to-gether. This will, in effect, create two "edges" to the seal. Your buddy should pull the two ends away from each other so that the latex is under a slight tension. You are actually cutting through two thicknesses of material at the same time. Some seals are manufactured with raised lines on them that serve as cutting guides.

Both "edges" of the seal must be parallel to each other. Use the sharpest, larg-est scissors you can find and trim the seal, removing a 1/4 inch ring of material at a time. Children's paper scissors are not up to this task.

Start your cut at the back end of the scissors, with the scissors as wide open as possible. When the scissors are about 3/4 closed, stop, open them up again, and move them forward. Make the longest cut possible as you trim to avoid nicks or rough edges. Try the seal on when you are close to the circumference you want to achieve.

When you get close to removing the final ring of material, stop! Try the seal on and see how it fits. You don't have to put the whole suit on, just don the seal by itself. If it is snug, but not uncomfortable you should try it as it is for a day of diving. Test the size of the neck seal with your chin up. This makes the muscles in your neck tighter and your neck bigger.

Be careful not to trim too much, because once you have gone too far it is im-possible to reattach the latex. If this happens you will need to install an entirely new neck seal.

Quick Replacement Seals

The latex seals are among the most vulnerable part of all dry suits. In the past, if your wrist or neck seal was damaged, your diving day was pretty much over. Today there are a number of seal designs that allow you to quickly replace these seals if they are damaged in the field.

One type of design for quick replacement wrist seals utilizes a hard plastic ring that is permanently attached to the suit, with a groove for a large o-ring to capture the wrist seal. The seal snaps over the plastic ring and a separate large rubber o-ring traps the wide end of the wrist seal in the groove. If your wrist seal is torn or

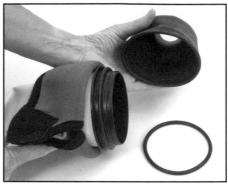

ZipSeals™ like this one are among the fastest and most convenient methods of rapidly replacing a wrist or neck seal.

Another way of quickly replacing seals that is easy and reliable is this ring system.

punctured, all you need to do is remove the o-ring, discard the damaged seal, and snap a new wrist seal in place.

Once you have the seal in position, the o-ring is stretched back onto the ring, locking the seal in position. This is a simple effective design for rapid seal replacement. The only drawback to this design is the large rigid ring is bulky and inconvenient for divers who engage in lobster diving or other activities where you need to reach into tight spaces.

Another design for rapid seal replacement is a system that uses two interlocking surfaces, similar to a Zip-Loc® bag. This type of system is among the easiest and quickest to use, and works for both wrist and neck seals.

To assemble these interlocking seals, a small amount of soapy water is used to lubricate the sealing surfaces. The seals are then pinched together tightly to help ensure a watertight seal. It's essential to make sure the seals are properly installed prior to diving to avoid any possibility of leakage.

Dry Suit Zippers

The zippers used in dry suits are very similar to the zippers used in an astronaut's space suit. Dry suit zippers must be both waterproof and pressure proof.

The zipper teeth are made from bronze. They seal by compressing a rubber sealing surface between the inner teeth of the zipper. Every dry suit zipper includes three essential parts; the slider, the teeth, and the tape.

Dry suit zippers should be as rugged as possible. Heavy duty zippers may last longer, but they are also more expensive. Selecting a dry suit zipper is a trade-off between durability and cost. Larger zippers may be a bit more durable, but they are also more difficult to close and more restrictive to your movement in the water.

Dry suit zippers can not be repaired if the tape is torn or the teeth "split" behind the slider. This means that once your zipper goes bad, it must be replaced. This is an expensive process, partly because the zipper is costly, and partly because it takes a qualified dry suit repair person to replace a zipper. The most common zipper failure occurs when the tape tears between the teeth. Sliders can also fail.

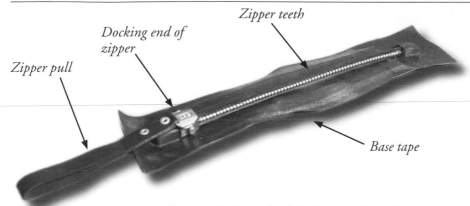

Zipper teeth

Docking end of zipper

Zipper pull

Base tape

Dry suit zippers will normally have all of the features shown here.

Optional Features for Dry Suits

Buying a dry suit is a bit like buying a car; there are many options available. The price you pay for a dry suit will largely be determined by the material, its capabilities, and the number of options you select. Generally speaking, the more options on the suit, the more expensive it will be. However, these options can make a big difference in how much enjoyment you get out of your dry suit.

Suspenders (also known as "braces" in Great Britain)

Suspenders are one of the features that can help make the difference between a truly comfortable dry suit and one that is just tolerable. On some dry suits suspenders are an option, while on others they are included as standard.

Most dry suits are cut somewhat loose and baggy. This is a necessity to give you the room to get your arms, legs, and head into the suit because most dry suit materials don't stretch. The extra room provides for changes in underwear thickness during different seasons. This also allows dry suits to tolerate changes in your personal body weight much better than wetsuits.

Once the suit is on, the suit hangs from your shoulders. Without suspenders, a substantial amount of material will hang down in your crotch. This excess material makes it more difficult to swim, walk, or climb a ladder. The effect of this excess material is roughly equivalent to tying a rope around your thighs and trying to swim. It's possible to move, but you don't have the same range of motion. Divers who use suits without suspenders usually pull their suits up around their waist just before they enter the water.

Suspenders help to make dry suits fit more comfortably.

Dry suits equipped with suspenders are much more comfortable to wear. You adjust the suspenders to pull the excess material snugly up into your crotch. This makes the dry suit fit and feel better. You will find you have greater freedom of movement while wearing a dry suit that comes with suspenders compared to a similar suit with no suspenders.

Another nice thing about suspenders is that they allow you to peel the top of your dry suit down between dives, without having the suit fall off. This makes it very comfortable to walk around on the deck of a boat or on the beach.

Ankle Straps

Ankle straps are another feature that will make certain types of dry suits easier to use and may help to increase your safety. Although they are not mandatory in a dry suit, ankle straps may also help some suits to fit better. The main purpose of the ankle strap is to help prevent your feet from coming out of the boots of your dry suit when you are inverted underwater.

Many dry suits today come with attached "soft" boots with hard soles. One of the important safety aspects of ankle straps is that they help to keep your feet secure in this type of dry suit boot.

If your feet pop out of your boots, your fins will pop off, making it difficult to regain control. This situation must be avoided. Proper training and diving procedures should prevent this from happening, but if it does it becomes an emergency of the highest order.

Dry Suit Boots

The majority of dry suits come with some type of attached boot. These boots usually are equipped with a hard sole and may be molded from a material that is

Ankle straps help to keep your feet more firmly in the boots.

different from the body of the suit. The most commonly used material for dry suit boots is some type of vulcanized rubber.

Soft Socks/Hard Boots

Many dry suits today are offered with an attached soft "sock" designed to be worn with a rugged overboot that helps protect the sock. This type of design is very popular.

The advantages of the soft sock/hard boot combination include:
• Superior foot protection for walking on rock surfaces
• Arch support for walking on dry land and climbing ladders
• Ankle support when you are carrying a heavy tank and weights
• No possibility of the feet of the suit

ballooning when the boots are on your feet
• Excellent protection for the dry suit boot from punctures
• Cheaper to replace when the boots wear out.

The disadvantages of this type of dry suit arrangement are that the boots require the largest possible fins and that you must remember to pack the boots along with the rest of your gear whenever you dive. If you forget your boots, your fins usually won't work with the dry suit "socks" by themselves.

Rugged boots like these are very popular on dry suits today.

Crotch Straps

Crotch straps usually come as standard equipment in dry suits that have a telescoping torso for self-donning. In a self-donning dry suit, the torso of the suit "telescopes" or extends to aid entry into the suit. Once the suit is zipped, the telescoping portion of the suit folds under and is held in place with a crotch strap. Underwater, the water pressure actually holds the suit in position.

Convenience Zippers

A convenience zipper is a small waterproof zipper mounted in the crotch area of a male diver's suit, to allow the diver to urinate on the surface between dives without removing the suit. It's essential to remember to close this zipper completely after use, not to use the zipper underwater, and to take care when closing the zipper to avoid catching your underwear or any delicate parts of your anatomy in the zipper!

Crotch straps are commonly found on self-donning suits.

Self-Don vs. Shoulder Entry

Another important decision is whether you want a "self-donning" dry suit (front zipper) or a rear entry suit. There are advantages and disadvantages to each.

Technical Diving with a Dry Suit

If you plan to engage in extended range dives, i.e., dives to deeper depths involving lengthy decompression, or shallow dives of long duration, you may want to invest in what is known as a "Pee Valve" for your dry suit. A "Pee Valve" does exactly what you would expect – it allows you to uri- nate while wearing a dry suit, and to vent the urine from the suit without fouling the inside of your suit. These valves are also sometimes referred to, in more refined circles than ours, as "overboard discharge valves." There is a female adaptation, but it is less comfortable to wear.

A valve for when you have to go....

The valve penetrates the suit and has an external vent control. The diver must wear a condom which connects to a hose that connects to the valve. As an alternative, male divers may use an external catheter that will hold a fixed amount of urine until it can be disposed of topside.

The only alternative to using a Pee valve is to wear adult diapers next to your skin, beneath your dry suit underwear. Since many divers find this practice distasteful, a Pee Valve is a good alternative.

Photo courtesy of Anthony Rue – Halcyon DIR Dive Systems

With a self-donning suit you can get in and out of the suit by yourself, pro- vided your body is flexible enough to do so. If you have a shoulder injury, this may not be possible. A male diver can also open the zipper and urinate topside without the need to remove the entire suit. The other disadvantages of self-donning suits are that they tend to be more expensive and are not quite as streamlined as shoul- der entry suits may be.

With a shoulder entry suit, you are dependent on someone else to assist you with donning and removing your suit. On the positive side, these suits tend to be less expensive and may be more streamlined.

Pockets

Depending on the type of diving that you do, a pocket may be a useful feature to have added to your suit. If you are an underwater photographer, a wreck diver, or a scientist, a pocket can be a useful place to store all sorts of accessories

Pockets should be self-draining so that they won't hold water after you have surfaced. They must he located where they will not interfere with other equipment.

Pockets can be mounted almost any place that is conve- nient for you. The two most common positions for pockets are on the upper thigh or on the chest.

Accessory pocket

Just be sure to avoid placing any large, sharp objects in your dry suit's pocket(s). Sharps objects can potentially puncture your dry suit.

Knee Pads

Knee pads are standard equipment on most dry suits. They are absolutely essential for all divers, but particularly important for underwater photographers, lobster divers, and wreck divers.

Knee pads on foam neoprene suits can be a problem, however, since the cells of the foam material break down under the knee pad. The material becomes spongy and impossible to keep dry.

Most dry suit knee pads are made from the same material as the base material of the dry suit itself, although some are heavier. Keep in mind that all knee pads restrict movement to a certain degree.

Custom vs. Stock Sizing

A dry suit need not fit you perfectly. Dry suits are designed to fit somewhat loosely, to accommodate a range of underwear combinations. If you have an "average" body, you probably can wear a stock dry suit. However if you are unusually thin, tall, short, or stocky, you may want a custom dry suit.

The advantage of a custom dry suit is that it can be tailored more closely to your body shape. A suit that is made for you will have a minimal internal volume and hold less air. For this reason, a custom suit will let you dive with considerably less weight than a stock dry suit. In addition, a custom suit will have less excess material to create drag, may provide more freedom of movement, and is more attractive.

Almost all dry suits can be ordered in custom sizes. However, some can be tailored from scratch where others (such as vulcanized rubber suits) can only be modified after the basic suit is assembled.

Doing Your Homework

Before you buy a dry suit, we recommend that you spend some time on the Internet and visit the web sites of the different dry suit manufacturers. It also pays to talk to other divers who do the same type of diving that you do, to see what their experiences have been with different dry suits. There are big differences between the various designs and materials that are hard to appreciate until you have some dry suit experience and have tried a particular suit.

Selecting a Dry Suit to Fit You

If you are buying a new dry suit, go to the dive store and put on the bulkiest dry suit underwear you anticipate using before you don the suit. This is very important, especially if the suit fits you snug.

Once you have the suit zipped up, test to see if you have complete movement in the suit. You should be able to freely squat, bend, kick, and reach. If your movement is hampered in any way by the suit or underwear, they are probably too tight. It is better to have a dry suit that is a little bit loose than one that is too tight. Most people give all of their attention to the fit of the suit without considering the underwear.

Dry suit valves should be rugged and have as low a profile as possible. Like most valves today, this one swivels so you can attach your dry suit hose from any direction.

Chapter 4
Dry Suit Valves

Dry suit valves vary greatly in type and performance. The placement, construction, age, and design of the valves on your suit will directly affect your ability to control the air in your suit. A good set of valves can make a big difference in your diving enjoyment.

Like the dry suit material itself, most dry suit valves are made by specialized manufacturers. Some of the key makers of dry suit valves include Apeks and A.P. Valves in England, SI Tech, and Poseidon in Sweden. Just as the same dry suit zippers may appear on competing manufacturers' suits, the same dry suit valves may also be found on several different brands of suits. Yet while they may appear outwardly identical, they may be manufactured to different specifications.

There are a number of types of dry suit valves that are used on contemporary dry suits. A dry suit inflator valve allows you to put air into your dry suit. Some manufacturers also refer to this type of valve as an "inlet valve." A dry suit exhaust valve will let air out of the suit. Certain manufacturers will refer to this type of valve as an "outlet valve."

Some manufacturers have added small additional exhaust valves to their suits on the wrists or ankles. These valves are appropriately known as "wrist valves," "cuff valves," "cuff dumps," or "ankle valves." Some valves of this design will not flow as much air as a regular exhaust valve, so be sure to inquire carefully regarding the performance of suits equipped with these types of valves. However, these smaller valves will allow the diver to vent the dry suit from awkward positions.

Most dry suit exhaust valves today are known as "automatic exhaust valves." Although this is a commonly used term, it is not entirely correct. The valves will exhaust "automatically," provided the valves are at the highest point on the dry suit and they have been properly adjusted.

Assuming the dry suit exhaust valve is mounted on the left upper arm, the proper position for venting automatic exhaust valves is for the diver to be upright with his arm bent at the elbow, and raised at the elbow, hand down. With correct adjustment and positioning, hands free operation is possible. In addition, most of these valves have a manual over-ride feature.

Not all dry suit inflator hoses take the same type of connector. Your suit should come with the correct hose when you buy it.

An older type of dry suit exhaust is the push-to-dump valve. This valve will vent only when you push down on either a button in the valve or the valve body itself. These are rarely used on dry suits today.

In discussing the force required to operate a particular valve, the term "pounds force" is the correct description of how much effort it takes to operate the valve. This is abbreviated as "pounds *f*", and is a measure of the force required to compress the spring in the valve. It is not realistic to use pounds per square inch, since some divers may use only a finger tip while other divers will use the palm of their hand. This results in a variation in the surface area of the valve button or head involved in its operation.

Dry suit inflator hoses should be easy to connect and disconnect when you're wearing gloves. Some hoses are equipped with a flange or wings to facilitate this.

While some manufacturers claim that their exhaust valves will dump air faster than their inflator valve can supply it, in the real world this is not always true. In most cases when an inflator valve sticks it is essential to disconnect the inflator hose, while simultaneously venting from the exhaust. It may also be necessary to open the wrist or neck seal to control the ascent in an emergency.

Dry Suit Valve Locations

The positions of the valves on your dry suit directly affect the buoyancy characteristics of your suit. Both the inflator valve and the exhaust valve need to be properly located in respect to the rest of your diving equipment.

The most common location for the dry suit inflator button is on the middle of the chest of the suit. This is a good location for several important reasons. First, it provides a solid base, your sternum (breast bone), to push the valve against to operate it. Secondly, this location does not interfere with most buoyancy compensators or other diving gear. Finally, it is a location that is easily reached whether you are right or left handed.

In the past, some dry suit manufacturers positioned the exhaust valve on the diver's chest, but today the most common location for the valve is on your left upper arm. With the valve located on the chest it is dif-

Like most inflator valves today, this one can swivel in any direction.

This very small exhaust valve has been mounted on the wrist of this dry suit.

ficult to get the excess air out of the suit. Notice we say, "the excess air," because it is not possible to get all the air out of the suit, and you would never actually want to do this. There will always be some air trapped in the underwear inside the suit unless the suit is completely flooded.

Another disadvantage to mounting the exhaust valves on the chest is that this forces you to assume an upright position in the water to vent the suit. If the exhaust valve is mounted on the arm you can vent the suit, as you continue to swim, by rolling down on your right side. For this reason, it is easy to see that the best position for the exhaust valve is on your upper left arm.

Dry Suit Valve Performance

While dry suit valve manufacturers are careful to provide excellent quality control, the reality is that no two valves will perform identically. Dry suit valves, like automobiles or scuba regulators, are manufactured within a certain range of tolerances. When they are assembled, they are tested and the valves must perform within a certain range to be acceptable for proper function. Other factors that will affect a valve's performance include the age of the valve, the type of underwear your are using, the fit of your suit, how well the valve has been maintained, the water temperature, and the gas used to fill the dry suit.

Ideally, a dry suit exhaust valve should vent as quickly as possible to help avoid an uncontrolled ascent. How quickly the valve will vent is determined by the spring setting in the valve and the size and resistance of the rubber membrane that the air must vent past to exit the suit.

Dry suit exhaust valves should vent faster than the inflator valve will supply air to the suit when the diver is in an upright position in the water.

Layering is a good dry suit insulation strategy.

Chapter 5
Dry Suit Undergarments

Without proper dry suit underwear, even the best dry suit will not keep you warm. Selecting the right dry suit underwear for your particular diving application is not hard, but it does require some knowledge and thought. There are several different types of dry suit underwear available. Each type of material has very different characteristics that will not only affect your warmth, but will also influence your buoyancy, mobility, and comfort.

The smart dry suit diver thinks in terms of insulation strategies for particular dives. Just as there is not one wetsuit that will keep you comfortable under all diving conditions, there is not one set of dry suit underwear that will be applicable to all divers under all situations. By developing a proper insulation strategy you will be able to put together the combination of dry suit undergarments for any dive.

The goal in developing an insulation strategy is to maintain the diver in thermal balance. The ideal situation is one where you are neither too hot nor too cold. Your body should be at a comfortable temperature when you dive.

Most people who participate in cold weather sports topside are familiar with the concept of layering. The term refers to wearing a selection of garments that will keep you warm, rather than one single garment.

When you dress in layers of clothing (insulation), you can remove some of the garments to adjust for changes in the water temperature or your exercise rate. While it is not possible to remove garments underwater, it is possible to adjust our insulation before the dive, based upon, our individual physiology, the water temperature, and, our planned diving activity (exercise rate).

As we have mentioned before, a dry suit with underwear works on the principle of passive insulation. The dry suit underwear traps a layer of air. The combination of air compartments in the underwear slows the heat transfer from your body to the water. Given two sets of underwear made from the same material, the thicker set will trap more air and keep you warmer.

Just because a set of underwear of one type is thicker than another type does not necessarily mean it will be warmer. It all depends upon the efficiency of the material from which the underwear is constructed. The ideal dry suit undergarment is the thinnest design that traps the most air in the smallest spaces. Certain materials, such as Thinsulate®, have much higher insulation efficiency than others, and depending on the type, still provide good insulation when wet.

For the Technically Minded

The efficiency of a dry suit undergarment is calculated in terms of a unit of measurement known as "Clo." One Clo unit is the amount of thermal insulation that is required to maintain an "average" resting man in thermal balance in an air environment where the temperature is 70 degrees Fahrenheit, the relative humidity is less than 50%, and the air movement is 20 feet per minute. These conditions approximate what we might call "room temperature."

From another perspective, the "average" person is comfortable when naked at a room temperature of 86 degrees F. A Clo unit represents the amount of insulation required for the 16 degree air temperature drop between the comfortable nude resting temperature and 70 degrees F.

As a further point of reference, a 1/4-inch thick wetsuit has a Clo value of approximately 1.8 Clo at the surface. However, at a depth of 100 feet, after the suit has been compressed, the Clo value of the same suit is only approximately 0.25 Clo.

Your body gives off moisture, even if you're not exercising and sweating. This moisture from your body will condense against the cold inner surface of the suit. How your dry suit underwear responds to this moisture will greatly influence how comfortable you will be in your suit. If the underwear soaks up this wetness you will feel cold and clammy inside your suit.

In this chapter we will compare different types of dry suit undergarments and provide you with the information to make predictions regarding your insulation needs. However, it is important to realize that each diver's insulation needs are different.

We caution you that our recommendations for insulation are guidelines only. They will provide the new dry suit diver with a starting point for selecting insulation. However, it is up to you to experiment and see what feels best to you. You may need more or less insulation than is recommended to be comfortable underwater.

Thinsulate® is a particularly efficient insulator.

Courtesy of Diving Unlimited International

The cut of this stretch Thinsulate® undergarment is very trim.

Problems in Comparing Dry Suit Underwear

Different manufacturers have used different systems for rating the thermal efficiency of their garments. It is recommended that before accepting a manufacturer's rating for your personal use that you investigate the following:

Check the basis for the rating. Ask the manufacturer what basis was used for the rating. Some manufacturers use more conservative rating systems than others. Remember that each person has a different heat production rate and heat loss rate.

Check the overall thickness of the insulation under compression. A quick way to do this is to just compress the underwear between your thumb and forefinger. A more accurate measurement can be achieved by preparing two squares of thin, stiff material, such as Plexiglas, measuring two inches by two inches square. Place one piece on either side of a piece of underwear and lay the whole assembly on a table. Place a 2-pound weight on the outside square. Measure the thickness of the underwear material between the two squares. Under these conditions you have the equivalent of approximately .5 P.S.I. suit compression, which is roughly equivalent to the pressure the underwear experiences during normal diving conditions.

Selection Factors to Consider in Choosing Dry Suit Underwear

Some of the factors that you will want to consider in selecting dry suit underwear include the following:

• What is the compression resistance of the underwear? Underwear that compresses less provides more insulation.

• What is the thermal conductivity of the material? More efficient underwear does not conduct as much heat away from the body.

• How much insulation does the garment provide once it becomes wet?

• How does the material feel against your skin? Is it comfortable?

• Does the material stretch, making it easier to don and remove and providing more freedom of movement?

Dry Suit Underwear is Available in Many Styles

While the material used in the construction of your dry suit underwear will have the biggest influence on your warmth, there are many other factors that will

Thinsulate® undergarment

affect your diving comfort. There are also certain other features that will make your diving more convenient.

Pockets are a feature that aren't essential to your comfort, but make your diving more convenient. Better quality dry suit undergarments are equipped with pockets.

Thinsulate®

Thinsulate® is made from polyolefin microfibers. The original material had no stretch, which made it less comfortable than some other materials. However, a new stretch Thinsulate® is available that is extremely pleasant to wear, but less water resistant.

Manufacturers of dry suit underwear use Thinsulate® in combination with other materials to produce their undergarments. The Thinsulate® is normally sandwiched between layers of other material. For example, the outside of the garment will usually be a nylon taffeta to help the dry suit to slide easily over the undergarment and make it windproof when you are on deck and not wearing your dry suit. The inside of the underwear may be a synthetic polyester "fleece" for comfort against the skin. The additional layers of material may also increase the Clo rating of the garment.

The greatest advantage of Thinsulate® dry suit undergarments is that even if your dry suit leaks, Type "B" Thinsulate® underwear still provides good insulation. While we do not recommend diving with a dry suit that has developed a leak, you will be much warmer with a Thinsulate® undergarment in this type of situation.

Thinsulate® comes in different weights so it's important to pick the garment that is appropriate for your diving location. Serious dry suit divers may own two dry suit undergarments, one for summer diving and one for winter, as well as a liner and vest, so they are prepared for any water temperature.

Thinsulate® batting is very dense. Any water that contacts Thinsulate® is broken up into very small droplets that are separated by these fibers. This action helps to prevent heat transfer since the water drops are not touching each other.

Booties made from Thinsulate® will absorb very little water, which is a big plus if you must remove your dry suit on a wet deck. Since the lower part of your dry suit usually suffers from the greatest compression, the consistent insulation provided by this material makes diving more comfortable.

While Thinsulate® fibers repel water, they "love" oil. When you sweat, the oils from your body will accumulate in Thinsulate® underwear. Dirt will stick to this oil, and water will be absorbed by the dirt. These factors combined will rob Thinsulate® of its efficiency. For this reason it is very important to launder your Thinsulate® underwear properly, and to use a liner like a cotton T-shirt underneath it to absorb sweat and body oils.

To properly launder Thinsulate® you must pay close attention to the care instructions provided with the particular garment you are using. In most cases, you can wash the underwear through a complete cycle with no soap but rather a cap of bleach to remove salt, body oils, and eliminate any odor. Just be sure to add the bleach after the washer is full to avoid damaging the material. If you use soap, use it sparingly and run the garment through three additional complete wash cycles without soap to remove all traces of the detergent.

Soap acts as a "wetting agent". Wetting agents allow the oils and dirt to be washed out of garments. If the soap is not totally removed during laundering

It's essential to launder your dry suit undergarment properly. This includes both washing and drying.

it will dry inside the garment and remain as a wetting agent during your dives. Since Thinsulate® is designed to be hydrophobic (repel water) this will reduce its capabilities.

Follow the specific drying instructions for your garment. If no instructions are available, allow the garment to air dry on a plastic hanger. Remember that most synthetic fibers are affected by heat, and Thinsulate® is no different. Drying Thinsulate® at a high temperature will cause the fibers to melt and destroy their effectiveness. It's best to hang Thinsulate® garments and allow them to air dry.

Wooly Bears

The term "wooly bear" has been used in dry suit diving for many years. It is a generic term that is used to refer to any dry suit undergarment that is made from a synthetic pile. Today there are many different synthetic materials available, so it is important to know what material was used to make the garment you select.

Most of the early wooly bears were made from nylon. While the material was reasonably comfortable, it was not as pleasant to wear as some of the polyester fibers currently sold.

One of the major disadvantages of older pile fabric was that the material had a tendency to form balls of lint, or "pill," after laundering. These balls of lint would break loose from the surface of the underwear and find their way into the dry suit exhaust valve. Some divers who have used nylon wooly bears have had the exhaust valves on their suits jammed by the lint produced by the garment. When lint jams an exhaust valve shut it becomes impossible to vent the suit properly. When lint jams an exhaust valve open the suit will not hold air properly and the diver will get wet.

Fleece Underwear

Synthetic fleece dry suit undergarments are popular, but do not offer the capabilities of advanced materials like Polartec® or Thinsulate®.

Many of the wooly bears today are made from polyester. Polyester has a nice feel against your skin and offers reasonable insulation. While some of the more expensive piles are quite comfortable to wear, they may not provide good insulation.

Polyester does not form lint like nylon. When polyester is wet it has very little insulation capability.

Most polyester undergarments can be easily laundered. Use warm water and a minimum amount of soap. Set your dryer to "no heat/air dry" or let the underwear dry on a plastic hanger.

Your dry suit underwear should be comfortable to wear and provide good insulation.

Polartec®

Polartec® is a synthetic fleece material manufactured by Malden Mills. It is an exceptionally good insulator with good stretch. This makes it quite comfortable to wear under a dry suit. Polartec® also dries quickly when wet. Several dry suit manufacturers offer dry suit undergarments from Polartec®.

Polartec® is a hypoallergenic material and maintains an attractive appearance for many years. Underwear made from Polartec® is very light weight. It also allows you to wear the least amount of weight of any dry suit underwear.

Follow the care instructions for your particular garment when laundering. The normal instructions for laundering call for Polartec® to be washed in cold water, without bleach or fabric softener, and dried on a line.

Polartec® is one of the most comfortable materials used to make dry suit undergarments.

Courtesy of Diving Unlimited International

Polyester Liners

A polyester or other mountaineering style liner can extend the temperature range of your dry suit underwear by as much as an additional 5 degrees F. The liner not only will add insulation, it will also help to wick moisture away from your body.

During the warmer summer months, a polyester liner and sweat suit may be sufficient insulation for some divers at water temperatures above 70 degrees F. Some divers even use their dry suit in the tropics with this lightweight combination! If you use sweats be sure they are synthetic rather than cotton. Cotton sweats saturate easily and will conduct heat rapidly away from the body when wet.

Try wearing a liner when you will be diving in colder waters for that extra bit of insulation.

A polyester liner should be part of your layering strategy for colder waters.

Vests

Some dry suit undergarment manufacturers offer vests that will help extend the comfort range of their outfits. By insulating your torso, you provide vital protection to your core. These vests are normally worn over your other dry suit underwear.

You can purchase a dry suit vest that is made from the same type of material as your underwear, or you may select a vest made from another insulating material. There's no rule that says that your vest must be made from exactly the same material as your primary undergarment.

Add a vest in colder waters or when you know that you will be making a dive where you will be less active. You can wear your vest with thick or thin underwear and it will add that extra bit of warmth to help keep you toasty.

Photo courtesy of Diving Concepts

Vests help to add insulation to your core.

Picking the proper accessories to compliment your dry suit is very important. This includes the right fins, BC, gloves and other items. Diver Mark Thurlow, shown here working on an IMAX film, is wearing a closed-circuit rebreather and other specialized gear.

Chapter 6
Dry Suit Accessories

Dry suit accessories range from those items that are "nice to have," to those that are "essential" to dry suit diving. The more diving you do with your dry suit, the more you will appreciate the convenience these accessories will add to your diving.

Gloves and Mittens

There are two types of gloves used for dry suit diving, wet and dry. Wet gloves are ordinary wetsuit gloves. Wet mitts with three fingers are also available. Wet hand protection is adequate in cool water, but not in water temperatures much below 50 degrees F. Wetsuit gloves compress at depth, resulting in a loss of insulation. However, they are cheaper to buy than dry gloves.

The best wetsuit gloves for use with a dry suit are those manufactured with a long gauntlet. The gauntlet is helpful because it also helps protect your dry suit wrist seal, by guarding it from objects that might puncture it.

Three fingered mitts offer greater cold water protection by decreasing the surface area of the fingers. They also tend to be thicker than the very thin neoprene used in wetsuit gloves. However, three finger mitts will decrease your ability to work with your hands, making it difficult to operate small camera controls.

Gauntlet gloves like these, made from foam neoprene, are preferred if you are not using dry gloves with your dry suit.

One cuff ring system that is commonly used with dry gloves includes an inner and outer ring.

Installing an outer ring on a vulcanized rubber dry suit.

Using a dry glove with the ring system shown above has the advantage that if the glove leaks, the wrist seal will still prevent water from entering your suit.

These form fitting dry gloves provide great manual dexterity.

Photo courtesy of Diving Concepts

Dry gloves and dry mittens are manufactured in several different styles. Whether you use dry gloves or dry mittens they are frequently designed to work with a set of cuff rings, or other quick replacement seal system.

Most dry gloves consist of two parts; an inner ring and an outer ring, and the glove itself. The inner ring is usually made from a rigid, machined plastic. The outer ring is usually made from a more flexible rubber. There are many different dry glove systems available and the assembly procedures vary from manufacturer to manufacturer. Some dry gloves are designed to mate to specific dry suits using the same quick replacement seal arrangement used for wrist seals, such as the ZipSeal™ system. This makes the dry gloves very easy to use.

Like your dry suit, most dry gloves and mittens are designed to be worn with some type of insulating material. A thin wool or synthetic liner is usually worn under the dry glove. The liner provides both insulation and protection from squeezes. Without a liner some dry gloves are extremely uncomfortable.

Some gloves are equipped with snug fitting round wrist openings known as "doughnut seals." These are designed to seal without any special type of ring system. Although they will stay "reasonably" dry, they can't be relied on to keep your hands completely dry.

Some divers like to equalize the pressure in their dry gloves by inserting a piece of surgical tubing, or open cell foam, under the wrist seal of their suit. This allows air from the dry suit to enter the gloves. Equalizing the gloves helps eliminate the possibility of a squeeze on your hands.

There are two problems that can happen when you equalize the pressure in your gloves. First, if the gloves leak, for any reason, water can enter the suit through the opening created by the tube or foam. Secondly, as you return to the surface at the end of your dive you must be sure to keep your hands low, so that the air in the gloves can return to your suit and vent through the exhaust valve. If you forget to do this there is a possibility that as the air inside your gloves expands it will blow the glove off your hand.

Dry gloves obviously will keep your hands warmer than wetsuit gloves. They arc highly recommended any time the water is colder than 50 degrees F. Whichever glove you choose, be sure you can operate all of your equipment and perform all emergency procedures with your gloves on.

Dry Suit Hoods

If the water is cold enough to wear a dry suit, you will almost certainly want to wear some type of hood. There are many types of hoods available and you should carefully evaluate which style best meets your diving needs.

The simplest hood arrangement is to use a separate wetsuit hood. Wetsuit hoods are relatively inexpensive and require little maintenance. They are easy to don and remove and comfortable over a wide range of water temperatures.

Most ordinary wetsuit hoods come with a bib that allows you to tuck them under a wetsuit jacket. On most dry suits, however, there is no way to tuck the bib of a wetsuit hood under the neck seal without causing the suit to leak.

One option found on some dry suits is a special "warm neck collar." This collar is mounted on the exterior of the dry suit, outside of the neck seal. The warm neck collar will allow you to tuck the wetsuit bib in between the body of the dry suit and the collar. This reduces the amount of cold water that comes up under the hood and adds quite a bit of extra warmth in colder waters.

If you already have a wetsuit hood with a bib, but your dry suit does not have a warm neck collar, you may want to remove the bib. This will help to keep the bib from floating up in your face. Use a large scissors to make a clean cut. Apply wetsuit cement to the ends of the stitching to prevent the seams from unraveling. You'll be more comfortable, however, if you buy a hood designed to be used with a dry suit.

Some manufacturers also make special dry suit hoods that are cut off square

Many dry suit divers prefer to use a separate hood made from wetsuit material with their dry suit.

at the collar. These are designed to seal on a neoprene neck seal.

If you use a wetsuit hood with your dry suit, you'll find that the most comfortable hoods are "vented." The vents are tiny holes in the hood that allow air that escapes from your mask or neck seal to drain out of the hood. A baffle system in the hood helps prevent water from circulating through the holes. Without vent holes the hood will fill with air, putting pressure on your mask. This makes diving very uncomfortable.

Some dry suits are equipped with neoprene hoods attached directly to the suit. This arrangement is warmer than a separate wetsuit hood, but also makes the suit more difficult to don and remove. In addition, most divers find an attached neoprene hood is very bulky out of the water when pulled back. It is usually more convenient to have a separate neoprene hood.

A dry suit can be equipped with a hood that will keep your head dry, too. Two types of dry hoods are available. The first is a simple latex hood, made from exactly the same material as wrist seals and neck seals. This type of hood can be glued directly to the suit or can be attached with a neck ring. An inner liner must be worn for the latex hood to keep you warm. The second is a Viking dry suit hood known as the "turbo hood."

Viking's Turbo and Magnum hoods are made from the same vulcanized rubber Viking uses for their suits. The hoods were designed for use in demanding diving conditions, such as search and rescue or contaminated water. They were not designed for casual sport diving.

Neither of the dry hoods will work properly if you have a beard. Beard hairs will break the seal allowing air to leak out and water to leak in. If you have a beard, an ordinary wetsuit hood may be your best option for use with your dry suit.

Latex dry hoods keep your head warm and your hair dry. If you have long hair this can be a definite plus. This type of hood must be worn with an insulating liner.

Slip-On Knee Pads

If the knee pads on your dry suit aren't heavy enough to hold up to sustained wear, you may want to use slip-on knee pads for additional protection. Slip-on knee pads are usually made from the same material used on the soles of hard sole wetsuit boots. The material is very rugged. When this type of knee pad wears out it can be easily replaced.

Slip-on knee pads are especially appreciated by underwater photographers or any other diver who spends a lot of time kneeling on the bottom. Keep in mind that any material placed around the knee creates some resistance and can interfere with your swimming ability.

Slip-on knee pad

Dry bags are very useful for transporting your dry suit underwear, especially if you are diving from a small boat. This bag rolls at the top and closes with a plastic buckle.

Dry Bags

Even if you already have a gear bag for transporting your gear to the dive site, your dry suit should have it's own bag for storage. This bag should also be used inside of your gear bag to help prevent your dry suit from damage from your other equipment.

It's odd, but many dry suits do not come equipped with a "dry bag" for transporting your suit to the dive site. By dry bag, we mean a bag that will keep your suit dry until you are ready to use it. If your gear bag is not waterproof, and most aren't, and your dry suit's bag is not waterproof, your dry suit could get wet inside before you're even ready to put it on, since the deck of most dive boats gets wet while the boat is traveling to the dive site. The same holds true to even a greater extent for your dry suit underwear.

If your gear does not come with a satisfactory bag, you can purchase waterproof river rafting or kayak bags that have a roll top that effectively seals water out.

A bag of this type is essential for transporting your dry suit underwear, especially if you will be diving out of a small boat. Once, you don your dry suit underwear, you can place your street clothes and other items in it to keep them dry while you are diving.

Weight Distribution Systems

Ankle weights are considered an optional dry suit accessory. They are not essential to dry suit diving. For the beginning dry suit diver, ankle weights give a sense of security and control, like training wheels on a bicycle. They can help you to regain an upright position if you are upside down, and the air in your dry suit rushes to your feet. However, if you are properly weighted for dry suit diving, and have a minimal volume of air in your suit, you should not need ankle weights to control your buoyancy.

Some dry suit divers use ankle weights to help distribute some of the extra weight they require for dry suit diving. Ankle weights allow you to remove some of the weight from your belt. Since a heavy weight belt can cause lower back pain this may be beneficial.

By placing weights on the ankle at the end of the leg, this may, in itself, cause lower back pain. Each time you kick you must move the mass of the ankle weight. This stress demands more energy from the diver.

Some divers also use weights strapped to their thighs, appropriately known as "thigh weights." If thigh weights are used they must never cover the knee or slip below the knee.

Many divers use special sport diving weight harnesses that are designed to transfer the load from your diving weights to the support provided by your shoulders and allowing you to also adjust your trim angle in the water. Any system of this type must provide a reliable quick release for your weights so they can be ditched quickly in the event of an emergency.

A well designed weight harness will give you the ability to ditch just half of your weights in an emergency. In many situations this will be sufficient to establish positive buoyancy without experiencing an overly rapid ascent.

Sport diving weight harness

Many divers find a weight harness particularly comfortable because they remove the weights from their hips. The weight pouches can also easily be removed and handed to the boat crew, making climbing a ladder much easier.

The ability to adjust your trim properly is very advantageous in most situations. Most divers swim in a head up attitude, with their feet much lower than their waist. A head up attitude can stir up silt if you are swimming close to the bottom.

In certain situations, such as cave diving or wreck diving, it may be more desirable to swim in a head down attitude, with the head lower than the feet. By using a weight system that allows you to adjust your trim you can assume the attitude that is best suited to the type of diving you are doing.

Buoyancy Compensators

Another alternative for distributing the additional weight you may need with a dry suit may be to use a buoyancy compensator that is equipped with weight pockets and a weight release mechanism. If you put weights in your B.C., you should only use a B.C. that is specifically designed to handle them.

By placing weights in the B.C., you transfer the distribution of weights from around your waist to across your back when you are swimming, and onto your shoulders when you are standing. This is a much more comfortable arrangement.

Choosing a buoyancy compensator to use with a dry suit involves some important considerations regarding the placement of the valves on your dry suit. Valve location will affect both the ease with which you can don your B.C. and your access to the valves themselves.

The easiest type of B.C. to use with a dry suit is one that has shoulder buckles that can be opened or adjusted. Jacket style adjustable buoyancy compensators put the buoyancy under your arms and tend to rotate you to an upright position.

The other important factor in B.C. selection is to ensure that none of the straps or bladder sections interfere with the operation of your dry suit valves. The B.C. must not cover any of the valves on your dry suit.

Many divers prefer low volume, back-mounted buoyancy compensators for use with their dry suits. Whatever B.C. you select, it should he capable of providing enough lift to give you positive buoyancy even when your dry suit is completely flooded and all of your other gear is still in place.

For surface swimming in your dry suit, it is much more comfortable to use your buoyancy compensator to establish positive buoyancy than to use your dry suit. When your dry suit is inflated enough to make you buoyant on the surface there will usually be excess pressure on the neck seal. This can be very uncomfortable.

In reality, most sport divers probably need no more than 30 pounds of lift from a buoyancy compensator for dry suit diving in cold water. Even if your suit floods completely you should not need much more buoyancy than this to establish positive buoyancy at the surface once your weight belt has been ditched.

Although a complete flood is rare, all of the dry suit manufacturers recommend that a buoyancy compensator should be worn with a dry suit under all diving conditions.

Your buoyancy compensator must work properly with your dry suit.

Dry suits will generally require you to use a fin with a larger foot pocket.

Fins

Most divers find they need a fin with a larger foot pocket than what they use with a wetsuit bootie. The combination of dry suit boot and dry suit underwear is quite bulky.

You may also want to add a short pull strap to your fin strap to help get them off after diving. Some fin straps are equipped with tabs for this purpose. However, with certain types of fins, it can be quite difficult to get the strap over a bulky dry suit boot. A short lanyard of braided nylon attached to the back of your fin strap can make this task much easier.

Necklace Ring

While you are on the surface, between dives, you may find your dry suit neck seal to be a bit snug. To relieve pressure on the neck seal while topside, you may want to use a necklace ring.

Necklace rings are made from plastic tubing. They snap together loosely around your neck at the level of your neck seal. By folding the neck seal over the necklace ring you pull the neck seal away from your neck.

Using the necklace ring also allows heat and water vapor to escape from your dry suit. Just be sure to remove the necklace ring and properly adjust your neck seal before you enter the water.

If the weather is cool and you want to keep your dry suit on topside, you can use a necklace ring to relieve the pressure from the neck seal.

Low-Pressure Swivel Adaptors

If you own an older regulator, the first stage may not have enough low pressure ports to accommodate your dry suit hose and your other low pressure hoses. If you use an octopus regulator, you will need at least 4 low-pressure ports to handle your dry suit, B.C., octopus, and primary regulator. Be sure to check the length of all of the hoses to make sure they are not under strain when you are fully suited up.

The low-pressure swivel adaptor may also be required even if you have enough ports, just to conform to the different angles your hoses must take. For example, if all your low pressure ports are clustered on one side of your first stage, you may not be able to make certain connections without kinking the hoses. If you must bend a hose to make a connection you need a low pressure adaptor.

LP Swivel

In most cases you will also be able to swivel the inflator valve on your dry suit to accept an inflator hose that must come from a particular side. Most dry suit inflator valves today will swivel to whatever angle is necessary to connect with the dry suit inflator hose.

Be aware that some valves may not swivel and may be sealed to certain dry suits with silicone sealant. If you swivel a valve that is sealed to the suit and break the silicone seal the suit will leak. See your dry suit dealer if you have this type of inflator and need to have the angle of the valve changed.

Argon Systems

Many technical divers use a gas mixture known as "tri-mix," which contains helium, oxygen, and nitrogen, on deeper dives. Helium is know for its extremely high thermal conductivity, and when used in a dry suit, it causes a much higher heat loss than air. In addition, divers breathing helium also lose more heat during exhalation than the same diver breathing air. To help reduce the heat loss from helium inside the dry suit, many divers inflate their dry suits with argon to help diminish this thermal drain.

In the past, there was some apprehension regarding the possibility of an increased risk of skin bends from the absorption of argon through the skin when using this gas inside a dry suit. However, based upon the experience of numerous tech divers using argon in their suits during the past ten years, it does not appear that this concern is warranted.

Some divers use argon even when diving with air for their breathing gas in cold water. You can improve your insulation by as much as 25% when you pre-purge your suit with argon prior to entering the water. Probably more argon systems are used in this type of application than are used for tri-mix diving.

Pure argon is a non-respirable gas and will not support life. Never breathe from an argon gas supply.

Note the small cylinder of argon that this Army Special Forces diver has attached to the thigh of his dry suit.

If you don't take the time to dress into your dry suit properly, you can damage your suit before you ever get in the water.

Chapter 7
Dressing in to Your Dry Suit

Think back to the first time you dressed into a full 1/4-inch wetsuit. If you have been diving for a long time you probably don't remember how difficult it was to perform that simple task. However, once you learned some of the tricks involved in effectively dressing into your wetsuit it became much easier.

Learning to dress into a dry suit is not difficult, but there are definitely some techniques that will make doing so much simpler. With very little experience, you will probably find that dressing into a dry suit is much easier than dressing into a full 1/4-inch wetsuit!

Many dry suit dives have been ruined before they even began due to improper dress-in techniques. Take the time to don your dry suit properly and your likelihood of having a good dive is almost a certainty.

Setting Up Your Dry Suit System the First Time

Once you have obtained all of the components of your dry suit system, it is still necessary to set them up correctly. You can have the best dry suit system available, but without proper harmony between all the pieces it will not function well.

Adjusting Dry Suit Seals

One of the most basic tasks in setting up your dry suit system is to make sure the seals on your suit are adjusted properly for you. If you don't take the time to do this, the seals on your suit will be extremely uncomfortable and possibly even dangerous. Be sure to trim the seals on your suit if they need adjustment, or have your dry suit instructor do this for you.

Regulator-Inflator Hose Geometry

Your dry suit inflator hose should only be connected to one of the low-pressure ports on your regulator's first stage. Never connect the low pressure hose to any port marked "H.P." (high-pressure). Connecting the hose to a high-pressure port could cause it to fail, injuring you and people around you. If you are unsure of how

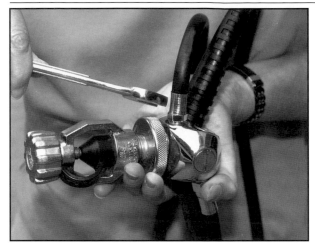

Your suit inflator hose must only be connected to a low-pressure port.

to do this, see your instructor or dealer and have them assist you.

If you do connect your dry suit inflator hose yourself, use the correct size wrench on the inflator hose and the plug in your regulator. Adjustable wrenches tend to slip, and can round the corners on brass fittings. This can make it difficult to achieve the proper torque in connecting a fitting or removing it later.

When you connect your dry suit inflator hose to your first stage, take a careful look at the angle and route it must take to connect to your suit inflator valve. It is very important that you do not stress or kink the hose to make the connection. Stretching the hose, or bending it to the point where it kinks, will create problems that could lead the inflator hose to fail.

Dry suit inflator hoses should follow a gently curving path to connect to your suit inflator valve. To achieve the correct angle it may be necessary to disconnect some of your other hoses and change the ports where they have been attached. Make sure all of the low pressure hoses are only connected to ports that are marked "L.P." (low-pressure).

Some regulators are equipped with a special large bore, low-pressure outlet for the second stage supply hose. In this situation, there may only be one low-pressure outlet available for mating to the second stage hose.

Your regulator may have a sufficient number of low-pressure ports, but with certain regulator and tank valve combinations the angles at which they join may make it difficult to properly route your low-pressure hose. If this is the case, you may need a low-pressure adaptor or swivel "T" to make acceptable connections.

Another important consideration may be the length of your low pressure hose. Again, certain valve and regulator combinations may make a long, low-pressure inflator hose desirable. Check with your dealer regarding the availability of extra-long inflator hoses. Certain manufacturers do offer this type of optional equipment.

Finally, you should be able to rotate the low-pressure inflator valve on your suit to a more comfortable angle. Most inflator valves today are designed to swivel easily. However, before you try turning the valve, check the manual that came with your suit to be sure that the valve is designed to swivel.

Estimating Your Weight Requirements

With most combinations of dry suits and underwear you will need anywhere from 4 to 10 pounds of additional weight compared to the weight you would wear with a full 1/4 inch wetsuit. How much weight you will need will depend upon your personal buoyancy, the type of dry suit you are using, the type of dry suit underwear you are wearing, the fit of your dry suit, the type of tank you use, and any accessory gear (such as cameras) you are carrying. Some divers are actually able to wear less weight with their dry suit system than with a 1/4 inch thick wetsuit.

The most important point to keep in mind is that all else being equal, your weight requirements will change most dramatically when you change the amount of underwear you use with your suit. This is particularly important if you dive in a location where you use an entirely different set of underwear during different seasons.

All scuba cylinders become more buoyant as the air inside the tank is consumed. This buoyancy varies depending upon the cylinder design. Check the manufacturer's specifications for your cylinder to see how the buoyancy changes from the time the tank is full until it is empty. Take this amount of additional weight with you when you dive your dry suit for the first time.

You should initially test your buoyancy in a swimming pool or other shallow, confined body of water. Of course, if you test your buoyancy in fresh water you will need a few more pounds to dive in salt water. To adjust for the change from fresh to salt water you will probably need to add anywhere from four to six pounds of weight.

If you must test your buoyancy in open water, position yourself in shallow water where you can stand on your fin tips if you need to, or immediately adjacent to the anchor line so you can stop your descent by grabbing the line. Be prepared to use your buoyancy compensator to re-establish positive buoyancy if you discover that you are grossly overweighted. Since each person has their own individual buoyancy and diving system it is impossible to predict here how much weight you will need to dive.

Most new dry suit divers have a tendency to use too much weight on their belts. This can cause serious problems in buoyancy control. A diver who uses an excess amount of weight must put a great deal of air in his suit to achieve neutral buoyancy. When this air shifts inside the suit, it can lead to buoyancy control problems for the untrained dry suit diver.

Your goal as a dry suit diver should be to dive with the minimum amount of weight possible and with the minimum volume of air inside your dry suit. You should wear only enough weight to allow you to make a 5 minute precautionary decompression stop at the end of your dive, at a depth of ten to fifteen feet, when you have 500 P.S.I. of air remaining in your tank.

Proper weighting is crucial for enjoyable dry suit diving.

Start Your Pre-Dive Check at Home

One of the most important tips to remember when using a dry suit is to check its condition before you leave for a dive trip. This check is especially important if you haven't used your suit recently. The pre-dive cheek should be performed several days before your trip to enable you to correct anything that might not be working properly. If you wait until the morning of your trip to discover that your neck seal has deteriorated, you may not have the parts or the time to properly repair it before the trip.

Start your pre-dive check with the zipper(s) on your dry suit. Open the zipper all the way. Carefully inspect all the teeth on the zipper to ensure that they are all present and that none of them are broken. Since the teeth are all symmetrically placed, any gaps in the teeth will immediately reveal that some are missing. You should not dive a suit that has a zipper with missing teeth. Missing teeth indicate a broken zipper. This condition could cause your suit to flood.

Examine the zipper further by grasping it on one side with your hands a few inches apart. Gently bend the zipper in an arc, but do not force it to bend any further than it will go naturally. If you notice any spots where the zipper bends at a right angle this indicates that the tape that forms the base of the zipper is torn. You should also look for frayed edges on the base tape of the zipper. These can be carefully singed with a match.

You should not dive a suit with a torn base tape. Damaged zippers can fail unexpectedly and cause your suit to flood. Frequent lubrication of the zipper will help prevent zipper damage.

If you think your suit may have leaks, you need to check it carefully. To leak test your suit, twist rubber bands carefully, but tightly, around the wrist and neck seals to close the seals. Next, close the zipper. If your suit has an automatic exhaust valve, screw the adjustment all the way "closed." Attach the inflator hose to your suit and inflate the suit until it is taut. Use a clean spray bottle and spray a dilute

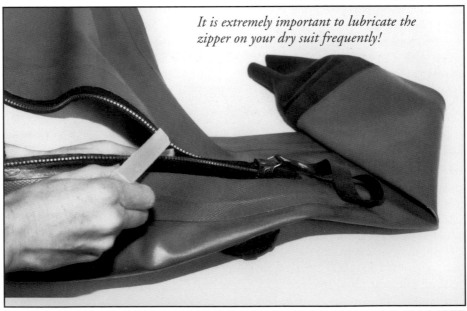

It is extremely important to lubricate the zipper on your dry suit frequently!

solution of soapy water on any sus-
pected leaks. Leaking air will form
bubbles on the suit and allow you to
detect leaks quite easily.

The seals of your dry suit must be
in good condition. Check the seals of
your suit for nicks or tears. Neoprene
seals can be repaired with wetsuit cement. Although you can dive them
shortly after repairing them, it is best
to wait overnight before use. Always
avoid temperatures over 100 degrees
F with any new neoprene repairs. For
wetsuit cement to fully cure it takes
at least 10 days. Heat will cause almost any newly glued seam to open.

If your suit has latex seals, carefully examine them for signs of
"checking" or cracking. Seals that are
gummy or sticky are on the road to

Leak testing a dry suit.

failure, too. If the seals are in poor condition they should be replaced before your
dive. Latex seals that are weak may tear during normal dress-in routines.

Test the valves on your suit to ensure they are working correctly. Hook up your
suit inflator and push the button several times. The button should not stick either
open or closed. If you are unable to make your inflator valve work properly do not
dive the suit until it is serviced or replaced. Salt crystals in the inflator mechanism
are the most common cause of a stuck inflator button. To correct this, try running
warm water through the valve followed by a brief squirt of silicone spray.

To test the exhaust valve you must seal your suit off with rubber bands like
you would during a leak test. Inflate the suit until it is rigid and let it stand fully
inflated to check for leaks from the valve. Next, operate the exhaust valve. Air
should flow freely through the valve when it is activated and reseal completely
when closed.

If the exhaust valve does not vent air properly, check inside the suit for lint or
other debris that may be blocking the valve. If there is no obvious obstruction it
may be that the membrane in the valve has dried and stuck to the valve body. Try
rinsing the valve and running water through it from the inside if possible. If you
are still unable to get the exhaust valve to open or close normally do not use the
suit until the valve has been replaced.

The importance of checking your suit several days before the dive can't be
stressed enough, particularly if your suit has not been used for a few months. This
is especially true if your latex seals are old, or you live in an area where there is
smog. High ozone levels in smog will cause latex seals to deteriorate faster than
usual.

The night before the dive it's a good idea to trim your fingernails if they are
long. This will help prevent you from accidentally tearing a latex seal.

At the Dive Site

Topside weather at your dive site will affect your pre-dive procedures on the day of your dive. If the weather is cold or rainy, it may be more comfortable to dress into your dry suit before you set up your other equipment. If you are diving through ice, it's usually safer to wear your dry suit on the surface than cold weather clothing and a life vest.

In warm weather you should set up all your other diving equipment before you dress into your dry suit. This means that your scuba system, weights, fins, mask and snorkel, and other accessories should be ready to go on the minute your dry suit zipper is closed. Most people find it very uncomfortable to stand around in a dry suit when the air temperature is warmer than 70 degrees F.

With certain types of dry gloves the cuff rings must be inserted into the dry suit sleeves before you dress into your suit. In fact, both the inner and outer rings should be installed in the suit when you set up the rest of your gear to dive. Some dry suit divers even install their cuff rings the night before the dive.

Some divers install their cuff rings permanently, by gluing them to the suit, although this practice can make it difficult to clean silt or sand from underneath the outer ring.

You can use soapy water to assist you in donning your wrist seals if they are heavy duty seals. Soapy water can be used to help you remove your wrist seals, too. Take along a small bottle filled with soapy water (15/1 dilution) for this purpose.

Silicone spray is **not** an acceptable lubricant for your dry suit seals. Although silicone spray will make it easy to dress in, it has a very negative effect when it is time to repair your suit. While some people claim that silicone spray will lengthen the life of your seals, we have seen no evidence of this. In the long run it is much easier and wiser not to use silicone spray, or any other commercially prepared "seal saver," on your suit or seals.

In the past, people used pure talcum powder to help don their wrist seals. This practice is no longer recommended because some medical authorities believe the inhalation of talc particles may be detrimental to your health.

If you are using a polyester liner underneath your dry suit underwear you should don this layer completely before proceeding any further. Most people wear a bathing suit under their dry suit underwear, but you could wear a pair of undershorts and a tee shirt if you prefer. Whatever you find comfortable is acceptable.

Soapy water may be used to help both don and remove your wrist seals, as shown here. You can use a dilution of fifteen parts water to one part soap.

Dressing into your dry suit underwear is much easier if you start by sitting down, especially if you are diving from a boat. Pull on the lower part of your underwear, then stand up to work your underwear over your hips.

If you are diving from a large boat, and the deck is wet, make sure your underwear boots and dry suit are close at hand. It can be uncomfortable if you must walk across a wet, cold deck in your bare feet. If your dry suit underwear is made from synthetic pile, walking on a wet deck will leave your underwear boots wet and cold for the rest of the dive day. Once you have your underwear on it is time to get into your suit.

General Techniques for All Dry Suits

Stop! Before you do anything else make sure that you have removed your watch and any jewelry that may catch on a seal and cause it to tear. This includes earrings, necklaces, rings, and bracelets. Anything that can tear a dry suit seal must be removed before you dress. More seals have been torn by divers getting dressed than have ever been damaged underwater.

When it is time to don your suit, it will be much safer and easier if you sit down to start the dress-in process. If your suit is equipped with suspenders make sure they are pulled out of the legs of the suit and properly aligned before you step into the suit. They should be pulled up and out to the side so they will be on the outside of your legs and body.

Pull the suit onto your lower legs and get your feet firmly into the boots before you stand up.

Pull the dry suit up to your hips and waist. Depending upon the cut of the suit, people with broad hips may have to work a bit to get the suit past their buttocks. This is one of the places where a custom dry

It's very important to remember to remove all jewelry as well as your watch before dressing into your dry suit.

Sit down to don the lower part of your dry suit underwear, then stand up to zip it closed.

Sit down to don the bottom of your suit.

suit really pays off.

If your suit is equipped with suspenders you should slip them over your shoulders at this time. Adjust the tension on the suspenders so they are taut but not tight They should be supporting the lower part of your suit. The suspenders themselves should still have stretch.

If your suit is not equipped with suspenders, just before you don the rest of your equipment, pull your suit up into your crotch as far as it will go. Bring your legs together to hold the suit up and don your weight belt. This will make your suit more comfortable and it will not feel as though it is hanging down around your knees.

At this point, if your dry suit underwear is equipped with thumb tabs, slip the tabs over your thumbs. This will allow you to slide your arm down the sleeve without having your dry suit underwear bunch up at your forearm.

Some divers prefer to grab the thumb tabs between their fingers rather than slipping it over their thumbs. Whichever method you use be sure to release the thumb tabs once your hand is through the seals and tuck them back inside the suit so they don't cause your wrist seals to leak.

Insert either arm into the sleeve of your suit first. When your hand reaches the wrist seal, keep your fingers extended but squeeze them all together (including your thumb). This creates the smallest diameter for your hand to go through the wrist seal.

Grab the outside of the wrist seal with your free hand and gently pull it over the hand inside the suit. Grab the wrist seal itself; do not grab the sleeve of the suit. If you pull on the sleeve to get your hand through the seal you will place a strain on the suit where the seal mates to the suit. Take special care not to dig your fingernails into the seals. Only use your fingertips for donning all seals.

Another method that some divers use for getting their hand through the wrist seals is to slip two or three fingers of their free hand inside the opening of the wrist seal and pull

Slip the suspenders over your shoulders.

If your underwear is equipped with thumb tabs, use these to help prevent your underwear from riding up your arm when you don the your dry suit. You can just hold the tabs between your thumb and forefinger and release them as soon as your fingers reach the latex inside the sleeve.

the seal over the hand inside the sleeve. This technique also works well. Again, just be sure you don't dig your fingernails into the wrist seal.

If your seals are well lubricated you can insert both of your arms in the sleeves and try to pop both arms through the seals at one time. This method works well as long as you suit has thin latex seals.

Once you have tucked the thumb tabs from your dry suit underwear back inside the suit, adjust your wrist seals. Most latex seals are designed to lie flat against your wrist. The seals should be as far up your arm as is required for them to seal effectively. There must be no underwear sticking out of the seal. Ideally there should be at least one inch of wrist seal material making direct contact with your wrists.

Neoprene wrist seals may either be cone shaped or designed to fold under. With a cone shaped seal, you need only check to make sure it is pushed far enough up your wrist to form an efficient seal.

Folding neoprene wrist seals are tucked back underneath themselves. With this type of seal there should be a minimum of two inches of material folded under the top layer of neoprene. As with other seals, there must be no underwear trapped under the seal to create a channel where water can leak in. Once your wrist seals are properly adjusted, it's time to don your neck seal.

If your suit has permanently attached gloves, you may want to don the neck seal first, provided you have the shoulder flexibility to do this. Otherwise, you will need to don the sleeves, and spread the neck seal with your gloved hands. Of course, you should have someone check your neck seal to be sure it is properly installed following this procedure and before each dive, even if you can dress into your suit by yourself.

Use care when donning your wrist seals.

Donning Latex Neck Seals

To don a latex neck seal, reach through the neck seal with both hands, keeping your thumbs on the outside of the seal and suit. Spread the neck seal by pulling against the palms of your hands. Avoid any bunching of the seal since this makes it more difficult to get it over your head. Do not dig your fingers into the latex or you may cut the seal. Pull the back of the neck seal over the back of your head then pull forward and down with your hands. Pull the neck seal gently, but firmly, over your head.

Divers with long hair may find it easier to don their neck seals if they wear an old nylon stocking over their head. Tuck your hair up into the stocking to get it out of the way. The nylon is quite slippery and helps to keep long hair from tangling in the seal. Some divers actually roll the nylon up onto their head like a cap, once they have the neck seal on. They leave the stocking in place when they dive so it is convenient to use again when they get out of the water.

Some latex neck seals are designed to be folded under on themselves, similar to the manner in which a neoprene wrist seal is adjusted. Other latex seals are intended to be worn straight up. Follow whichever method the manufacturer of your suit recommends. However, regardless of the design, all latex seals should be worn as low on your neck as possible for maximum comfort.

Like any other seal, neck seals must be free of any interference that might interrupt the seal. Dry suit underwear collars and long hair can create leaks in neck seals if they are not properly adjusted. In addition, divers with long hair on the back of their neck may experience leakage due to hair interfering with the neck seal. If this is a problem you may want to have your hairdresser shave the back of your neck.

It's very important to spread the neck seal properly.

If you have long hair, an old nylon stocking will help make it easier to don a latex neck seal. It will also make it easier to remove the seal, too.

Note how the diver's hands are not digging into the latex. The latex is spread by pulling against the palms of your hands. Try to keep your fingers flat and do not bunch up the neck seal.

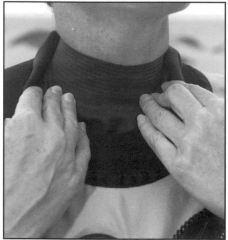

The neck seal must be adjusted so it lies flat against your neck and as low on your neck as possible. There must be no hair or underwear protruding out from under the seal.

Donning Neoprene Neck Seals

Neoprene neck seals are also easy to don and adjust, although the procedure is slightly different from a latex seal. Although neoprene seals do not tear as easily as latex seals they can be damaged and take longer to repair. It's better to don your seal properly than to miss out on diving while you make a repair.

Pull the upper end of the dry suit over your head and position your head at the opening for the neck seal inside the suit. With your hands on the outside of the neck seal, use the friction of your hands on the neoprene to slide

Donning a neoprene neck seal.

the seal over your head. Push your head up through the neck seal while pulling down with your hands.

Stop when the top edge of the neck seal reaches your chin. Grab the edge of the seal and turn it down and in on itself, just as you would a reverse turtle-neck sweater, with the smooth "skin" side of the material against your neck.

Neoprene neck seals must be folded down and in, like a reverse turtleneck sweater.

General Instructions For All Waterproof Zippers

If you did not lubricate your dry suit zipper after you used your suit the last time, take the time to lubricate your zipper before you use it again. The extra minute it takes to lube the zipper will pay off in longer zipper life and smoother zipper action. Dry suit zippers are expensive and it's worth the effort to take good care of them.

To properly lubricate the zipper, first close the zipper all the way. Most zippers are lubricated with either paraffin wax or bee's wax. Keep in mind that cold surface temperatures will make it difficult to use paraffin wax.

Do not use silicone spray or silicone grease on your dry suit zipper. If you use either of these lubricants they will work their way into the base material of the zipper tape. They can make it difficult or impossible to replace the zipper if necessary. In an emergency, if no wax is available, you can use a bar of soap.

Lubricate the outside of the zipper with a thin film of wax. Never lubricate the inside of the zipper with wax. If you lubricate the inside of the zipper with wax it will collect dirt and other debris that can cause the zipper to fail.

Some manufacturers use a separate liquid lubricant for the inside of their zippers. If your manufacturer provides this type of lubricant be sure to use this as directed by the manufacturer.

If you have a shoulder entry dry suit, you will be dependent on your dive partner to close the zipper of your suit. If they are not familiar with how to operate a dry suit zipper, show them how it works before you don the suit, so that you can assure yourself they will do the job properly.

Instruct your dive partner to put their finger inside the loop on the zipper pull before they close the zipper. Some zippers may be equipped with a T-bar on the end to help ensure a positive grip. If the person assisting you just grabs the pull casually they can lose their grip and possibly hurt themselves. Also, if they lose their grip this can cause the zipper to jerk, possibly causing it to accidentally jam under-wear in the zipper. Make sure they understand how you want them to do it.

Be sure they tuck all dry suit underwear out of the way before they close the zipper. Have them pull the tab out and forward to close the zipper.

Be sure your dive partner understands how to close the zipper on your dry suit.

Anything caught in the zipper will cause it to leak. In addition, any fabric caught in the zipper may damage it. If your zipper does jam on your underwear, have them work it very gently but firmly back away from the jam. Be sure they do not force it.

Always ensure that the zipper slider is hard up against the stop. You can see this even if you are wearing a shoulder entry suit. Even the slightest gap between the slider and the docking end of the zipper will cause the zipper to leak. Double cheek the zipper to make sure it is correctly closed. Your partner's final tug should be firm, but smooth. Make sure they do not jerk the zipper!

Additional Hints for Closing the Zipper On Self-Donning Suits

Pull the torso of the suit down and fasten the crotch strap first, if your suit is equipped with one. This will make it easier to close the self-don zipper. Put your finger in the loop on the zipper pull and close the zipper with a smooth action.

After you have closed the dry suit zipper, close the outer protective zipper, if your suit is equipped with one. This outer zipper will help to prevent sand and other material from getting into the waterproof zipper.

Closing the zipper on a self-don suit.

Additional Hints for Closing Back Mounted Zippers

For dry suits equipped with back mounted zippers, it is wise to have your buddy assist you in closing the zipper. While it's possible to attach a long string to the zipper pull, so you can close the zipper yourself, this is not a good idea. There is a strong possibility if you do this that you will catch your dry suit underwear in the zipper.

To close a back mounted zipper, lift your elbows to the height of your shoulders. Bring your arms forward until your elbows are just in front of your chest. This creates a gentle curve in the dry suit zipper that is the perfect angle for closing it.

Adjusting Dry Hoods

Dry hoods must be properly adjusted before you go in the water. Just as it is essential to make sure nothing interferes with a wrist seal or a neck seal, the same considerations hold true for the face seal on a dry hood. Remember, if you have a beard, a dry hood will not seal on it.

Latex dry hoods are designed to be used with a liner to provide insulation and give the hood shape. Never use a latex dry hood without the liner. It will not keep your head warm and the hood could seal over your ear causing a squeeze.

Most of the hood liners are equipped with a chin strap that fastens onto the liner itself with Velcro®. Older liners did not have chin straps, but were equipped with Velcro® tabs in the back of the suit. This arrangement did not work well. If your suit has these tabs you may want to remove them and purchase a liner with a chin strap. It is much more comfortable.

Fasten the chin strap securely under your chin and tuck your hair up inside the liner. Make sure the liner is centered on your head and not crooked. Next, grab the dry hood with both hands and stretch it up and over the liner. If the liner shifts forward or to the side you may need to reposition it. Make sure the liner is not covering your forehead and that there are no stray hairs sticking out from under the dry hood.

Donning the liner for a latex hood.

Latex hoods will keep your head dry only if they are properly adjusted.

Your face mask is meant to seal over the latex hood. The bottom of the latex dry hood should be under your chin, unless you are using a full-face mask. With a full-face mask, the bottom of the dry hood should be covering your chin.

Adjusting Foam Neoprene Hoods

Some dry suits are designed with a special feature known as a "warm neck collar." This allows you to tuck the bib of a foam neoprene hood underneath a special collar so there is no gap between the bottom of the wetsuit hood and the neck seal on your dry suit. You will probably need some assistance to properly tuck the hood in underneath the warm neck collar in the back. The bib of the hood goes between the collar and the body of the suit.

Squat down to vent the air out of your dry suit prior to donning the rest of your gear.

Venting The Dry Suit

Once you have closed the zipper on your dry suit, you should vent your suit before you don any other equipment. This will make your suit more comfortable to wear on deck and will increase your control when you enter the water. Entering the water from a height when your suit is full of air can cause your neck seal to vent air and leak.

To vent your suit, squat down, fold your arms across your chest, and manually open the exhaust valve. This will force the excess air out of your dry suit. You can also achieve the same effect by opening the neck seal with your fingers, but if you are not careful you can unknowingly get underwear trapped under the neck seal this way.

If the weather is warm, enter the water (or stand under a cold shower) to cool off before donning the rest of your gear. You don't want to overheat!

Have Your Buddy Help You Don Your B.C.

When it is time to don your tank and buoyancy compensator, have your buddy assist you. Donning your B.C. by yourself when you are wearing a dry suit can be difficult and there is a good chance you may damage your neck or wrist seals. Have your buddy hold your tank up or rest it on a bench as they steady it for you.

To don your B.C., loosen all of the strap adjustments to their widest opening. Insert your left arm first through the left B.C. shoulder strap, taking care that your dry suit exhaust valve clears the strap. Then insert your right arm through the right shoulder strap. If your arm catches on the strap do not force it through.

It's best to have your dive partner assist you in donning your tank.

Instead, allow your buddy to clear it and guide it through the harness. More than one dry suit diver has torn a wrist seal by forcing their arm past a B.C. strap or buckle.

After you have put on your tank and B.C. double check to make sure your weight belt has a clear drop path. Connect your suit inflator hose and secure your submersible pressure gauge to your B.C.

Test Your Dry Suit Inflator & Exhaust Valve Before You Enter the Water

Always take the time to test your dry suit inflator valve before you enter the water. Push the button several times to be sure it is operating freely and does not stick. It is better to discover a problem on the surface than to find out your valve is not working correctly once you have started to descend.

Be sure that all components of your system are working properly before you enter the water.

Pre-Dive Checklist for Dry Suit Diving
(Note: This list will vary depending on the type of suit you own.)

- *Have you completed dry suit training with a qualified dry suit diving instructor?*
- *Is your dive partner familiar with the operation of your dry suit?*
- *Are the seals on your suit trimmed to fit you?*
- *Have you inspected the seals and zipper on your suit to make sure they are in good condition?*
- *Have you conducted a buoyancy check with all of the gear you will use to dive?*
- *Do you have a BC that works properly with your dry suit system?*
- *Are you weighted properly to conduct a hovering safety stop at the end of your dive?*
- *Is your dry suit inflator hose connected to the correct port on your regulator and attached to your inflator valve?*
- *Do you have the correct size fins to use with your dry suit?*
- *Do you have the right amount of insulation for your intended activity during the dive?*
- *Have you donned your neck and wrist seals correctly?*
- *Is your dry suit zipper closed all the way with no underwear or hair trapped in the zipper?*
- *Have you tested both your suit inflator valve and exhaust valve prior to entering the water?*
- *Is your hood properly adjusted?*
- *Have you vented most of the air from your dry suit prior to entering the water?*
- *Have you practiced your dry suit emergency skills recently?*

Always use a lift bag to raise heavy objects underwater. Never use your dry suit for this purpose.

Chapter 8
Dry Suit Diving Skills and Techniques

Learning to dive with a dry suit is not difficult, but you will need to perfect a few new skills. Although this book is as comprehensive as possible, you should not attempt to dive a dry suit until you have completed a dry suit training course. This book is not a substitute for in-water training and experience. You must complete in-water dry suit training from a certified diving instructor who is knowledgeable in dry suit diving techniques, before you dive your dry suit in open water without supervision.

Most people find that controlling their buoyancy while wearing a dry suit is much simpler than they expect. It's especially convenient if your hands are busy holding a camera to be able to vent excess buoyancy by merely rolling on your side and having the suit vent automatically, rather than having to locate the power inflator on a BC and having to manually manipulate the exhaust button.

How Much Weight Do You Need for Dry Suit Diving?

Most people find that they do not need to add a great deal of extra weight to their weight belt for diving with a dry suit compared to diving with a wetsuit. In fact, some people can actually dive with exactly the same amount of weight (or less) with their dry suit as they do with a wetsuit.

As a general rule of thumb, we tell most people that they will probably need an additional four to six pounds of weight while diving with a dry suit compared to what they wear with their normal thermal protection, diving in the same waters. Each person will have different needs depending on their personal buoyancy, the type of dry suit they are using, the fit of the suit, the type and thickness of the underwear they are wearing, the buoyancy characteristics of their scuba cylinder, and any accessories they are carrying. An experienced dry suit instructor is essential to help you determine your individual weight requirements.

Two people of the same size may require very different amounts of weight depending on the gear they use. A person wearing a snug fitting crushed neoprene dry suit with thin Polartec® underwear and a high-pressure steel cylinder will require less weight than a person wearing a baggy urethane coated dry suit, thick Thinsulate® underwear, and a low pressure cylinder.

Your goal as a dry suit diver is to dive with the minimum amount of weight possible, and the minimum volume of air in your dry suit. Your suit should feel as though it is hugging you gently but firmly over your entire body. This is normal. If it's not, you have too much air in your suit and you will have a difficult time controlling your buoyancy. Your suit should not feel like it's hurting you, or making it difficult to move, but it should feel snug up against your body.

In a mistaken attempt to control their buoyancy, some divers add lots of extra weight to their belt to try to hold themselves on the bottom. If you do this, you will have to add a large amount of air to your suit. When this bubble of air shifts in your suit as you move underwater, it is uncomfortable and potentially dangerous, and can lead to a hazardous situation if you are unprepared to cope with it.

Entering the Water

Entering the water in your dry suit is not much different from entering the water in your wetsuit. If you are diving from a large dive boat, get as much air out of your suit as possible before you make your entry. Vent the suit properly on deck before you hit the water.

To assure yourself of being buoyant after your entry, add just enough air to your buoyancy compensator to allow yourself to float. A couple of puffs of air should be all you need if you are properly weighted.

The first thing you will notice after you enter the water is that when you are upright (vertical) on the surface, there will be more pressure on your feet than on your chest. This is due to the pressure differential caused by the water over the length of your body. Air migrates inside the suit to the highest point on your body, and most of it will be up around your shoulders.

This phenomenon is known as an "underpressure," and is common to all dry suits. If you turned upside down in your dry suit you would experience an "underpressure" on your chest. Technically speaking, an underpressure is a squeeze, but proper dry suit underwear, and the use of the suit inflator as you descend, will help prevent any discomfort or injury.

Whenever you enter the water with your dry suit always take a moment to check the system for leaks. Concentrate to determine if your suit is taking on

Whenever you are upright in the water in a dry suit, whether you are on the surface or underwater, you will feel greater pressure on your legs than on your chest.

It's easy to achieve neutral buoyancy in a dry suit. This diver is using a metal detector as she swims just above the bottom.

water at any point. If your suit is leaking, for any reason, take the time to get out of the water to correct the problem. A small leak on the surface may not get worse underwater, but it will continue to leak throughout your dive. You will get very wet if the problem is not fixed and you continue to dive. Do not dive if your suit is leaking.

Checking Buoyancy (Getting Neutral) for the Sport Scuba Diver

Testing that you're neutrally buoyant in your dry suit is almost identical to testing for buoyancy in your wetsuit. The principles are all the same; you just have to deal with the additional volume of air in the dry suit.

Your first buoyancy check with your dry suit should take place in a swimming pool or other confined body of water. Enter the water by climbing down a ladder or swimming out into the water to a point where you can still touch bottom by standing on the tips of your fins. Position yourself close enough to the ladder or a descent line so that you can instantly stop your descent if you are too negatively buoyant.

First, put your regulator in your mouth and breathe normally. Vent all the air out of your buoyancy compensator. You should still be floating at this point.

Next, vent all the air out of your dry suit. In reality, although we say, "vent all the air out of your suit," there will always be some air left inside the insulation in your dry suit.

If you have a manual exhaust, raise the valve to the highest point possible and push the button, if the valve is mounted on your chest, lean back in the water so the valve is on or near the surface.

If you have an automatic exhaust valve, which is the most common, it will probably be mounted on your left arm. Open the exhaust all the way. On most automatic exhaust valves, the head of the valve is turned counterclockwise to open it, and clockwise to close it. With the exhaust valve all the way open, lift your left elbow out of the water to vent the dry suit. Even if you are unable to see the valve, due to your equipment, you should be able to hear air hissing out of the valve and feel it bubbling. When all the air is out of the suit, you still should not sink at this time.

Take a deep breath, fill your lungs, and do not exhale. Hang motionless in the water in a vertical position with your head up. If you are properly weighted, or neutral you should be floating with your eyes at the water level. If you are sinking at this time you are heavy, or negative. If you are floating higher than eye level you are too buoyant.

While you are still vertical in the water, exhale all the air in your lungs. You should start to sink very slowly. If you do not sink, you are too buoyant. If you sink rapidly you are too negative. Add or subtract weights as needed so that you float at eye level. Now you are weighted for being neutral, but you have not finished your buoyancy adjustment. You must still make adjustments for your precautionary decompression stop.

For your first dry suit dive, add 2/3 the weight of the buoyancy change of your scuba cylinder from full to empty. For example, if your tank experiences a 6 pound shift to positive buoyancy as it empties, add 4 additional pounds of weight to your belt. You will probably need to adjust this weight by a little bit either way, but this is a good place to start.

Try this on your first dive, and make your ascent at the end of your dive next to a weighted line. See if you are able to make the necessary precautionary decompression stop. If you find yourself too buoyant at 15 feet with 500 P.S.I. of air in your tank, be prepared to stop your ascent by holding onto the weighted line. You should still be capable of becoming neutral at a depth of 10 feet when it is time for you to exit the water. Add or subtract weight on your next dive to fine tune your buoyancy. Remember, your goal is to dive with the minimum amount of weight possible and the minimum volume of air inside your dry suit.

Once you think you are weighted properly, another test you can employ is to extend your right arm above your head while you are underwater and shift your body so that all of the air in the suit goes up into your right sleeve. If you can feel air in the suit below your elbow (i.e., the sleeve of the suit feels "loose" below the elbow), you probably have too much air in your suit, which means you are probably carrying too much weight. When you are properly weighted, it really takes very little air in the suit to achieve neutral buoyancy for sport diving.

Proper Descent Technique

To start your dive, position yourself next to the anchor line so you can stop your descent if you need to do so. Vent all the air out of your buoyancy compensator. Next, vent the excess air out of your dry suit by using the exhaust valve. If you have an automatic exhaust valve, open it all the way and leave it open throughout

Technical Diving with a Dry Suit

Technical diving is a type of recreational diving that goes beyond the scope of sport diving. It typically involves deeper depths and gas mixtures other than air. Tech divers frequently dive in what is known as an "overhead environment," where it is not possible to make a direct ascent to the surface, such as inside a cave or shipwreck. The majority of technical dives require staged decompression stops.

Due to the long bottom times involved in most technical dives, a dry suit is almost essential to help reduce the risk of exposure (hypothermia) and decompression sickness, and make the diver more comfortable. In colder waters, it's virtually impossible to make most technical dives without a dry suit.

Technical divers must normally wear more than one cylinder in order to carry all of the gas they will need to make their dive and complete their decompression. Alternatively, they may wear a closed-circuit rebreather which recycles their breathing gas, adding oxygen and eliminating CO_2. Either way, their dives are usually much longer than the typical sport dive.

Wearing multiple high-pressure cylinders will usually give most tech divers enough negative buoyancy that they may not need to wear a weight belt underwater. For this reason, unlike most sport divers, tech divers will routinely use their dry suits in conjunction with their buoyancy compensators underwater. They use the suit inflator to relieve suit squeeze and the BC to control their buoyancy. This means that they must vent and control the air in two separate compartments during their ascent. This is an advanced skill.

The typical tech diving buoyancy compensator also usually has far more lift than the BC worn by recreational divers.

"Typical" technical diver with multiple cylinders, dry suit and "wings" BC.

Add air to your dry suit in short bursts by pushing the inflator button on your chest.

your dive. Exhale the air from your lungs and you should slowly start to sink, feet first.

After you have dropped down a few feet you will notice that you will start to descend even faster. This happens because even though you got "all the air" out of your dry suit, the remaining air inside the suit has started to compress. As you continue to descend, your body will naturally rotate to a more horizontal position and eventually most people turn head down. This will allow you to observe the bottom below you more completely.

As you begin to feel the "squeeze" on your body, push the inflator button on your suit using short bursts to add enough air inside the suit to relieve the pressure. Add just enough air to relieve any uncomfortable suit squeeze and control your descent. You should be able to stop your descent at any time by adding just enough air to make yourself neutral at that depth.

If the boots on your suit feel uncomfortable due to squeeze, turn head down and raise your feet above your shoulders so air can migrate into the boots. Once you turn back to a head up position, keep your legs slightly bent when you are hovering to help maintain air in the boots.

Proper Dry Suit Trim Underwater for Sport Diving

Once you reach the bottom, adjust your buoyancy using only your dry suit so that you are neutral. Do not add air to your buoyancy compensator to adjust your buoyancy. It is very difficult to control your buoyancy when you have air in two separate compartments at the same time, i.e., the B.C. and your suit. Controlling both air compartments is an advanced dry suit diving skill and is not recommended for the novice dry suit diver.

If you pick up additional weight during your dive, such as a small anchor or

Leave the exhaust valve on your dry suit all the way open.

lobsters in excess of 5 pounds, consider using a small lift bag attached to your goody bag to raise the load. This is much safer than trying to use your buoyancy compensator to lift this weight. The danger of using your B.C. is that if you lose control of the object you will suddenly have a great deal of positive buoyancy. This can cause an uncontrolled ascent leading to decompression sickness or lung over-pressure injuries, such as air embolism.

To raise heavy objects, like a porthole or anchor, use a large lift bag. Do not attempt to raise heavy objects using your dry suit and/or B.C. This procedure requires special training.

The feel of your dry suit on your body will seem unusual at first, but will be less noticeable as you make more dives with your suit. The sensation is quite different from wearing a wetsuit. However, there should be no discomfort from the suit.

There should not be a large bubble of air inside your suit, nor should you notice massive air shifts if you change position in the water. There should only be a minimum volume of air inside the suit.

We recommend that while you are underwater, if your suit is equipped with an automatic dry suit exhaust valve, that you leave the valve all the way open, or at most, close it not more than one quarter of a turn. You can vent your suit as you swim up a gradual slope or over a wreck by rolling onto your right side so that the exhaust valve is at the highest point on your body and air will vent from the suit. You should be neutrally buoyant at your new depth without needing to add air to the suit.

Hovering in a Dry Suit

Just as in using a wetsuit, weights, and your buoyancy compensator to achieve neutral buoyancy underwater, you can do the same thing using a dry suit and weights. You can actually fine tune your buoyancy more precisely in a dry suit, once you have practiced a bit.

For example, if you want to hover horizontally, we sometimes find that by allowing our knees to bend a bit and having our feet slightly above the rest of our body, we can hold a bit of air in the calves of our suit, which provides more control for hovering in this position. When you are using ordinary open circuit scuba (as opposed to a rebreather) you can further fine tune your buoyancy by controlling the volume of air you are breathing in and out. Large, full breaths give you more buoyancy than smaller, shallower breaths. Of course, you must never hold your breath while you are breathing any type of compressed gas while you are underwater.

Some people mistakenly believe that it is unsafe to turn upside down while they are wearing a dry suit. In reality, if you are properly weighted, you can actually hover upside down in a dry suit. Author Steve Barsky has actually used this technique many times while performing marine biological surveys for the National Park Service, when it is critical not to disturb the creatures on the bottom in order to get an accurate count. Again, the trick is to be properly weighted and use a minimum volume of air inside your suit. To recover to an upright position, you simply exhale fully, tuck your knees to your chest, and roll back to upright.

Dry Suit Leaks

It is not uncommon during the course of a dive to sometimes get a little bit of water inside your dry suit, even if your suit is working perfectly. The usual points of entry are at the wrist seals and the neck seal.

Some divers have very pronounced tendons at their wrists. If you flex your wrist underwater, to operate a camera or other piece of equipment, this can create a channel for water to enter your dry suit. Normally this should be no more than perhaps a tablespoon of water. This is a very common event and almost all divers will experience this from time to time. Pushing the seal above the exposed tendons can reduce this effect.

Any seal that is not adjusted properly will leak, too. This can occur when underwear or hair is trapped under a seal. When a seal is pinched or twisted it will almost always leak. Another cause of an occasional leak is through the neck seal. If you twist your neck at an unusual angle the tendons on your neck can also contribute to water leakage. Again, most divers will have this happen to them occasionally.

The most common dry suit leaks are from a zipper that has not been closed completely. Punctures can also occur if an inflator valve stem is jammed against the suit during transport. The sharp edge of the stem can cut through some dry suit materials and create a leak.

While it is rare to tear a dry suit, pinhole punctures are the most common source of leakage and damage. Sea urchins in particular can go through almost any dry suit. Sharp pieces of metal on shipwrecks will penetrate most dry suits with ease if you are careless while exploring a wreck.

You can manually override most dry suit exhaust valves by pushing down on the top of the valve to make the valve vent faster. However, some valves will actually vent more slowly when you do this depending on the type of underwear you are using and the design of the valve. Test the valve on your dry suit to see how it behaves.

For extra protection, serious wreck divers will sometimes wear a pair of cotton coveralls over their dry suits. This is acceptable as long as the coveralls do not interfere with the operation of the valves on your suit. Also, be aware that the coveralls will add weight and drag to your diving system and will make swimming more difficult.

Ascending in Your Dry Suit

When you are ready to ascend, if you have an automatic exhaust valve, check to be sure that the valve is open all the way before you begin your ascent. Raise your left upper arm so that the valve is as high (shallow) as possible in relation to the rest of your body, and ascend slowly. Do not extend your hand above your arm since this will trap air above the valve, between the valve and your wrist, where it cannot vent. If you are using a "push-to-dump valve," raise your arm so the valve is at the highest point and push in on the valve with your other hand.

Your first few ascents and descents should be conducted next to a weighted line to allow you to stop your descent if you need to do so. Monitor your dive computer carefully to help ensure you are not exceeding the recommended ascent rate.

If you have a manual valve you should keep one hand on the valve at all times during your ascent and vent air as needed. Air does not vent through a dry suit as fast as it does through a buoyancy compensator. The air must travel through the underwear to escape through the valve. Some of the more "earthy" divers we know refer to venting air through your dry suit exhaust valve as "passing gas."

If you are using an automatic exhaust valve and find yourself ascending faster than you should, lift your upper arm higher and the valve will vent faster. If the valve is still not venting enough air, push down on the top of the valve with your right hand to vent the valve manually. Keep in mind that some valves actually dump slower when manually depressed since you are compressing the valve against the underwear and that may block the valve. You may also want to stop your ascent by holding on to the line until you can vent off any excess air.

You can also slow your ascent by using your fins. By holding your ankles rigid with your fins parallel to the surface you can slow your ascent dramatically. The fins act as "dive brakes." To maximize this effect, arch your back and hold your arms out parallel to the surface, too. This technique is known as "flaring."

Flaring will slow a rapid ascent, but it will not stop it completely. Another technique used to slow an ascent is to swim horizontally, so your body presents a greater surface area to the water.

As you get closer to the surface, exhaust more air from your suit, particularly as you near 20 feet. Remember that most dive computers call for slower rates of ascent the nearer you get to the surface. Watch your depth gauge/dive computer carefully so you do not overshoot your precautionary decompression stop.

Once you have reached the surface, immediately inflate your buoyancy compensator just enough to give yourself positive buoyancy. It is far more comfortable to snorkel back to the boat this way than by making yourself positively buoyant by inflating your dry suit. If you put enough air in your dry suit to give yourself positive buoyancy you will create uncomfortable pressure on your neck seal from air in the dry suit. You will also find it awkward to move around on the surface.

Dry suit diving is fun!

Exiting the Water

If you are diving from an inflatable boat you will probably want to remove your weights and cylinder before you try to climb back aboard. Remove your weight belt first and hand this up. If you must leave your weight belt on, be sure your exhaust valve is closed and there is enough air in your suit to provide you with positive buoyancy after you have removed your tank and B.C. Disconnect the inflator hose from your suit, remove your tank and B.C., and hand your tank into the boat.

Diving from a large boat is usually a bit easier when it is time to exit the water. On some charter boats, the crew members will actually help you to remove your fins once you are back on the swim step. Once you are back on deck, disconnect your suit inflator hose and have your buddy help you remove your cylinder.

Beach diving in a dry suit requires more care than other dive locations, particularly if you are diving from a sandy beach. Be especially careful to avoid getting sand in your dry suit zipper and valves. If at all possible, don't remove your suit until you are standing on a clean towel or paved parking lot.

Practice all of your dry suit skills frequently, including your emergency skills, so you feel confident in your abilities.

Chapter 9
Dry Suit Diving Emergency Techniques

Modern dry suits are very reliable, but you should always be prepared for the unexpected to happen underwater. During your dry suit training course, your instructor should show you how to deal with any potential problem that might arise when using a dry suit. Although these incidents are rare, you will be able to dive with greater confidence knowing that you are prepared to handle these emergencies. To maintain proficiency, you must practice your emergency skills on a regular basis under controlled conditions. We recommend that you practice your emergency skills frequently.

How to Deal with Malfunctioning Valves

If you do not properly maintain your dry suit, one of the situations you may encounter is an inflator valve that sticks open. If this happens, your suit will inflate continuously. The first thing you should attempt to do if your inflator valve sticks open is to disconnect your inflator hose immediately, and vent excess air through the exhaust valve at the same time.

You will only be able to do both actions simultaneously if your suit is equipped with an automatic exhaust valve. If your suit has a manual exhaust and you must choose one action over the other, disconnect the suit inflator hose first. Then vent the manual exhaust.

If you are unable to disconnect the power inflator, but manage to control your buoyancy by using the exhaust valve, stop and get control of the situation before you ascend. Although some dry suit exhaust valves are purported to vent air faster than their accompanying inflator can supply it, certain underwear, suit, and harness combinations may inhibit this from happening.

Even if you are able to control the suit with a stuck inflator valve while you are submerged, you may be unable to maintain control during your ascent. In any case, you should be prepared to vent air by opening either your wrist seal or neck seal during your ascent. Of course, you will get wet if you are forced to take this emergency action.

Poor quality pile underwear may produce balls of lint when the suit rubs against the underwear. When an exhaust valve gets clogged with lint it may be

In an emergency, you can vent air through a wrist seal or a neck seal. Of course, you will get wet if you do this.

blocked to the point that it will not exhaust air properly. If the valve jams open, your suit will not properly hold air and you will probably get wet. You will be able to trap some air above the valve, in the neck and shoulders of the suit, particularly if you keep your right shoulder high. In this situation you should abort your dive and get out of the water.

Should your exhaust valve become fail to vent, you probably won't notice this until it is time to ascend. If you notice that your exhaust valve is not operating properly you should immediately stop your ascent, if possible. If your suit is equipped with an automatic exhaust valve, try rotating the valve or operating it manually. If your suit is equipped with a manual exhaust there will probably be little you can do to get it to work if it is clogged.

Exhaust valves must be properly maintained. Any contaminants that have dried in the valve, could effectively seal the rubber flapper in the valve to the valve body. This would prevent the valve from flowing air.

In the event your valve will not exhaust properly, try to make your ascent on the anchor line, on a kelp stalk, or by following the bottom contour if possible. Stop and vent your suit through the cuff or neck seal every few feet. As long as your air supply will hold out, it is better to get a little wet than to violate your ascent rate and possibly suffer from decompression sickness, or a lung over-pressure injury.

If you must ascend in mid-water, with nothing to slow your ascent, be prepared to vent your suit rapidly through the wrist or neck if need be. Yet while you must be able to vent rapidly, you also need to control your ascent so that you don't lose so much buoyancy you start to sink again.

How to Deal with a Lost Weight Belt

Losing your weight belt underwater while wearing a dry suit will result in becoming very buoyant with an extremely rapid ascent. In this situation it is doubtful you will be able to vent enough air through the exhaust valve to get control of this predicament. Work to control your ascent by flaring and be prepared to vent air from your suit from the wrist seal or neck seal.

Rather than losing your weight belt you should try to maintain an awareness of what is happening with your gear at all times while you are underwater. The experienced diver can concentrate on his or her dive, yet immediately knows when any piece of equipment is not acting right. Learn to develop this awareness. You should instantly know when your belt is loose or has slid off center from your waist.

Recovering from an Inverted Position (Upside Down)

Most divers who experience buoyancy problems with dry suits encounter this difficulty because they have worn too much weight. Too much weight on your belt forces you to add a large volume of air to your suit. When this air shifts to your feet it can cause problems for the untrained dry suit diver.

A properly trained and weighted dry suit diver has no problem in assuming any position they want to in the water. As long as you have a minimum volume of air inside your suit it is possible to turn upside down or do somersaults underwater without difficulty. However, if you are wearing excess weight, and have a high volume of air in your suit, righting yourself from an upside down position can be tough to do.

If you are upside down and have excess air in the feet of your dry suit, it can be difficult to regain an upright position. If your suit is not equipped with ankle straps or laced boots, it can cause your fins to pop off. Once that happens, regaining control is almost impossible.

Righting yourself from an upside down position is usually not too difficult if you are not excessively buoyant. Ordinarily, all you need to do is tuck your body into a ball, give one or more strong kicks, and roll to an upright position. Once you are right side up immediately vent your suit through the exhaust valve to regain control.

If you are properly weighted, recovering from an upside down position should not be difficult.

If you are upside down and find yourself floating off the bottom, kick hard towards the bottom, bend at the waist, and push off the bottom to achieve a heads up position. Push in whichever direction will help you turn right side up. Again, vent your suit right away to get control of your buoyancy.

In a worst case scenario, if you are upside down, unable to right yourself, and headed toward the surface, all you can do is flare out in that position. You will undoubtedly exceed the ascent rate required by the dive tables and/or your dive computer. Be sure that you are exhaling in this situation to avoid a lung over-pressure injury. Monitor yourself once you are back on the surface for any signs of decompression sickness.

How to Deal with a Flooded Dry Suit

Keep in mind that as most dry suit underwear gets wet, it becomes less buoyant. A little bit of water won't make much difference. However, if you completely flood your suit, you may need to either ditch your weights, or add air to your B.C., to maintain positive buoyancy at the surface.

Only in extremely rare cases does a dry suit ever flood completely. We refer to this as a catastrophic dry suit failure. These cases might occur with the complete failure of a zipper, blow-out of a neck seal, or the destruction of a valve. If you get a little bit of water inside your suit (and everyone does occasionally) that is not a flood. On the other hand, if your suit is completely full of water, and will not hold air properly, that is a serious situation.

Should your dry suit become full of water, depending upon the type of suit and underwear you are wearing, you will probably become negatively buoyant. In most eases, depending upon the volume of your buoyancy compensator, you

can return to the surface by inflating your B.C. Even in a completely flooded dry suit, with the zipper fully open, you can usually trap some air in the upper part of the suit (unless the neck seal has failed). This will be enough to give you slight positive buoyancy if you have ditched your weight belt.

This dry suit was flooded intentionally by opening the zipper to test buoyancy changes when a suit floods.

With most dry suit/underwear combinations, if the suit is completely flooded, and all the air escapes from your suit, you will not become positively buoyant even if you drop your weight belt. However, you will probably not be excessively negatively buoyant once you ditch your belt. You will probably be able to swim to the surface under your own power, but you should be prepared to use your B.C. in this situation if you find yourself still negative.

One of the most dangerous aspects of a flooded dry suit is that a suit in these circumstances will hold a great deal of water. The weight of the water inside the suit can make it very difficult to exit the water whether you are diving from the beach or from a boat. It may be necessary for your buddy to carefully make a small hole with his knife in each of the legs of your suit to drain the water out before you can climb a ladder or stand up. If you don't have a knife, you'll need to tip your body sideways on the ladder, or lie down on the swimstep to allow the water to drain out of the upper part of the suit.

If you dive from a small, wet boat, you'll probably leave your dry suit on until you get back to shore.

Chapter 10
Between Dives and Removing Your Dry Suit

Removing your dry suit properly is just as important as donning it properly. If you are careless about the way you handle your suit while you are removing it, it's easy to damage it. If it's warm topside, you'll probably want to remove your suit shortly after you return to the surface. Just be sure to take your time and do it right.

Opening the Zipper After the Dive

While you are out of the water, between dives, you may want to open up your dry suit to avoid overheating. This will generally be true for most people any time the air is warmer than 65 degrees F. Some divers may actually want to remove their entire dry suit, or at least peel down the upper portion. You may also need to remove at least part of the suit to use the toilet.

If your suit is equipped with a back mounted zipper, have your buddy open the zipper for you. Be sure to remind them to put their finger in the loop on the zipper pull. Make sure the zipper is open all the way.

When you are wearing a suit with cross-chest zipper, it's a simple matter to unzip the suit yourself. If that action does not provide sufficient cooling you may want to get out of the top portion of the suit.

Be sure that the zipper is completely open. This is important because if it is not open all the way and you try to remove the suit you may damage the zipper.

Depending on the air temperature and the wind, you may only need to open your suit to cool off. However, if the weather is really warm, you will probably want to remove both the suit and underwear.

Removing a Latex Neck Seal

For divers with cross chest zippers on self-donning dry suits, be sure to release the crotch strap on your suit and pull the torso up before you remove the neck seal. Get the suit as high on your body as possible before removing the neck seal.

With your fingernails against your neck, slide the fingers of each hand down between the neck seal and your neck. Keep your thumbs on the outside of the

The real beauty of a self-donning dry suit becomes apparent when it's time to remove your suit.

Photo courtesy of Diving Concepts

neck seal. Grasp the neck seal firmly with both hands, but make sure you are only grabbing the neck seal, that you don't have a handful of underwear, too. Spread the neck seal by pulling it against the palms of your hands. Tuck your chin to your chest and lift up with your arms. The neck seal should slide over your head easily.

Smaller divers may need assistance getting the neck seal over their head. Your buddy can help you with this. Have your buddy grab the suit at the zipper, on the side of the zipper closest to your head. Have them lift the zipper gently over your head. They must understand that they cannot pull hard on the zipper or put a strain on it. If they pull hard on the zipper this can cause the tape to tear.

Be sure to spread the neck seal by pulling against the palms of your hands when it's time to remove your suit.

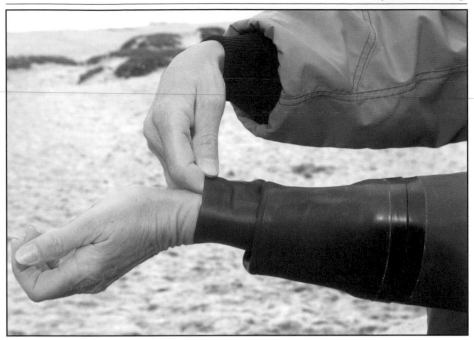

Insert your index finger and middle finger under the wrist seal with your fingernails against your wrist. Then grab the wrist seal between these fingers and your thumb and pull the seal over your wrist.

Removing Latex Wrist Seals

Grasp the sleeve of the suit just above the wrist seal by slipping your index and middle finger under the seal and holding the sleeve between your thumb and fingers. Pull your right hand through the wrist seal and into the sleeve. Pull your arm out of the sleeve and repeat the operation for the other wrist seal.

An application of soapy water or dish soap to your wrist can make it easier to remove a wrist seal, particularly if your suit is equipped with the heavy duty seals used on commercial suits. Sometimes it is easier to remove heavy duty seals with the aid of a buddy. Have them slide their thumbs in on either side of the wrist seal and grab the sleeve of the suit between their thumbs and fingers. They can then spread the seal and slide it over your wrist.

Divers with shoulder mounted zippers may be tempted to turn a sleeve inside out to aid them in removing a wrist seal. Don't do it! This action places a heavy strain on the docking end of the zipper and could break it.

Smaller divers may need assistance removing their suit. You can help by placing one hand one their shoulder (on the underwear) to stabilize them and gently pulling the zipper with your other hand. Note that if the suit has a latex attached hood, the hood needs to be up to remove the neck seal.

Another way you can assist a diver with a latex attached hood is to place one hand on their shoulder (on the underwear), grasp the latex hood in your hand, and gently pull with a steady pressure. This method places less strain on the zipper than pulling on the zipper itself.

Some suits have thicker latex seals than others and some divers may need assistance removing them. You can help by sliding your thumbs under the seal, grabbing the seal, and spreading it, then holding steady as the diver pulls their hand through the seal.

Removing a Neoprene Neck Seal

Unroll the neck seal so it is no longer turned under on itself. Grab the leading edge of the neck seal with both hands, with your fingers inside and your thumbs on the outside. Do not dig your fingernails into the seal. Pull the neck seal up until the leading edge of the seal is at your chin and as high on the back of your head as you can.

The edge of the seal should be in the joint between your thumb and forefinger. Grasp the seal firmly, tuck your chin, and pull the seal up and over your head.

Removing Neoprene Wrist Seals

To remove a fold-under neoprene wrist seal, start by pulling the sleeve of your suit up your arm to allow the seal to invert. Turn the seal so that the nylon lays flat against your wrist. Insert the fingers of your opposite hand into the sleeve. With your fingers on the inside and your thumb on the outside, grab the sleeve just above the point where the wrist seal meets the sleeve. Pull the sleeve off your arm. To remove a cone-shaped neoprene seal, have your buddy put their thumbs inside the seal, spread it, and pull it over your wrist.

Between Dives

A suit equipped with suspenders will stay in position between dives, even if you have peeled the top down, while you walk around topside. For a loose fitting dry suit without suspenders, you may want to tie the arms in a knot in front of you, or tuck the arms inside the dry suit (only if they are dry). If this action is not taken your suit will gradually slide down your body, making it difficult to walk.

You can also use a weight belt without weights or a bungee cord around your waist to hold the suit in position. If you use a bungee cord make sure the ends of the hooks are wrapped with tape to prevent them from cutting your suit or seals.

Be sure to drink non-alcoholic fluids like water, non-caffeinated beverages, or sports drinks between dives. Many dry suit divers try to avoid drinking fluids because they want to avoid the need to urinate while underwater in their dry suits. The reality is you need to drink fluids to stay properly hydrated to help avoid decompression sickness.

As long as you drink fluids in moderate amounts and observe reasonable surface intervals between your dives, you should have time to urinate before entering the water again. In addition, because you are diving with a dry suit, even those of us with relatively small bladders find we can normally make it

It's important to stay hydrated when you are diving.

If you have been diving off the beach, be sure to rinse any sand off your suit before you attempt to remove it.

through a one hour dive without an overwhelming need to urinate. Of course, you'll probably want to use the bathroom fairly soon after you return to the boat! On the positive side, you won't smell like you urinated in your wetsuit on the drive home!

Keeping Cool Between Dives

On warm days it can get very hot inside a dry suit. If you must keep your suit on between dives you should take care not to overheat. There are several techniques that can be used to solve this problem. The simplest solution is to remove all of your other diving equipment except your fins and stay wet.

Other cooling methods to be considered are keeping your hands in a tub of ice water, or flowing cold water over your head and suit. A wet towel wrapped around the head can also be effective. Periodically dunk the towel in cold water and reapply it as needed. Always take care not to overheat.

Overheating in a dry suit is very dangerous. Your body has no way to cool down because you can't lose heat through evaporative cooling (sweating).

Removing the Bottom of the Suit

If it's a warm day, or you're finished diving, you will probably want to remove your dry suit completely, even if you have peeled the top of the suit down.

To remove the suit completely (after opening the zipper and removing the neck and wrist seals), find a suitable location where you can sit down on a dry surface and where you are out of the path of other divers coming back aboard the boat who may still be wet.

First, slide the suspenders over your shoulders. Lower the suit until it is just past your buttocks and sit down. If your suit fits loose, it will probably just slide down until it is in a pile at your ankles and you can just step out of it. If your suit fits snug, you may have to work the suit down to your feet and pull the boots off. It's not uncommon to have the boots from your dry suit underwear remain inside the boots of your dry suit. You'll want to retrieve them so they can be stored with the rest of your underwear.

If you will be diving again that day, you'll probably want to leave your suit out of the bag, with it's zipper open, especially if it is damp at all inside the suit. If you're diving from a large boat, you can probably find a safe place out of the way to hang your suit over the side. Just be sure not to leave it there while the boat is underway! If you're diving from a small boat, you may have no alternative but to roll the suit up and store it back in your dive gear bag.

When you're done diving for the day, if your suit is still wet on the outside, you'll want to roll it up with the zipper closed for the boat trip home. Keeping the zipper closed at this time helps to prevent any water from getting inside the suit while you are transporting the suit. Be sure to avoid dropping any heavy equipment on your dry suit when the zipper is closed.

Drying Damp Underwear Between Dives

Wet or damp dry suit underwear should be dried between dives. Wooly bears and other types of underwear may also be wrung out. If no drier is available you can also try twirling the underwear in a circle over your head to spin the water out using centrifugal force. If the weather is warm enough, the underwear can be dried by hanging it on a hanger although this can take quite some time depending upon the type of underwear. Some dive boats have driers on them that you can use for this purpose. Remember, if your underwear contains Thinsulate®, do not use high heat for drying.

Larger ships may have blower systems to vent engine room air. Hanging your underwear in front of a blower vent will allow it to dry quickly. Wet dry suit undergarments can be wrung out and worn again even if they are damp. Most quality underwear will still retain a good deal of its insulation value even if it is damp, once it has been rewarmed by your body. Of course, if you find that you aren't warm enough underwater wearing damp underwear you should exit the water as soon as it is convenient.

Be sure to carry a dry bag to stow your underwear when you aren't wearing it and to keep it dry for the trip home. If the inside of your suit is wet or damp, turn the suit inside out and allow it to dry, too. This is especially important with suits with a fabric lining that may take quite a while to dry.

Maintain your dry suit properly and you will never have to worry about it not being ready for your next dive.

Chapter 11
Maintenance & Repairs for Your Dry Suit System

Dry suits require a bit more maintenance than wet suits. No one will deny that fact. However, that little bit of extra maintenance is well worth it when you hit the water knowing you will be warm and your suit is in top condition. The few minutes required to properly maintain your dry suit will pay off in fewer repairs and a longer lasting suit.

Checking Your Suit After the Dive

Once you are out of the water, after your dive, as a matter of routine you should check your dry suit when you first open the zipper. If your dry suit underwear feels or looks wet, look for possible points of water entry.

Most "leaks" are the result of an improperly adjusted seal or a channel created by the tendons in your wrist or hair at your neck. A damp underwear cuff or water around the collar of your underwear is a good clue that water entered at those points. Wet spots on your stomach or legs may indicate a puncture. Water on your left arm may indicate a leaking exhaust valve. Water on your underwear where the zipper closes may mean that your zipper was not fully closed.

Take the time to examine your suit while you are still wearing it if you suspect your suit is damaged. This action will save you time later when you must locate the damage to make the repair.

After you have removed your suit, feel down inside the bottom of the suit, all the way down to the boots. Even if your suit didn't leak, the inside of your suit may still be damp due to condensation from your sweat.

On a warm day, most people will sweat a bit inside their dry suit and may never realize it. Although the upper body of your suit may be dry, the sweat from your body will usually accumulate on the walls of your suit and then drain into the boots and lower legs. If this is the case, you will probably want to rinse the inside of your suit when you get home to prevent any mold or mildew from growing inside your suit. Check your suit after the dive and check it again when you get home.

Rinsing Your Suit After Diving

When it is time to rinse your suit after diving be sure to do a thorough job, especially if you have been diving in salt water or there is sand on your suit. Dry suit valves and zippers must be thoroughly rinsed after ocean diving.

You can close the wrist seal and neck seal of your suit with rubber bands to prevent water entry while rinsing your suit (unless your suit is already wet inside which makes this unnecessary). Close the zipper on your suit, too. Rinse the exterior of the suit completely, paying particular attention to the valves and zippers.

Run water over it to help remove any sand or grit that you may have picked up on your suit during the dive.

Operate the valves as you run water over them. If your suit has an automatic exhaust valve, rotate the head of the valve as you run water through it. Push the inflator button several times as you run water over the outside of the mechanism.

It isn't possible to run fresh water directly through most inflator valves. To get water through the valve you need to flow water in the inlet and hook up your inflator hose. Depress the valve button and allow the water in the nipple to spray inside the suit. You can also lubricate the valve with a small amount of pump silicone liquid this same way. Dried salt crystals and corrosion inside an inflator valve are a major cause of stuck inflator buttons. Be sure that there is no salt remaining between the valve button and the valve body.

If your suit is wet or damp inside you should rinse the inside of the suit, too. Run fresh water inside the suit and drain it out several times. This is especially important if you have a vulcanized rubber suit with a fabric lining.

Latex seals should be periodically washed with mild soap and water. This procedure will help to remove body oils that will destroy the seals prematurely.

Cleaning the Zipper

Dry suit zippers need special attention if you want to get the most life from them. They should receive an extra cleaning at least once a year, or more frequently if you dive often.

To clean a dry suit zipper, use a mild soap solution (such as Ivory) and an old toothbrush. Scrub the zipper teeth vigorously, inside and outside with the toothbrush. This will help to remove corrosion from the zipper and allow it to slide more easily. Brush between the teeth to remove old wax and grit.

Always rinse your dry suit thoroughly after diving.

Latex seals should be periodically washed in a mild solution of soapy water to remove body oils.

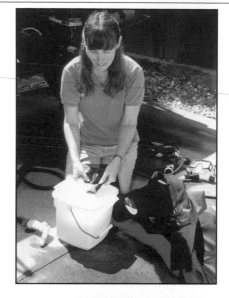

Clean the zipper on your dry suit with a mild solution of soapy water and an old toothbrush.

Hang your dry suit in a cool, dry location and allow it to dry completely before storing it.

Proper Drying

Your dry suit should be hung over a line, out of the sun where it will receive good air circulation. Vulcanized rubber dry suits, TLS suits, and pack cloth suits will dry very quickly on the outside, but other types of dry suits may take some time for the exterior to dry. If your suit is equipped with ankle straps or suspenders, hang it from these devices. This will help the inside to dry more quickly than if you drape the entire suit over a line or rod.

After the outside of your suit is dry, carefully turn it inside out. Avoid stressing the docking ends of the dry suit zipper when you do this. Allow the inside of your suit to dry thoroughly. Suits with nylon knit linings may take several hours to dry thoroughly.

Check your suit when you think the inside is dry. Pay particular attention to the inside of the boots. These are hard to turn inside out on most suits and water may be trapped in them if you are unable to completely expose them.

When your suit is completely dry, both inside and outside, turn it right side out again. Take extra care with the zipper as you do this.

Zipper Lubrication

It's a good idea to lubricate your zipper before you put your suit away for storage. Bee's wax is the lubricant recommended by most manufacturers. Just be sure to wipe away any excess lubricant before you store your suit.

Proper Storage

As we've mentioned before, never apply silicone spray to the seals of your dry suit. This will not help extend the life of your seals and makes repairs more difficult.

Inspect your suit before you put it away. Look at the seals and stretch them to detect signs of aging or cracking.

Your dry suit should be rolled for storage with the zipper left either open or closed, depending upon your manufacturer's recommendation. Some people feel there is less stress on the zipper when it is left open. They believe it is less prone to breakage if the suit is dropped, or if anything heavy (like a weight belt) is dropped on the zipper.

Some manufacturers recommend that you roll your suit up with the suit lying on its front, while others recommend that the suit be on its back. Again, follow the recommendations for your suit.

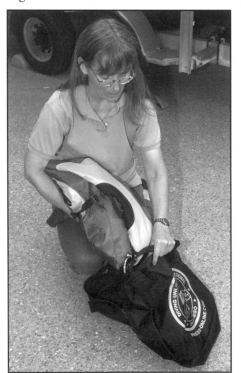

The important point is that you roll the suit and cap your inflator valve if it has a metal stem that may contact the suit. Inflator valve stems can puncture a dry suit if they are not capped before you roll your suit for storage. If you roll your suit with the inflator valve on the outside you will not puncture your suit with the valve stem.

After you have rolled up the body of the suit, fold the arms of the suit over the body. Place your suit in its storage bag. If no bag was provided with your suit, put it inside a plastic trash bag and seal it up.

Proper storage will help prolong the life of your dry suit.

The goal of proper storage is to prevent ozone and sunlight from damaging your suit. Ozone is a chemical that will attack all rubber and latex seals. Correct storage will extend the life of latex seals greatly, especially if you live in a smoggy environment such as southern California. If the bag provided with your suit does not seal well you may want to place the suit and bag inside a plastic trash bag and seal it tightly.

Store your suit in a cool, dry place, away from electric motors or gas water heaters, both of which produce ozone, Ultraviolet light is also detrimental to suit seals.

Laundering Dry Suit Underwear

Don't forget to take care of your dry suit underwear, too. Follow the manufacturer's directions for laundering. Generally you'll want to use only a small amount of soap, if any, cold water, and a gentle cycle. The usual reasons to launder your underwear are to remove any salt or odor, so in most cases soap is not necessary.

It's usually best if you allow the underwear to air dry.

Repairing Your Dry Suit

Repairing a dry suit is no more complicated than repairing a wetsuit. The techniques are very similar, they just aren't as widely known. The most important elements of dry suit repair are to have all of the correct repair materials, to take your time, and to be patient.

Locating Punctures

Punctures are the most common type of damage that dry suits sustain. Even a small puncture can leave you wet. However, a puncture will rarely, if ever, cause your suit to flood.

Locating the puncture is the first step in repairing your suit. There are two methods that you can use to reliably locate punctures. You can either inflate the suit, or use what we call the "flashlight method."

To locate a puncture by inflating the suit, you will need three heavy duty rubber bands and a spray bottle full of soapy water. To start, seal off the wrists and neck seal with heavy duty rubber bands. Close the zipper on the suit and the exhaust valve. If your suit has an automatic exhaust, screw the valve in all the way. Attach the suit inflator hose to your suit and blow up the suit until it is stiff (approximately 1 P.S.I. of pressure inside the suit).

Spray the suit with a solution of soapy water. Anywhere where there is a puncture, the surface of the suit should "bubble." You may also even be able to hear air escaping out of the leak, too. Mark the spot with a ball point pen by drawing a small circle around the puncture so you will be able to find it when you are ready to apply a patch. Be sure to rinse the soap off before you do any repair work.

The flashlight method of locating leaks also works well. The only item you will need to perform this test is a flashlight and a dark room. Take your suit into the darkened room and sit on the floor where you can spread the suit out comfortably.

Professional repair facilities use tanks like this to leak test dry suits.

Hold a bright flashlight inside the suit and turn it on. Hold the lens of the flashlight against the inside surface of the suit and move it around in the area where you suspect the puncture to be located. The light will shine through the hole making the puncture very apparent in most cases.

In an emergency, you can patch most punctures with duct tape. Depending upon the type of suit or seals that you have, this may not always work well. Use duct tape only when you have no other patching material available and you must dive to perform a rescue. Be sure to remove the duct tape immediately after you have completed your dive so that it doesn't leave a sticky residue on your suit.

Patching Vulcanized Rubber Suits

Vulcanized rubber dry suits can be patched very quickly, provided you have the proper patch materials with you. Most manufacturers have patch kits available for their suits that contains the glue and patches you will need to repair your suit. Be sure to follow the directions in the manual provided with your suit and/or repair kit.

Keep in mind that most glues have a shelf life and few are usable after 2 years, even if the container has not been opened. Also, many glues get thicker once the container has been opened and become difficult or impossible to use. Be sure to replace the glue in your repair kit periodically or it may not work when you need it.

⚠ WARNING

Most dry suit glues, cements, and solvents are highly toxic. Use adequate ventilation, gloves, and eye protection when working with these materials. Always read the Material Safety Data Sheet (MSDS) for any chemicals you use to make repairs.

Patching most dry suits is relatively quick and easy.

For example, Viking's patches and glue are specifically designed to work together. The glue provided with the patch kit actually consists of two parts. One component is in the tube of glue while the catalyst is on the back of the patch itself. If you try to use the glue supplied with a Viking repair kit with an ordinary piece of latex, or suit material, it will not stick because the catalyst is not present.

The most important point in patching a vulcanized rubber suit is to dry the suit surface. Use a towel to dry the outside of the suit quickly. Viking also recommends that you rough up the area where the patch is to be applied. Don't worry about the inside of the suit as long as you are only repairing a puncture.

Repair kits for vulcanized rubber suits include a piece of coarse sandpaper specifically for preparing the surface of the suit for patching. Rub the area vigorously where the patch is to be applied. Most manufacturers will recommend that you actually remove the shiny surface layer of rubber and get down to the base material underneath, but be sure to read the instructions for your specific suit. For most suits of this type, unless you prepare the surface in this way, the patch will not stick. The area you prepare should be slightly larger than the patch itself since it is almost impossible to get the patch down with 100% precision.

Once you have applied the patch, rub it down vigorously. Although you can use your thumb for this, a wallpaper roller works much better. Be sure to rub around the outside edges of the patch.

Follow the directions on the glue provided with your patch kit regarding how long you should wait until you can dive again. With most repair patches and glue you can dive again after 5 minutes, but it takes several days for most adhesives to completely cure. Be sure to neutralize any excess glue per the manufacturer's instructions to avoid getting glue on other parts of your suit.

Patching TLS and Other Coated Nylon Suits

TLS suits and other laminated materials can be patched very quickly. The materials you will need to repair a TLS suit include a small nylon brush, a rag, surface preparation solvent, glue, and a clean tin can (like an empty coffee can).

Patches on these suits are normally applied to the inside of these suits rather than to the exterior nylon. The surface is prepared using the cleaning solvent recommended by the manufacturer. To clean the surface, rub it vigorously with the rag dipped in the solvent. Allow the solvent to dry. Then apply the glue recommended by your suit's manufacturer. You won't need more than 1/6 cup of this mixture to apply a small patch.

Coat the area where the patch is to be applied and the patch itself. Allow the first coat to dry for 5 minutes. Apply a second coat and allow it to dry for 10 minutes. Apply the patch and rub it down with your thumb. The patch should be allowed to dry for at least 5 more minutes before you go back into the water.

Seam leaks in TLS or other urethane backed dry suits should be coated with a mixture of 50% Cotol and 50% Aquaseal. Apply 3 coats, allowing time for each coat to dry (usually 15-20 minutes). Allow the coating to dry until it is no longer tacky before you go back into the water. The drying time will vary with the temperature and humidity. This procedure also works well for sealing punctures in most dry suits.

Patching Foam Neoprene

Repairing foam neoprene suits can be a bit more difficult than other types of dry suits. First, the suit must be completely dry before any permanent repair can be made. Due to the thick, cellular nature of this material, water and air don't always move through punctures in foam neoprene in a straight line. In addition, high wear areas in these suits, such as knees or armpits, often become spongy, making it necessary to replace whole sections of material.

Some repair facilities have developed special techniques for plugging leaks in foam neoprene suits. They use a large, heavy-duty syringe to fill the puncture holes with Aquaseal®.

Repairing Crushed Neoprene Suits

Crushed neoprene dry suits can be patched and seam leaks repaired very easily, using a 50/50 mixture of Cotol® and Aquaseal®. Patches and seam repairs are normally made to inside of the suits for both aesthetic and for functional reasons.

Most dry suit manufacturers can supply you with a repair kit.

The nylon jersey is lighter on the inside and is much easier to seal, i.e. blocking the wicking action of the nylon filaments.

The area to be repaired needs to be completely dry. Repair work should be done in a well ventilated space or outdoors.

Mixing the Cotol® and Aquaseal® must be done in a something other then a plastic container because plastic will dissolve. Wax paper cups, glass, ceramic, or metal containers work well. Small metal acid brushes or natural bristle paint brushes with wood handles work are satisfactory for both mixing and applying the mixture.

Mix only small batches at a time. Repairs require three coats with minimum of 30 minutes between coats. A new batch of cement will be required for each coat. Select a patch of the appropriate size from the patch kit.

To repair a puncture, apply the first coat in a one-inch diameter circle around the affected area and to the patch. Allow to dry for 30 minutes, with 30 minutes between each of the two additional coats. If the area to repair is more then a single point, establish a one-inch boundary outside the affected area which can be marked out with a crayon or piece of bar soap. Then apply the three coats within the marked area again allowing 30 minutes between coats before applying the patch.

Seam repairs use the same mixture and same number of coats. Apply the mixture to the affected seam area, plus a one-inch margin on both sides of the seam.

Though the mixture takes a full 24 hours to cure, you can use it in two and a half hours after the last coat has been applied. Just be sure to apply talcum powder to the surface of the repaired area. The powder eliminates the tackiness of the surface and prevents it from sticking to other surfaces. It's advisable to wear a particle mask when working with talcum powder due to potential health risks.

Enjoying the Dry Suit Experience

Over the years, we've met many people who have told us that they only dive in warm, tropical waters. They complain that the visibility is too poor, there isn't enough to see, you have to wear too much equipment, and the water temperature is too uncomfortable to enjoy cold water diving.

Those of us who dive in cold water, however, know there is no substitute for many of the great diving adventures you can enjoy only in these special environments. To swim through a towering kelp forest in California, to dive with penguins in Antarctica, to explore the deep wrecks off the east coast of the U.S. or Scapa Flow in Great Britain, are all experiences that are best appreciated in a dry suit. When it's raining topside, or the wind is blowing hard, a dry suit can make diving a completely enjoyable experience. We all enjoy diving in the tropics, but there are just as many memorable moments to be had diving in cold water. Given that there are more cold water diving areas than warm ones, you're missing much of what the underwater world has to offer if you don't dive in cold water.

We hope that you will get as much enjoyment from diving with a dry suit as we have experienced.

*For diving in polluted water,
a dry suit is essential.*

Chapter 12
Contaminated Water Diving:
When Staying Dry is Essential

What Is Contaminated Water?

One of the more critical applications for dry suits is in contaminated water diving. We define contaminated water as any underwater environment that contains biological, chemical, or nuclear pollution that may be harmful to the diver. Harmful pollutants are those that will injure or kill the diver when taken into the body either directly through the skin, through breathing, or through accidental swallowing. The purpose of the dry suit is to help keep the contaminants completely away from the diver's body, when used with appropriate breathing gear.

Contaminated water diving is not for the amateur. It should only be undertaken by highly trained professional divers who have a specific reason for entering a polluted water environment. Divers who are not properly prepared for this type of diving have died from exposure to contaminated water environments. Others have developed medical problems following these types of dives.

Who Dives In Contaminated Water?

The need to dive in contaminated water environments varies from mission to mission. Water quality biologists may need to dive in contaminated water to take biological or chemical samples, or to make observations. Law enforcement divers regularly dive in polluted water to recover evidence, make rescues, or save lives. Fire fighters may be required to fight fires under piers where burning pilings release creosote or other chemicals. Fire fighters are also frequently called upon to deal with toxic spills.

Military divers may be required to deal with biological or chemical warfare agents. Commercial divers must frequently dive in polluted harbors or other waterways to do their work. Some commercial divers also regularly work inside nuclear reactors.

Professionals who deal with hazardous materials on a regular basis have developed classifications for both the hazards and the level of protection required to deal with specific hazards. Exposure to certain biological or chemical agents may have short term effects, such as causing diarrhea, nausea, or chemical burns.

Other chemicals such as cancer causing agents, or radioactive materials, may have long term chronic effects. Certain other chemicals or biological materials may cause death after very short exposures.

Determining what equipment the diver should wear for a particular hazard requires the dive team to evaluate the effects of that hazard. Diving in contaminated water requires a coordinated team of highly trained divers and support people. It is not an activity that can be conducted by a single diver. Depending upon the scope of the incident and the resources available, more support personnel may be involved than divers.

To dive in contaminated water requires, at a minimum, a dive team and support personnel with the following assignments:
- Primary diver
- Standby diver
- Primary tender
- Standby tender
- Dive control system operator
- Diving supervisor
- Preliminary decontamination wash down team (2 people)
- Definitive decontamination wash down team (2 people)
- Back up decontamination team (2 people)
- Medical support personnel
- Haz-mat (hazardous materials) supervisor and/or Incident command
  supervisor

Contaminated water diving operations require highly trained personnel. This suit is made from a chemically resistant polyurethane.

Photo courtesy of Whites Manufacturing

Basic Equipment Decisions for Contaminated Water Diving

On dry land, unless you are dealing with a toxic substance that creates fumes or penetrates the skin easily, haz-mat personnel may only be equipped with little more than a "splash suit" and a respirator. Topside, this is considered "Level C" protection by haz-mat personnel. If you add a self contained breathing apparatus to the basic splash suit, then you have graduated to "Level B" protection. Incidents that demand complete encapsulation of topside personnel are said to demand "Level A" protection.

Underwater, however, where toxic substances are dispersed by the water, the contaminant may be suspended in solution and completely surround the diver. For this reason, a dry suit with attached boots, hood, and gloves is always required when diving in polluted water. The only other equipment variable that usually remains to be decided is whether to use scuba or surface-supplied air, and whether to use a full-face mask or a helmet. If a helmet is used it must connect directly to the suit.

Most public safety divers use full-face masks when diving with dry suits in contaminated water.

Scuba operations in contaminated water are typically conducted with full-face masks. With this type of equipment there is always the risk that the mask will come loose and leak. Communications with full-face masks usually do not match the quality of those possible with a dry helmet. For these reasons, scuba operations in contaminated water with full-face masks should be limited to those situations that present hazards that would not cause more than short term illness or injury.

Full-face mask scuba equipment is not recommended for most contaminated water diving operations for several reasons. Most critical is the fact that if you run out of air during a scuba operation there is a very serious risk of exposure to contaminants if you remove your mask to share air or breathe once you break the surface. Since most contaminated water diving operations tend to take place in environments with limited visibility, there is also a very real chance of entanglement.

Any contaminated water diving operation that presents the risks of chronic disability, carcinogens, or death should only be conducted with a dry suit that mates directly to a full coverage helmet, such as the Kirby Morgan® 37. This equipment is designed to be used in the surface-supplied mode, the preferred method for all contaminated water diving operations.

Surface-supplied diving equipment has several major advantages over scuba for this type of work. The advantages include an unlimited air supply, hard wire communications, back-up breathing systems, topside depth monitoring, and a direct link to the surface.

The minimum diving equipment required for a surface-supplied dive in biologically contaminated water includes a topside air supply with backup, an air supply manifold for controlling the air supply to the diver, a hard-wire communications system, a diver's umbilical, a diver's full-face mask or helmet, bail-out bottle, vulcanized rubber dry suit, and mating dry gloves. The standby diver must be equally equipped with an equivalent mask or helmet, bail-out bottle, suit, and gloves.

Dry Suit Essentials for Contaminated Water Diving

Many tests have been conducted on dry suits and diving helmets for use in contaminated water diving operations. For diving in biologically polluted water, the type of dry suits that have been traditionally recommended by the Environmental Protection Agency (EPA) and the National Oceanic and Atmospheric Administration (NOAA) are those made from vulcanized rubber.

Vulcanized rubber dry suits provide a very reliable level of protection in biologically contaminated water. They are especially easy to decontaminate due to their slick outer surface. After proper decontamination, and once they have dried, there is very little chance that bacteria or other organisms will continue to grow on this material. In contrast to this, suits with an exterior nylon coating are very difficult to decontaminate properly. Polyurethane coated suits also show good promise for diving in biologically contaminated water (and possibly other environments).

Any dry suit that is used for contaminated water diving should be equipped with hard sole, attached boots. Latex socks are not acceptable for contaminated water diving because the risk of puncture, even with protective neoprene booties over them, is unacceptably high.

Divers with thin faces may have difficulty getting a proper seal between the full-face mask and a latex hood. If this happens, the mask may inflate the hood making it very uncomfortable. Before you use this equipment in any location other than a swimming pool be sure to test it to see if this is an issue for you. If it is, you should have your dry suit dealer install the smallest hood available and it will probably solve the problem.

Although attached latex hoods are considered the minimum for diving in contaminated water with a full-face mask, an attached dry hood made from the same material as the suit itself, is the preferred option. The hood is glued directly to the body of the suit so that no part of your neck or face is exposed. The pressure inside the hood must be equalized to prevent ear squeeze, but also must be vented upon ascent. The full-face mask must mate directly to the hood with no gaps.

Not all dry suits are compatible with all chemical environments. Divers who do this type of diving must choose the proper suit for their particular application.

Dry gloves, like those worn by this diver, are an essential piece of gear for contaminated water diving.

Dry gloves are another essential piece of equipment for dry suit diving. Dry gloves, or mittens, are part of a system that consists of several parts. These parts include:

a) A set of inner cuff rings (one for each sleeve)
b) A set of outer cuff rings (one for each sleeve)
c) A set of dry gloves or mittens
d) Liners for gloves or mittens

If you are diving with a full coverage helmet, such as a Kirby Morgan® or a Desco®, your suit must be equipped with a special yoke so that the helmet will mate directly to the suit. The yoke eliminates the gap that would exist at the neck if a conventional neck dam was used with the helmet.

It must be kept in mind that there is no one dry suit material that will be compatible with all chemicals under all conditions. Every chemical hazard varies with the nature of the chemical, the concentration of the chemical(s), time of exposure, and temperature. The diver must not dive unless he knows exactly what hazards are present, their effect on the body and equipment, and what decontamination procedures must be followed. However, divers should keep in mind that even a mild chemical exposure can alter equipment in ways that are not easily detectable. These exposures can cause the equipment to fail unexpectedly in chemical environments that otherwise might be considered acceptable.

Most commercially available vulcanized rubber dry suits are made from a combination of synthetic and natural rubber that is easily assembled. However, dry suits can be made from other combinations of materials that will give an equally smooth outer surface.

Due to the stringent requirements for this type of diving, at a minimum, one third of all equipment used in contaminated water diving should be scheduled for replacement on an annual basis. Depending upon the chemicals involved, certain items of diving equipment may need to be replaced after a single exposure.

Basic Contaminated Water Diving Procedures

To fully understand contaminated water diving we can best illustrate the procedures involved through an imagined hazardous materials incident. The procedures and methods presented here do not begin to cover all of the details in handling a hazardous materials incident. In addition, as technology changes, some of these procedures will be revised. We present this example to give the reader an idea of the complexity of a hazardous materials incident where divers are involved.

Our hypothetical scenario involves a truck carrying toxic waste that has gone off a bridge into a shallow lake. The driver is dead and trapped inside the cab underwater. One side of the truck can be seen from the bridge

The dive team that is dispatched to respond to the incident is part of the fire department's hazardous materials team. They have all of the proper equipment for decontamination. The local police department has also been dispatched to provide control of the area.

At the site, the fire department uses tape to cordon off the area. The lake itself is considered to be the center of the "hot zone", the center of the contaminated site. The incident command post is set up on the upwind side of the bridge. In the event the truck starts to leak and release hazardous fumes, the public safety personnel should not be downwind of the fumes.

From the chemical warning labels on the side of the truck the divers can determine who owns the vehicle, and contact the owner of the vehicle to get information on what chemicals the truck is carrying. They determine that their diving gear is compatible with the chemicals in the truck.

The decontamination equipment is set up so that the divers can be properly washed down after the dive. There is the proper equipment on hand to collect all of the water and chemicals used in the washdown process.

The diver is dressed into a vulcanized rubber dry suit with a mating helmet. Surface-supplied equipment is chosen due to the fact that one of the chemicals is a carcinogen.

The tenders who will handle the diver's hose are also dressed into the appropriate haz-mat gear for topside protection. Since they will be directly handling the wet hose they will need a very high level of protection.

Once the diver is dressed in, he enters a small portable water tank filled with clean water to leak check his gear. After it has been determined that the diver's equipment is working properly he is led to the side of the bridge. The diver and tender pass from the support zone, where the diver was dressed, into the contamination reduction zone. To do so, they go through a cordoned off area where the decontamination will take place. Plastic tarps are spread on the ground to catch the chemicals and water used during the decontamination process.

Entry and exit from the water is always made at the same point, the access control point. Objectives for the dive will be to recover the driver of the truck and determine if there is any chemical leakage into the lake.

The diver enters the water and removes the body of the driver. The driver's body is placed in a body bag and removed from the lake. The diver determines that none of the drums of chemicals appear to be leaking.

With his tasks completed, the diver exits the water. At the top of the ladder, the diver is given a preliminary wash with fresh water. He then is led to the decontamination area, more properly known as the contamination reduction corridor.

The diver is carefully washed down before any equipment is removed. This should take place in some type of portable pool where the waste water can be captured for removal.

The nature of the contamination will determine what decontamination solutions are used. In the case of biological contaminants, some of the more common solutions used include a variety of soaps. In the case of chemical hazards, the decontamination solution selected must be one that neutralizes the specific chemical(s).

After the diver's equipment is removed, it is bagged for a more complete breakdown and cleaning later. The diver then proceeds to a special trailer where he removes any remaining clothing and showers. After drying, the diver disposes of his towel in a special bin and proceeds to a second shower. The diver then dresses and is examined by medical personnel. It should be obvious at this point to do this type of diving, a high level of training is required.

Diving in contaminated water requires a great deal of specialized training. The divers must be trained in both dry suit and surface-supplied diving techniques. Equipment maintenance for this specialized gear is essential. First aid training is also required. In addition, the divers should also be trained in topside hazardous materials incident response.

Regular training in simulated hazardous materials incidents involving diving must be conducted to maintain proficiency. At a minimum, we recommend at least four training dives per quarter. It is unreasonable to expect a dive team to learn how to use the equipment, but not use it again until an actual incident many months later.

Regular training is essential to keep divers prepared for contaminated water diving.

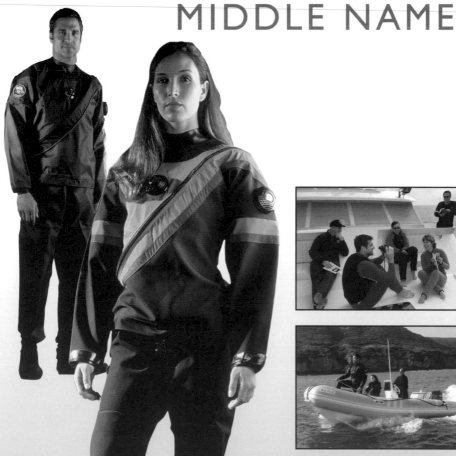

THE COLD WATER SPECIALISTS

WHITES
SINCE 1956

DIVE DRY

THE FUTURE OF HAZMAT IS HERE
ictoria.bc.canada 250.652.8554 www.whitesdiving.com

DIVING CONCEPTS RAPID CUFF REPAIR KIT™

You ripped your latex wrist seal and now your day of diving or your multi-day trip has come to an abrupt end! Frustration abounds and you are done!

Maybe not.

Not if you had the foresight to purchase a Diving Concepts Rapid Cuff Repair Kit™.

Save your diving day! The Diving Concepts Rapid Cuff Repair Kit™ will allow you to install a new rolled cone latex wrist seal or dry glove.

The Diving Concepts Rapid Cuff Repair Kit™ will work on latex seals <u>on any drysuit</u>. No advanced modification of your drysuit is required!

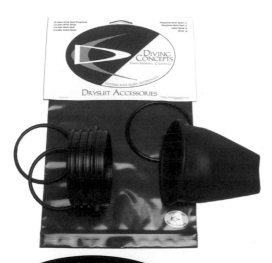

DIVING CONCEPTS, INC.

P.O. BOX 80222, SANTA BARBARA, CA 93118
(805) 692-2001, FAX (805) 692-1651
E-MAIL: INFO@DIVINGCONCEPTS.COM
WEBSITE: WWW.DIVINGCONCEPTS.COM

CUSTOM AND STOCK DRYSUITS AND UNDERSUITS, DRYGLOVES AND DRYSUIT ACCESSORIES

About the Author
Steven M. Barsky

Steve Barsky started diving in 1965 in Los Angeles County, and became a diving instructor in 1970. His first employment in the industry was with a dive store in Los Angeles and he went on to work for almost 10 years in the retail dive store environment.

Steve attended the University of California at Santa Barbara, where he earned a Masters Degree in Human Factors Engineering in 1976. His master's thesis was one of the first to deal with the use of underwater video systems in commercial diving. His work was a pioneering effort at the time (1976) and was used by the Navy in developing applications for underwater video systems.

His background includes being a commercial diver; working in the offshore oil industry in the North Sea, Gulf of Mexico, and South America. He worked as both as an air diving supervisor and a mixed-gas saturation diver, making working dives down to 580 feet.

Barsky was marketing manager for Viking America, Inc., an international manufacturer of dry suits. He also served in a similar position at Diving Systems International, now called Kirby Morgan Dive Systems, Inc., the world's leading manufacturer of commercial diving helmets.

Steve is an accomplished author and underwater photographer. His photos have been used in numerous magazine articles, catalogs, advertising, training programs, and textbooks.

A prolific writer, Barsky's work has been published in *Diver Canada, Sea Technology, Underwater USA, Skin Diver, Offshore Magazine, Emergency, Fire Engineering, Dive Training Magazine, H2OPs, Searchlines, Sources, Undersea Biomedical Reports, Santa Barbara Magazine, Selling Scuba, Scuba Times, Underwater Magazine,* and many other publications.

He is the author of the *Diving in High-Risk Environments, Spearfishing for Skin and Scuba Divers, Small Boat Diving, Diving with the EXO-26 Full Face Mask, Diving with the Divator MK II Full Face Mask, The Simple Guide to Snorkeling Fun*, and a joint author with Dick Long and Bob Stinton of *Dry Suit Diving: A Guide to Diving Dry*. With his wife Kristine, he wrote *California Lobster Diving* and *Careers in Diving* (also with Ronnie Damico). With Mark Thurlow and Mike Ward, Steve authored *The Simple Guide to Rebreather Diving*, the first widely distributed book on the topic.

Steve also wrote and produced four books for Scuba Diving International; *Deeper Sport Diving with Dive Computers - Wreck, Boat, and Drift Diving - Easy Nitrox Diving -* and *Underwater Navigation, Night, and Limited Visibility Diving*. Working with co-author, Dr. Tom Neuman, Steve produced *Investigating Recreational and Commercial Diving Accidents*. With fellow author Bob Christensen, he wrote *The Simple Guide to Commercial Diving*. With Lance Milbrand and Mark Thurlow, Steve wrote *Underwater Digital Video Made Easy*.

In 1989 Steve formed Marine Marketing and Consulting. The company provides market research, marketing plans, consulting, newsletters, promotional articles, technical manuals, and other services for the diving and ocean industry. He has consulted to Light and Motion, Dräger, AquaLung/U.S. Divers Co., Inc, Zeagle Systems, Inc., Diving Unlimited International, Kirby Morgan Dive Systems, Inc., DAN, NAUI, Nuvair, and numerous other companies. He also investigates diving accidents and serves as an expert witness in dive accident litigation.

Steve has taught numerous workshops on contaminated water diving, dry suits, small boat diving, spearfishing, and other diving topics. He has also conducted specialized diving courses and programs for organizations like the Canadian Navy, Universal Studios, the U.S. Bureau of Reclamation, the City of San Diego Lifeguards, the National Park Service, NOAA, and the American Academy of Underwater Sciences. In 2004, he was invited to speak at two hyperbaric medical symposiums in Japan, one of which was sponsored by the Undersea and Hyperbaric Medical Society (UHMS), where he delivered papers on diving accidents and contaminated water diving.

In 1999, Steve and his wife Kristine formed Hammerhead Press to publish high quality diving books. Marine Marketing and Consulting, Hammerhead Press, and Hammerhead Video all operate under the umbrella of the Carcharodon Corporation.

Steve is also a partner in Scuba-Training.Net, one of the first on-line training programs in the scuba industry. The web site provides the academic portion of diver training including text, photos, animations, and full-motion videos. Both quizzes and exams are administered and graded instantly on the site.

Steve has produced five professional video projects including a CD-ROM for Viking dry suits and DVDs on *California Lobster Diving, Dry Suit Diving in Depth, The Simple Guide to Boat and Wreck Diving,* and *California Marine Life Identification*. All of these projects were produced by Hammerhead Video.

Steve lives in Ventura, California, with his wife Kristine, and they regularly dive at the Channel Islands.

About the Author
Dick Long

Dick Long is one of the pioneers of the diving industry and the founder of Diving Unlimited International. He is one of the few executives among the diving equipment manufacturers who regularly gets in the water to dive.

Dick started diving in 1958 and attended the very first NAUI instructor course held in Houston in 1960. At the time, he remembers reading the U.S. Navy diving manual in the closet with a flashlight, because he thought it was classified material and had such good information! He later became certified as an instructor for both PADI and the YMCA.

In 1965, he worked as a contract diver for the U.S. Navy in the Arctic, and from 1965 through 1972 he operated his own commercial diving company. He also worked with the Navy on the development of equipment for the Underwater Demolition Team's divers doing lockouts from submarines during this same period.

Dick was an equipment designer for the Navy's Sea Lab II experiment in saturation diving. He subsequently went on to develop the hot water suit which has made modern saturation diving possible.

Dick started Diving Unlimited International in 1963 as a sport diving store and custom dive equipment manufacturer. He sold off the retail division in 1977 and has concentrated on the manufacture of diver thermal protection equipment since that time. The company has become the undisputed world leader in the development of dry suits and thermal protective systems for underwater use.

The recipient of numerous awards and honors, Dick has received the NOGI award for education, the DAN Rolex Diver of the Year Award, has been inducted into the NAUI Hall of Fame, and received the DEMA Reaching Out Award. In 2006 he was inducted into the Commercial Diving Hall of Fame for his work on hot water suits.

Dick's passion for diving is infectious. He has introduced thousands of divers to dry suits and other advanced equipment concepts. He is well respected for his advocacy of diver safety and was instrumental in the development of the Responsible Diver program.

From 1995-1999 he was on the board of directors of the Diving Equipment and Marketing Association (DEMA) and is currently the chairman of the San Diego Ocean's Foundation. His consuming passion during the last few years has been the management of the sinking of the *Yukon*, a former Canadian Navy ship, which has become an artificial reef for divers. He is actively involved with the Ships-to-Reefs program which works to acquire decommissioned naval vessels and prepare them as artificial reefs.

About the Author
Bob Stinton

Bob is a native San Diegan who grew up in and on the water, fishing, snorkeling and surfing. Bob's first introduction to non breath-hold diving took place off La Jolla Cove in 1964 when he and his fellow free divers came to the aid of a boat with a fouled anchor. The owner of the boat had a Johnson Air Buoy, a gasoline powered compressor mounted in an inner tube which supplied two free flow masks via an umbilical. The boat's owner did not know how to dive so Bob and his friend volunteercd.

After freeing the anchor, the boat owner let Bob and his friend use the Air Buoy for several hours. Bob was hooked; it was almost like being Mike Nelson (the hero on the first scuba diving TV series in the 50s). This launched Bob's interested in the development of diving equipment. Bob and his friends had to have one of these air buoys, but could not afford one. The alternative was to build one from what could be scrounged up. After two years of advanced garden hose diving, Bob became a certified scuba diver in 1966.

Bob's affiliation with Diving Unlimited International (what was the former Skin Diving Unlimited store) began in 1965 when Bob joined the Junior Unlimiteds, a club sponsored by the store. This was an interesting period of time at Skin Diving Unlimited; Dick Long was developing and perfecting the free flooding hot water suit and system to support the needs of the Navy's Man in the Sea program and the growing offshore oil industry. This development effort meant there was always a need for test divers, tenders and gofers to try something new. This gave Bob an opportunity to dive a wide range of equipment form the tried and true heavy gear of the time such as the Navy MK V and Yokohama dress, to the latest and sometimes experimental lightweight helmets and band masks.

Bob joined the Navy in 1969, and after boot camp he proceeded to Hospital Corps School at Balboa Navel Hospital. After school Bob spent most of the remainder of his enlistment on the staff of the intensive care unit at Balboa. Bob joined DUI full-time after separation from the Navy.

At DUI, Bob worked in every aspect of the growing business including retail sales, instruction, government and commercial sales, and manufacturing. Bob moved from dabbling in product development work, to doing it full time in the late 70s. At that point he took the lead position in the development and integration of a hot water suit system and gas heaters for use with the EIP-5. The EIP-5 was an early return-line helmet system which recovered the diver's exhaled breath and returned it to the diving bell where it was scrubbed for CO_2 and oxygen was added before it was pumped back to the diver. This development work let to a series of dives which were conducted at the French Naval Station at Toulon to depths of over 1,000 feet of sea water.

Bob has been involved a number of ongoing Navy diver programs including diver thermal protection, helmet integration and closed-circuit systems. Bob has also been active in the aviation community, where he has worked with NAVAIR, Rockwell, and McDonnell Douglas on advanced crew protection systems.

Bob is currently the Vice-President of Engineering at DUI and his biggest disappointment in life is that it appears that there are no diving destinations on Mars for which to prepare. However, he takes solace in the fact that there may still be water-filled caves on Mars; and if this does not pan out there are still diving opportunities on Europa....

About the Model
Kristine C. Barsky

Kristine Barsky is a senior marine biologist and diver with the California Department of Fish and Game. She holds a bachelor's degree in biology from Humboldt State University with a minor in botany.

An avid diver since 1970, Kristine's diving experience includes dives along the entire California coast, the Coral Sea, throughout the Caribbean, Hawaii, and Mexico. Kristine worked on the Department of Fish and Game's abalone project for 8 years, logging over 250 dives annually at the Channel Islands and along the coast. She is currently the Department's senior marine invertebrate specialist, dealing with the management of lobsters, shrimp, sea urchins, sea cucumbers, squid, and numerous other species throughout the state of California.

If Kristine looks familiar, it's probably because you've seen her photo many times. As a model for her husband Steve, Kristine's image has appeared in numerous diving catalogs, books, and ads, including those for Force Fins®, Viking, Zeagle Systems, Poseidon, DUI, and AquaLung/U.S. Divers Co., Inc.

Kristine is qualified in numerous types of advanced diving equipment including full-face masks, rebreathers, and dry suits. She is an extremely versatile diver.

Kristine has authored numerous scientific papers, articles, and several books. She also is an avid photographer and video camera person. She has been the producer for four video projects including *Dry Suit Diving in Depth, California Marine Life Identification, The Simple Guide to Boat and Wreck Diving,* and *California Lobster Diving.*

Index

Symbols

3M Corporation 24

A

A.P. Valves 49
accessories 61–69, 76
acclimation
  to cold water 27
active heating system 20
activity level 27
adaptor
  low-pressure 72
  low-pressure swivel 68
advanced dry suit diving skill 94
air 15, 17, 28, 29, 51, 53, 63, 64, 69, 73, 90, 92, 95, 96, 102, 103, 104
air consumption 27, 28, 31
alcohol 27
anchor line 73, 92
ankle straps 103, 117
Apeks 49
Aquala 18
Aquaseal 122–123
argon 69
ascent 92, 102, 103
  uncontrolled 51
ascent rate 97, 102
Avon 21

B

B.F. Goodrich 20
back mounted zipper
  closing 84
bacteria 128
bag
  dry 65
bail-out bottle 128

ball point pen 119
bathing suit 76
battery technology 16
beach diving 99
bee's wax 82
Bel Aqua 18
beverages 111
  non-caffeinated 111
biologically polluted water 128
blower vent 113
boat 77, 90, 99
  inflatable 99
body
  surface area of 28
body fat 27, 28
body mass 27
body temperature 27
boots 68, 77, 113
  attached 34, 128
  drying inside 118
  hard 44
  overboot 44
  underwear 77
bottom 66, 104
bottom time 28
braces. *See also* suspenders
Bradner, Dr. Hugh 18
breath 92
British Navy 17
bubbles 16
bungee cord 111
buoyancy 15, 34, 53, 73, 89, 90, 102, 104
  change 92
  check 91
  control 21, 73
  negative 92, 93, 105
  neutral 73, 94
  positive 67, 73, 92, 95, 98, 103, 104